GROWING UP GOOD

GROWING UP GOOD

Policing the Behaviour of Girls in Europe

edited by Maureen Cain

⑤SAGE Publications
London • Newbury Park • New Delhi

First published 1989

SAGE Publications Ltd
28 Banner Street
London EC1Y 8QE

SAGE Publications India Pvt Ltd
32, M-Block Market
Greater Kailash – I
New Delhi 110 048

SAGE Publications Inc
2111 West Hillcrest Drive
Newbury Park, California 91320

British Library Cataloguing in Publication Data

Growing up good: policing the behaviour of girls in
  Europe.
  1. Girls. Social behaviour
  I. Cain, Maureen, *1938–*
  305.2'35

ISBN 0–8039–8021–3
ISBN 0–8039–8022–1 Pbk

Library of Congress catalog card number 88–64111

Typeset by Photoprint, Torquay, Devon
Printed in Great Britain by J.W. Arrowsmith Ltd, Bristol

Contents

Acknowledgements

As always in the production of a book there are a great many people to be thanked. And as always a lot of the people who contributed in the most important ways, by boosting one's self-confidence and general feeling of energy and well-being, cannot be included in a list of those more directly involved. So let me say thank you first to my friends and my family, hoping they will all know who they are.

Of the people who helped with the project I must first mention Lisa Alisi and Caterina Fanfani-Bühler who shared the administrative workload with me, and Angela Sheffield who helped with the typing. I want also to express my appreciation to the Italian Ministero dell'Interno for its most generous financial support which enabled this contribution to the United Nations Year of Youth (1985) to occur. Il Ministero della Grazia e Giustizia also assisted with statistical information and attendance at the conference on which this book is based, held at the European University Institute, Florence, in November 1985. Joseph Weiler, the Director of the European Policy Unit, supported me generously and I have greatly valued his help and good judgment. Gunther Teubner and colleagues in the Law Department at the European University Institute were a constant source of intellectual stimulation, as were my friends in the Women's Group without whose laughter and insights I would never have come to see my own life space and theirs as continuous with those of the girls we write about in this book. The administrative and ancillary staff of the Institute deserve every accolade for making the conference itself such a productive and happy occasion, as do the participants. Although many of the contributions to the Conference could not be included, it must be said that all our discussions have informed the 'second drafts' for this book. And the chairpeople merit a particular word of thanks in that regard, for steering us so graciously on to such fruitful topics.

Finally, I must express my very real gratitude to all the people, mostly women, whom I harried for information on my preliminary visit to the UK in January 1985, and on my 'grand tour' of the EEC countries (excepting Greece and Luxembourg) later that year. The hospitality was so warm, the help so generous, and the whole series of expeditions exhaustingly unforgettable. I can only hope that I have done you justice in these pages.

M.E.C.

Contributors

Rosa Andrieu-Sanz is a social scientist and is at present a research worker and journalist in Bilbao, Spain.

Caterina Arcidiacono is a psychologist and consultant in girls' penal institutions in Italy. She has worked in health and welfare centres for women and families and is involved in training programmes for public health personnel and welfare workers and in studies on gender identity.

Maria Blom carried out sociological research into heroin prostitution from 1981 to 1986, finishing a study of South Moluccan heroin users in the Netherlands at Groningen University in 1987.

Anthony E. Bottoms is Wolfson Professor of Criminology and Director of the Institute of Criminology in the University of Cambridge, UK. He is currently directing a large-scale research project on intermediate treatment, funded by the Department of Health and Social Security.

Maureen Cain is Professor of Sociology at the University of the West Indies, St Augustine, Trinidad. She is author of *Sites of Judgment: Essays in the Sociology of Civil Law* (1989), *Marx and Engels on Law* (with A. Hunt, 1979) and *Society and the Policeman's Role* (1973), and is co-editor of *Disputes and the Law* (with K. Kulcsar, 1983).

Roberta Cipollini teaches at the Department of Sociology of the University of Rome, Italy. She has published extensively on the sociology of work and organization.

Franca Faccioli teaches at the Department of Sociology of the University of Rome, Italy. She has published work on the sociology of deviance and criminology.

Gabriella Ferrari-Bravo is a psychologist working in juvenile penal institutions and educational centres for teenagers in Italy. She has been involved in training programmes for public health personnel and is a UN Social Defence Research Institute consultant for the Street Children project in Argentina.

Annie Hudson is a Lecturer in Social Work in the Department of Social Policy and Social Work, University of Manchester, UK. She has long maintained an interest in connecting feminist perspectives with issues of social work policy and practice.

Barbara Hudson is Research Officer for the Middlesex Area Probation Service and also does some teaching on the MA Social Services Planning course at Essex University, UK. She is author of *Justice through Punishment* (Macmillan, 1987) and has published articles on criminal justice in general and issues concerning young women in particular.

Joachim Kersten is a Lecturer in Criminology at the University of Melbourne, Australia. He previously worked in Berlin and Munich. His research interests include gender-specific patterns of institutionalization; masculinity and crime; law and order and the crisis of the welfare state.

Jean-Charles Lagrée is Director of Research at the Centre de Recherches ITS in Paris. He is an anthropologist by training and specializes in ethnographic work with young people. Most recently he has been engaged on a comparative study of unemployed youth in Manchester, Rome and Paris.

Sue Lees is Co-ordinator of the Women's Studies Unit at the Polytechnic of North London, UK. Her book *Losing Out: Sexuality and Adolescent Girls* (Hutchinson, 1986) analyses the importance of sexual reputation to feminine identity. She is currently researching the ways in which allegations about the victim's sexual reputation are used in rape and homicide trials.

Paula Lew Fai is a research worker at the Centre de Recherches ITS in Paris and co-author (with Jean-Claude Lagrée) of a major ethnographic study of deviance and control published in 1985.

Virginia Maquieira is Associate Professor of Anthropology at the Autonomous University of Madrid, Spain, and researcher at the Centre for Research on Women at the same university. She is co-editor of *Mujeres y Hombres en la Formación del Pensamiento Occidental*.

Edna Oppenheimer is a Senior Lecturer at the Addiction Research Unit, Institute of Psychiatry, London, UK. She has participated in numerous long-term follow-up studies of people with alcohol and drug problems. She is co-author (with Gerry Stimson) of *Heroin Addiction: Treatment and Control in Britain*. Her current research interests include addiction problems in women and help-seeking processes.

Tamar Pitch teaches at the Institute of Cultural Anthropology of the University of Perugia, Italy. She has published work on the sociology of law and social movements.

John Pratt is a Senior Lecturer in Criminology at the Institute of Criminology, Victoria University of Wellington, New Zealand. After graduating in Law, he undertook research at Keele and Sheffield universities and then became senior research associate on the DHSS Intermediate Treatment Evaluation Project at the Institute of Criminology, Cambridge, UK.

Ton van den Berg carried out sociological research on heroin prostitution in the Netherlands from 1981 to 1986. He now works as an adviser in advertising and in setting up new firms.

Karmele Vasquez-Anton is a social scientist who works as a journalist and freelance researcher in Bilbao, Spain.

Introduction

Feminists transgress criminology

Maureen Cain

Few, if any, survive their teens. Most surrender to the vague but
murderous pressure of adult conformity. It becomes easier to die and
avoid conflicts than to maintain a constant battle with the superior forces
of maturity.

Maya Angelou, *I Know Why the
Caged Bird Sings* (1984: 264)

Shug say, Albert. Try to think like you got some sense. Why any woman
give a shit what people think is a mystry to me.
  Well, say Grady, trying to bring light. A woman can't git a man if
peoples talk.
  Shug look at me and us giggle. Then us laugh sure nuff. Then Squeak
start to laugh. Then Sofia. All us laugh and laugh.
  Shug say, Ain't they something? Us . . . slap the table, wipe the water
from our eyes.
  Harpo look at Squeak. Shut up Squeak, he say. It bad luck for women
to laugh at men.

Alice Walker, *The Color Purple* (1982: 208)

Delinquent girls

This book started in response to a request from the Italian Ministry of
the Interior to organize a pan-European project on juvenile delinquency. First, given the ten-month time-span for the completion of
this project, I decided that it could only take the form of a conference
of people who had done original research. Secondly, I decided that
our discussions would be restricted to girls.[1] My own experience as
an unmanned woman, a middle-aged spinster, indeed, connected
directly with emerging evidence about the pressure on girls to couple
and to be manned by a single, particular male (for example, Griffen,
1985; Lees, 1986; Leonard, 1980). Moreover, feminist criminologists
had begun to point out the continuity between the ways in which
women and girls are pressured and schooled to conformity by the
criminal justice system and the ways in which they are controlled by
a myriad of other institutions and structures in society at large
(Heidensohn, 1985). Also, Eaton (1983, 1986) had demonstrated the
importance of the rhetoric of the couple for both women and men
caught up in the penal process. From its inception, therefore, the

conference aimed to transgress the concerns of conventional criminology.

One such major concern of feminist criminologists has been whether women and men are treated in the same way by police and courts and social workers (for example, Casburn 1979; Chesney-Lind, 1977, 1978; Datesman and Scarpitti, 1980; Elzinga and Naber, 1987; Farrington and Morris, 1983; Hancock, 1980; Nagel, 1981). A second, more recent concern has been with female crime and women criminals. Self-report studies (for example, Campbell, 1981; Shacklady Smith, 1978) and the life stories of offenders (Carlen, 1985) have attempted to reveal what women 'really do', in all its rich variety – a variety so rich, as Carlen argues, that it cannot be theorized at all.[2] A third dominant issue has been concerned with women as victims of crime (for example, Dobash and Dobash, 1979; Pizzey, 1974).

The equal treatment studies are, however, inherently problematic. The treatment of males is presumed to be a norm or yardstick against which the treatment of females may be judged. But such a concern with equity leaves unanalysed the substance of what is being equalized. The working brief of the agencies involved is not called into question. Furthermore, the connections of the control agencies with the rest of society are not questioned, either empirically or theoretically. So, even if women and girls were treated no worse than boys and men, the largest part of the political problem (how people *should* be treated) and of the theoretical problem (how we can make sense of the agencies' actions) would remain untouched.

Even without this theoretical critique, however, equal treatment theorists had found their limits by increasingly sophisticated empirical work. Eaton, for example (1983, 1986) found sameness of treatment according to all the usual criteria, but argues that the courts hold conventional gender relations in place by the extra-legal ideologies and rhetorics which they deploy.

Criticisms of self-report studies are similar. Once again what boys and men do is treated as a taken-for-granted standard. This not only makes it impossible to question what boys and men do but also leaves us with no way of making sense of what girls say they do. And the self-report studies, like the equal treatment studies, define women as secondary, as unable to set their own standard or be understood in their own or any non-masculinist terms, from the outset.

Life stories bring us closer to the concerns of this volume. They redirect our attention to the projects of those whom we are studying; and one such study, *Criminal Women* (Carlen, 1985) avoids what has often seemed to me an overwhelming criminological concern with female sexuality. Before the publication of that book, it had begun to seem that feminist researchers had themselves adopted the male view that what matters most about women is their sex! Moreover, life histories provide us with empirical routes into a range of penal and welfare agencies; they also reveal the ideological connections between these agencies and other people – families, friends, and so on. Heidensohn (1985) too argues that there is a continuity of control in women's offending and non-offending lives.

Studies of girls and women as victims point in the same direction. Rape, violence, incest, even getting burgled, emerge as articulated in a range of ways with problems of the private sphere more generally, and of the permanent potential vulnerability of women within it. Already it becomes clear that the solutions suggested by conventional criminology, however sympathetic to the plight of women, can do harm rather than good. A strengthening of the criminal law reinforces the pretence that the problem is not structural but individual; severe punishments imply that it is only exceptional bad men who victimize women. In contrast, feminist work has demonstrated that the problem and the solutions arise from social relationships, or structures: the problem is powerlessness (isolation, economic and emotional dependence); the solutions are working to maintain networks of girlfriends in the early days of a partnership, help lines, refuges, crèches, and work. Feminism begins to transgress criminology. There is also ideological work to be done on the 'fearful' concept of the unmanned woman, to which we shall return.

Thus the work of Heidensohn and Eaton, Carlen's life histories, and the victim studies all begin to point in the same direction – towards an understanding of 'women and crime' in terms of a theory which is far more general in its implications and applications than 'criminology' or the 'sociology of deviance' can ever be. Crimes, criminals, victims; courts, police officers, lawyers, social workers may be objects of investigation, but our explanations must reach beyond and encompass all of them, as the life histories and the victim studies, the continuity studies and the ideology studies already strain to do. I am arguing that, in a sense, feminist *criminology* is impossible; that feminist criminology disrupts the categories of criminology itself.

Instead of criminology, the authors of this book are concerned with the forms of expression of a discourse which is not particular to crimes, criminals, victims of crime, or penal and welfare sites. We are concerned with the complex ways in which these discursive practices and the sites of their constitution and expression interlock or are independent.

We focus on girls and women but, at a theoretical level, we can and must reintroduce men, not in the liberal sense of maleness as a given status or a mode of treatment to be caught up with or attained by the non-men, but as problematically constituted people too (Cousins, 1980). Men, as males, have not been the objects of the criminological gaze. Yet the most consistent and dramatic finding from Lombroso to post-modern criminology is not that most criminals are working class – a fact which has received continuous theoretical attention – but that most criminals are, and always have been, men. Instead of asking how the maleness of men connects with this result, with this hugely unexplained finding, we ask why women do not offend, as if even the criminogenic properties of maleness were normal compared with the cheerful and resigned conformity of women. This is because the *criminological* gaze cannot see gender; the criminological discourse cannot speak men and women. We left criminology, perhaps, when we left libeɪalism: certainly we are outside it now.

Yet, in spite of the limitations of criminology and our resentment that girls are seen only in terms of their sex, this book is in large part and paradoxically both about the sexuality of girls and about their encounters with the criminal justice system. These choices therefore need justifying.

On our girlish preoccupation with sex: strategies of transgression

The contributors to this volume are frequently, though not exclusively, preoccupied with the sexuality of girls for at least three very good reasons, the most overwhelming of which is that everyone who comes into contact with girls, *including other girls*, seems to be preoccupied in just this way.[3] Sexuality first, and beyond that a range of gender-approved ways of behaving such as mothering and caring, are what girls and boys, mums and dads, teachers, judges, social workers, prison guards, the medical profession, and just plain men and women talk about to any researcher interested in girls. For us to give primacy to another aspect of girls' lives would involve ignoring this fundamental and near universal discourse in terms of which girls are constituted and in large part constitute themselves. To know the girls we are studying we have to work through and within that discourse. But we have also to be aware of the fact that that is what we are doing. This is the strategy of *reflexivity*.

Secondly, this discourse of sex can be used to justify penal practices, that is, to cause authorized pain to both girls and boys, albeit in different ways and sometimes by its own silence. The discourse and the ways in which it is integral to these practices must be *recognized* and analysed before its relevance in such a context can be considered and before political choices about how girls (and boys) should be treated can be made. This is the strategy of *deconstruction*.

Thirdly, there is evidence in these pages that some girls, some times, become aware of a discrepancy between the discourse and themselves, between who they are told they are and who, in some inchoate way (because lacking a conventional language of expression) they feel themselves to be – at least as a forever possibility, closed off but whimsically and fleetingly grasped. This may produce insanity (the records suggest that it often does for married women; see Mathiesen, 1980). A few of the permanently marginalized remain angry: some Spanish prostitutes do (Andrieu-Sanz and Vasquez-Anton, this volume; see also McLeod, 1979). But most of the girls we write about resolve the contradiction by resignation and compliance.

The essays published here reveal why and how this outcome was achieved. But a description of how 'social control becomes effective cannot be an adequate reason for research when one is working from the standpoint of the controlled, of women and girls in this case, and when there is evidence that they feel trapped and unhappy (Cain, 1986a; Cain and Finch, 1982; Finch, 1986; Hartsock, 1983; Smith, 1980). As Gouldner pointed out so long ago (1973), such descriptions can rather readily be used to make the control more effective. So the third good reason for focusing, after all, on the discourse of legitimate and illegitimate sexuality is to find ways to help girls to reach outside it or beyond it and to begin to imagine an alternative. We must find ways of creating spaces in which girls can start to think of themselves and who they might be in new and, hopefully, far more varied ways (a moment's introspection might tell us that we all need that). This is the hazardous strategy of *reconstruction* which justifies, we hope, the writing of this book.

On penal practice and the constitution of women

The justification for looking at the criminal justice (or, as mainland Europeans more appropriately call it, the penal) system is more humdrum: our sponsors asked us to and then very generously gave us a free hand. However, by 1985, when we met to discuss these issues, we were already beyond criminology. It was therefore clear that it would be more useful to our sponsors, as well as more theoretically interesting for us and more politically valuable to girls, if we were to trace some of the continuities and discontinuities between the ways girls are constituted (and so come to 'control' themselves and each other) in their more typical daily lives, and the ways in which (as it appeared) these practices are distorted and writ large in welfare agencies, the courts and correctional institutions.

Another argument which I would have used before our meeting is that it is within the penal system that girls are subjected to the greatest pain. There are therefore humanitarian grounds for making it a first object of study as a prelude to transformative or, in this case, even reformative political action. While still sympathetic to this point of view I now recognize that women suffer psychic and physical pain in many spheres of life, and who is to say which is the worst? So now I can only offer the weaker form of this argument, that girls and women certainly do suffer within the penal system, and one has to start somewhere.

What we have done is to displace not a practical concern with what goes on in penal institutions, but the traditional criminological discourse about these practices. Effectively we ask in many of these essays, 'how is gender constituted in these sites; how do these sites and modes of constitution of gender connect with other sites and modes; what are the effects of these practices for women and for human self-fulfilment?' Thus we start with a large question and then hone it down to the sites and practices which have typically been the province of criminology. Criminology, however, starts with the sites and practices which are 'given' to it by the criminal law and its administration. So while it has always, whether in conservative, liberal, or radical guise, been concerned with social class, for example, it has rarely posed class relations and their constitution and reconstitution as its central question;[4] rather it has seen class as impinging on what goes on within its central area of concern. As Garland (1985) has indicated, the objects of its interest are borrowed from the language of penal administration. So I am not arguing here that no one should ever study the police, the criminal courts, the prisons, and sentencing agents again. I am arguing that we should approach these institutions with theoretical and political concerns which are far more general in scope, and which will accordingly enable us to make better sense of those institutions in terms of their now theoretically visible relations with the rest of society.

In the end, however, the chapters and the argument must stand as justification for retaining some focus on penal practice, while at the same time attempting to go beyond criminology. The chapters constitute an uneven argument, with emerging and re-emerging themes which I shall attempt to draw out here.

From everyday life to the prison: a journey with discontinuities

'Everyday life' was a concern of the early sixties which it is worth holding on to. The term implies a lack of reverence for those sociologies which focus on institutions as relatively enduring structures and a preference for the fluid and the mobile. It also implies that the normal, the routine with its minor surprises is far more important than the Big Event. What the chapters in the first two parts of this book have done is precisely to analyse the patterning of the normal. Sue Lees and Virginia Maquieira discuss two very different groups of teenagers: the British ones, hopeless and already resigned; the Spanish ones, resisting their approaching fate as adult women in an articulate and imaginative way. But they too acknowledge the inevitability of their destiny, and anticipate their own future resignation.

The girls whom Lees describes are preoccupied in their talk with sexuality, and in particular with the injustice of the way in which they are controlled by boys. The lack of specific content of the abusive term 'slag' means that girls are in a permanent state of vulnerability: they can be policed by the boys for dressing too sexily (or too drably), for talking to too many boys (or not being friendly enough), for having too many sexual encounters or for being 'too tight', for making too much noise or . . . the litany goes on. Their only security against abuse and a bad 'reputation' is to find and confine themselves to a single sexual partner. Their only active resistance to this policing by the boys is denial in the individual case ('it's not true'). Solidarity and a collective denial of the validity of these boyish criteria has not even occurred to them. They accept the criteria, they accept that girls *should* 'love' one boy (or one at a time, with not too frequent changes). Thus in the end they assist the boys in the policing of the other girls: become God's police in north London (Summers, 1975). They deny their own experience in relation to marriage too: their mothers may have been tired, bored, unhappy, but marriage is 'alright'. In various ways, and especially by choosing carefully, they will make it all right for themselves – they hope. Lees' discussion ends, as do most of the chapters, with some likely-to-be-effective, short-term policy suggestions. These girls' destinies will probably be fixed before this book is published. We are all acutely aware that the millennium will be too late. This does not mean, however, that the immediate recommendations are not theoretically grounded; they are, and none more clearly than those which Lees offers on the basis of her research.

Maquieira's girls were from a cross-section of social classes, but Spain appears a more articulate (or a less de-schooled) culture than Britain, and she assures us that the youth culture she describes is not a middle-class one. Indeed some class differences between the girls do emerge in the course of her analysis, but they are not many. What is most striking about these young people is their active disassociation from, and resistance to, adult society, which they see as hypocritical, lacking in authenticity, and substantively unsatisfactory for both men and women. In contrast, they have created a set of social spaces for themselves in which honesty, 'being oneself', and experimentation play a major part. In Maquieira's pages they sound happy. But the unity of the youth group disrupts along gender lines when the girls' again – seen-as-inevitable – destiny as wives and mothers is discussed. The boys say the girls have an easy time of it as dependants. The girls are angry, and united. The form of their resistance here as elsewhere is a pragmatic accommodation to what they believe cannot be changed, an accommodation which is instrumental and detached and which leaves them enough space in which to 'be themselves'. These girls believe that their future is hopeless. Given their solidarity and the emphasis on innovation which they shared, I am more optimistic for them.

All this massive weight of circumscription of girls' behaviour, and of girls' sexual behaviour in particular, takes place within the field of the everyday. Routes to illegality (the title of the second part of this volume) also start in the everyday, wherever they may lead. In this sense, the discussion of socially marginal youngsters by Jean-Charles Lagrée and Paula Lew Fai provides a useful link. For one point that emerges is that it is the boys' policing of the girls – forcibly taking them home on occasions when trouble is brewing – that keeps them out of the criminal statistics. This may be good for the police and the state, even for the boys, but the girls' crimelessness is in this context just further evidence of their subordination. These girls are at the bottom, in gender terms, in class terms (none had a job), often in race terms, and in age terms. Wherever they turned they were not their own people. The only realistic target for them, that of joining the French working class, was cut off by their unemployment. Lonely and isolated they found company in the boys' street groups, on strictly subordinate terms. The boys too were experiencing a disrupted transition to adulthood. They could not spend money in the authorized carefree years of 16 to 18; they could not begin to find their way from 18 to 24, or envisage 'settling down' thereafter. While they acknowledged these stages as the proper route (normatively evaluated) to being a working-class adult, they were helpless to achieve them. The stages were not quite the same for the girls, given that their only viable economic opportunity was to be the wife of a good wage earner. The inconsequential years of 16 to 18 could carry consequences if they did not manage the sexual encounters with sufficient sophistication. They could reduce their marriage prospects, that is, the social status within the working class of the partner they could expect. Indeed, the gang membership on which they depended might already have done that. These girls had a doubly disrupted transition to adulthood: they could become neither young workers nor young wives.

Lagrée and Lew Fai, therefore, remind us of the economic underpinning of the boys' so effective policing. In the segmented labour markets of Europe boys are girls' destiny because boys are girls' livelihood. Although those who are not dependent share the values, the male hegemony has a very clear economic underpinning.

The other two chapters in this part deal with prostitution, and both show how false are male theories of the phenomenon, and how inappropriate are male suggestions for dealing with it.

Maria Blom discusses heroin-prostitutes in Holland. By dint of careful, sympathetic and concerned research she is able to show how the girls' routes to their present life-style, and that life-style itself, are inextricably bound up with their love lives and emotionally strong friendships. In this context, 'addiction' and 'prostitution' make sense, for both girls and researchers. And of course, each person makes a unique sense. Blom has stylized these life histories into five types to make both understanding and policy making simpler. What stands out very clearly is that *none* of the girls comes into heroin-prostitution in the way that masculinist theories of 'peer group influence', for example, predict. Importantly too, Blom is able to show how a girl's attitudes, relationships and patterns of using as a complex 'life' connect with whether or not she is interested in coming off drugs, and the kind of treatment programme she is prepared to use.

The Spanish chapter by Rosa Andrieu-Sanz and Karmele Vasquez-Anton takes prostitution rather than heroin abuse as its focus. Again its value is that it does not start with preconceptions about the lives of the women interviewed and observed. Indeed, popular (male) preconceptions are shown to be totally out of place in contemporary Spain. The authors examine the changing nature of prostitution from a totally marginalized 'red-light district' activity to an easily obtained service that is taken for granted. The women practitioners vary too: some are professional; some are part-timers who use the extra money to 'do up' their homes, to be closer to the ideal housewife; some are bitter about their public image, others are not – and so on. Beyond the description the authors argue that the male cannot be constituted without the female, who is therefore secondary in her inception. The good woman cannot be constituted without the bad one, who is therefore tertiary in hers. While this means that prostitution as an idea is necessary so long as patriarchy persists, the authors are sympathetic to liberal reform proposals, which at least can make life easier for the girls and women involved.

At this stage (part three) the book changes setting: we move to the more formal atmosphere of the juvenile courts, starting with Barbara Hudson's review of the literature on equal treatment, and comparison of developments in French and English sentencing practice. She argues that the rate of incarceration for girls is increasing faster than the rate for boys and considers French and English strategies in relation to juvenile imprisonment. Importantly, and in this context, she considers that the so-called 'justice model' of tariff-related sentencing would not benefit girls, since their actual offences would be reinterpreted in a gendered way; the welfare model which is arguably preferable on other grounds should therefore be retained.

In the first research of this kind ever carried out in Italy, Roberta Cipollini, Franca Faccioli and Tamar Pitch remind us once again of the ways in which class and race cut across an analysis of gender. 'Girls' are not a gynogeneous category. Restricting this part of their analysis to girls, the marked tendency in Rome to arrest and detain gypsies, whereas Italian offenders are summonsed, is revealed. We have really made rather little headway in theorizing gender and race interconnections; such a theorization depends on a great deal more careful empirical mapping of just this kind.

Part four deals with the ways in which girls experience their sentences. Two chapters deal with carceral sentences, and the third with 'intermediate treatment' in the UK. Some themes in the first two chapters are similar, and both describe the institutional environment in vivid detail. Both are concerned primarily with the gendered discourses in terms of which the girl and boy inmates are constituted, and with the practices which embody, give rise to and express these discourses. For the Italian girls the ultimate obscenity was that their resistance was seen as confirming this discursively constructed femininity. The German girls did not resist, at least for the duration of the research.

Joachim Kersten's careful ethnography reveals not just how girls in secure institutions in the Federal Republic of Germany are encouraged to become conventional females, but also how boys are constituted as male. For the girls, the image of what not to be is the heterosexual prostitute. Their salvation will lie in finding a good man, in becoming part of a couple. Thus in institutional discourse it is 'natural' for girls to linger longingly by the telephone for the call of some boy they have met at a disco; it is not so natural to go down to the pub with a group of girls. For the boys 'real' homosexuality is the taboo, inscribed in all the institution's practices. It lies behind the fear of the expression of affection, the disguising instrumentalism of the way things get done. But the collective denigration of the female sex, which Kersten tells us is normal among males, does not connect with the not-male of homosexuality. This is a rehearsal of a discourse of power, waiting to be brought into play on release into 'normal' society.

Caterina Arcidiacono and Gabriella Ferrari-Bravo also indicate, albeit obliquely, that the gendering of males is at least one half of gendering – a point that comes through strongly in the earlier chapters but is briefly lost sight of in the section on the juvenile court. Their essay describes and analyses the life history of an attempt to integrate girls into a hitherto male prison at Eboli, in Southern Italy. For obvious reasons, the prison chosen for this experiment had the most liberal staff that could be found. Yet there was a revolt, and it was decided that the girls were unsettling the boys! What went wrong? The authors argue that what went wrong lay outside the prison, in the discourse of 'woman' and the practical, taken-for-granted subordination of women in everyday life. To the prison officials a mirror image of this everyday stratification inside the prison would constitute integration. To the rebels and, more consciously, to the researchers, true integration involved equality, and was only achieved in the moment of the revolt itself.

Intermediate treatment (I.T.) in England and Wales being closer to and a part of 'everyday life' does not yield, as the two institutional settings did, that massive discursive caricature which enables life outside the institution suddenly to become clear as a result of analysing life within it. But Tony Bottoms and John Pratt have not only provided a useful survey of the debates surrounding this practice but also highlighted an important contradiction which connects with life in the girls' wing of the medieval prison at Eboli, discussed above. The study by Bottoms and Pratt discusses the finding that girls favour mixed groups rather than the single-sex groups that feminist social workers have advocated as likely to be better for them. This is the old debate about populism versus radical leadership in a new form. Using an editor's privilege of theorizing connections between the contributions (and going a bit beyond the authors' arguments in the process) it seems that the girls are being realistic. They want to improve their chances of marrying a good man: they need to practise their allurement skills with men in order to do this, and in any case, as we have seen, working-class girls largely achieve their identity and their status through male contact. As in the Eboli prison, where girls demanded male teachers, women and girls cannot give status to each other. Girls think, and possibly other staff think so too, that girls' groups are lesser, are secondary. On these grounds too, of course, girls want to be with the boys. So what is the way to transcend populism without being authoritarian? There is a role here for theory and for us as interpreters of it. We must come up with the ideas – with the girls as far as possible, but also without them. They will say whether or not the ideas fit: usually by voting with their feet. The trouble is, of course, that we are talking about aspects of a penal system, and the element of compulsion makes even this negative form of democracy impossible for some of them.

So, the chapter poses for us an important dilemma, the same one that recurs throughout this volume: working-class girls really do need to make a good marriage; their lives are very intelligently directed to that objective. They are also policed towards that objective by other girls, by boys, by social workers, courts and the police (and presumably also aunts and uncles, teachers and parents, clergy and the mass media). Coupling is their destiny and their salvation, that is the message which is both true and untrue. For as women have been pointing out for well over a decade (Delphy, 1977, 1984; Barrett and McIntosh, 1982) the couple is not a wholesome relationship for women. Within families, and within 'the' relationship in particular, women and girls may be molested and raped, beaten up and driven mad, de-skilled and required to work long hours, after hours. These things happen less often to unmanned women: they are not imposed on coupled women by strangers and friends but by sexual partners and kin. So we have an interesting theoretical problem and, given the wasted lives, the pain, the diminution of what people might be, an important political motive for unravelling it. The theoretical problem is how is an ideology which is so widely discrepant from reality so widely and deeply believed in? And what can or should be done about it?[5]

The final section of the volume addresses the second of these questions. Like Sue Lees, both Edna Oppenheimer and Annie Hudson are looking for practical solutions, things that could be done at once rather than things that depend upon some larger change of consciousness in relation to women. Indeed, the doing of these immediate practical things can and should become part of that larger change, as Annie Hudson argues.

Edna Oppenheimer confronts exactly the same dilemma as Tony Bottoms and John Pratt. After an account of the competing discourses governing the way drug addicts are dealt with in the UK she considers the particular problems and dilemmas of the system in relation to girls and young women. For example, young women do have special needs as mothers: this is often a real and strong emotional experience and, of course, child-care facilities in treatment units are essential. Yet these special needs can be used by men to police women into becoming the kind of mother that men approve of, otherwise the child may be taken away. This threat can also be used to induce other kinds of conformity. If the policing fails, the mother who fails to fit the mould because she is a junkie may be permanently marginalized. Oppenheimer brings a range of sources to bear revealing the pain and psychic damage to these young women if their children are taken from them, more so if internalizing their own unfitness is a condition of getting the children back. The dilemma is that advocating special facilities which women really need can reinforce those images with which they may be policed. What is missing is a clear image of the alternative of what *else* women might become.

Like Blom, Oppenheimer points out that, without research on why and how women come into the system, any appropriately designed treatment is likely to be a pure fluke. But in addition to her wise list of suggestions she offers, from her young women subjects, one solution to the Bottoms and Pratt populism problem. What her young people liked best was women's groups *within* mixed institutions. Like all true insights, it does sound obvious!

Annie Hudson's concluding chapter reminds us powerfully of the centrality of sex in social workers' judgments. Even more important, and once again picking up one of the themes of this collection, she warns us against empty slogans as prescriptions of the way forward. 'Empowerment' is all very well and we are all in favour of it, but what precisely does it mean for a girl who needs help at least tomorrow if not today? In part it means putting one's own house in order, and getting rid of patriarchal management practices in social work which marginalize both consumers (girls) and those with most contact with them. Moreover, within the family too inequality and power differentials must be challenged. Further, womanhood and emotionality must be redefined, and girls' statements about themselves must be taken seriously. Running away is such a statement which must be correctly read. All this involves not just help to girls but also help to the would-be helpers of girls, to liberal-minded social workers in particular. Mindful of Eboli and the crises that liberals can precipitate without such help, the benefits of having this analysis for social workers are plainly considerable. It is followed by a set of even more practical suggestions. I hope that social workers at all levels will read and pay attention to them.

The book concludes with an Appendix compiled by 11 people,

and drawn from originally collected as well as official statistics in both northern and southern Europe. While the theoretical problems of comparison are not discussed at length here (but see Cain, 1983, 1985) the practical ones of different systems, different classifications and so on are inevitably still with us; not to mention the absence of data bearing on one or more topics in several countries, including the UK. Given all this, we have kept the materials simple, using them to address just three questions derived from the foregoing and other 'feminist criminological' theory:

1   Are sentences the same for girls and boys?
2   What is the trend in imprisonment for girls and boys?
3   What are the employment prospects for girls and boys?

While the similarities revealed between countries with radically different political economies must finally challenge any notion that the sex-gender structure is in any sense a function of economic relations, comparative work also ensures that no false unity is created for either women or feminism.

Why girls?

One question not posed at the beginning, but demanding an answer none the less, is 'why girls?' Or rather, 'why only girls?' These pages have done much to make that clear. The answer to the question, 'why girls *only*?' is linked with the point made most explicitly by Rosa Andrieu-Sanz and Karmele Vasquez-Anton: women do not need to be compared with men in order to exist. Everywhere woman is defined as that which is not man. In her inception she is difference, as far as our pervasive male common sense is concerned. In her inception, therefore, she does not exist for herself or as herself but only as what she is not. Any consideration of women and men together, in a comparative way, runs the risk of recreating this non-existence, because the question posed is 'how are women different?' It is necessary instead to ask *who* women are, and how do they become who they are. These are the questions addressed by the contributors to this collection, amongst whom all the women discuss only girls.

Who women are, again as we have seen, is not a simple question, because of hegemony and because of variation. By hegemony I refer to a common sense of absolute pervasiveness in terms of which women are constituted and constitute themselves and each other. It is an active process. This is why in the course of their struggles to be in society, women have insisted on the need for their own spaces in which a new language to capture their own incapable-of-being-thought experiences can be brought to consciousness in a supported process of giving them voice. This making it possible to speak the unspeakable is difficult, because each new naming is a creative invention and an emotional release. One such new object in the world, one such new experience which we can now have, is sexual harassment (Harding, 1983). And then, after the discursive invention, we have a politics of naming which is a crucial moment in the struggle to change those practices which oppress: domestic-(ated) violence and assaults sound tame; wife beating is a music hall joke; but talk of beating or assaulting *women* embarrasses us, it sounds positively criminal!

These discursive inventions are difficult and emotional because in their absence nothing could be said. Indeed, but worse, women could not be certain of the 'experience' they had had. This is the ontological argument for realist philosophy: the social relationships,[6] the linking spaces between people in terms of which those people are constituted, can exist independently of anyone's consciousness, either that of the people constituting the relationship, other people in their society or social researchers. And one or other of these may 'recognize' a relationship without the others doing so (see Cain, 1986a, 1986b, 1987).

This may sound recondite. But we need such a philosophy to resist the denial of our emergent discourses. It means, for example, that women had to be experiencing and disliking work relationships *before it was possible* for sexual harassment to be invented. How frighteningly uncertain women must have been before they could know or say or 'recognize', and therefore confidently *have*, that experience. Women knew the bruises inflicted by husbands and lovers, but before Erin Pizzey's brave work they had only a male discourse to make sense of them in – a discourse which all too frequently compounded pain with guilt. This is our answer to the question why (only) girls.

All this exhausting and inventive work must be done before women can *be* positively; and the lack of it and the struggle towards it emerge time and again in these pages where we have tried to capture who girls and women are. They are what they are thought to be: preoccupied with men and marriage, concerned about children and about making a good home. They are also already and in the process of becoming who they might be, refusing to be locked into what can be spoken, what is socially possible, as we record their lives and hopes. Their revolts are inarticulate, because there is no language. Their revolts are negative: they refuse to leave the block, they do not attend for therapy or treatment. Or they make futile gestures: they go out to fight, but the boys take them home; they believe their marriages will be different, but know they won't be. Everywhere, if they are foreign, they are tormented more. They know that those who help them hinder them. The helpers' lives, their modes of organization, the activities they encourage, the justice they offer, speak of how the helped can be held in place. But girls, or some girls, develop circuitous strategies for salvaging autonomy, they develop a cynical, often amused distance from male society or respectable society, however they see it. And – the most political act perhaps in any woman's life – they make friends. When women talk to women anything can happen: all the emperors' nakednesses can be revealed.

These are the reasons we have studied girls and what happens to them, and written about the world as they see it. Our efforts were not co-ordinated. They do not stem from a planned comparative study. But they do reveal why comparative work is important, because they reveal that neither girls and women nor the things they believe in nor the politics of the situations they are living in are the same. The politics of prostitution in Spain is not the same as it is in Holland. Growing up as a gypsy girl in the Campana is not the same as growing up as a Moroccan girl in Paris. The progressive women staff of Eboli prison are not the same as those advocating girls' only groups in Britain, and are different again from the secular women officers in the high-security girls' sections in the FRG, who differ also from the men doing the same job. And their charges differ too. So there is not one woman: it is a male myth that they have rich and various characters but we are all the same. Neither is there one feminism, nor one politics, nor one way of life we all should want.

> Comparative work helps women to retain a respect for each other, and for other women's political objectives . . . Some of these concerns seem contradictory, others complementary: what is important is to retain the discovery that originally made possible the unity of housewomen and employed women – that there is no one true way; and to recognize that what unites these struggles is a concern by women to create spaces in which to develop their own theory of themselves, sites from which a struggle against male hegemony can be waged, sites from which women in their various and doubtless contradictory ways can make a claim. The causes in which that power will be used will of course change historically and culturally. (Cain, 1986b: 11)

All these are timely warnings. But there *are* experiences in common and therefore a politics in common too. And let it be noted that both emerge from comparisons between groups of women, not from comparisons between women and men, which would forever close such experiences off from the possibility of being known. (And how boring would be a book about whether the difference between women and men was greater in north London than in Italy or Denmark!) If we abstract from these case studies, then what emerges most clearly as an experience in common is that of *denial* (Laing and Esterson, 1960). To make this clear I want to return again to a very short story about me, for it is this which helps me to know denial, and it probably was similar experiences which made it possible for the contributors to this volume to hear denial when the girls were telling them. The story has the form of a dialogue:

> *Maureen:* One thing these weeks of living together has taught me is that I don't want to do it. I've been alone too long. The price is too high.
> *Reply:* Why do you keep claiming me?

I argue that this experience of one middle-aged spinster is *the same* as the experience of Madridian girls when their boys tell them that 'really' they have the best of things as dependants, or of Neapolitan girls who are told that their prison revolt is proof of their disturbing femininity. The experience of the female is simply *not allowed to exist*, unless it is in accord with the prevailing co-man sense.

And the huge taboo in this co-man sense, which most of us largely share, is the happy, fulfilled, complete woman spinster. If she were allowed to exist there really would be no image left to police the poor girls with. I suppose the argument for sequential or monogamous coupling would then have to depend on the economic vulnerability of women: but women already have evidence of their long hours of unpaid labour (Oakley, 1974) and could use economic arguments back, as well as those about equal rights in employment, with even greater force. No, unless women can be persuaded to go on feeling sorry for the middle-aged unmanned woman, unless men can successfully present spinsters as predatorily desperate to be coupled, unless women who choose singularity can be characterized as themselves unchosen (as passive creations of male un-desire), then as the economies of Western Europe expand again more girls may choose to grow up to be their own adult woman, either coupled, trebled, or single, but never policed with the terrifying and mythological imagery of unmanned life.

I do believe I have written myself into a position where my own politically most important act is simply to exist. For that new pride I have to thank the girls of Western Europe and their many and richly different interpreters.

Notes

1   I am grateful in particular to Tony Jefferson, who officiated at the birth of this insight.

2 Smart (1976) first drew attention to the distinction between the images and the realities of which crimes are female. Reviews of the self-report literature can be found in Box (1981) and Morris (1987).

3 The Rome Juvenile Tribunal alone is not analysed in these terms. The authors' data base – the records – gives no indication of how far sexual as opposed to gendered concerns play a part in the decisions. See Cipollini et al., 1987: the chapter in this volume does not consider boys.

4 One obvious and exemplary exception here is Hall et al. (1977).

5 This is, of course, directly analogous to the belief, also both true and untrue, in salvation through getting a job and becoming a wage-worker.

6 See Cain (1987) for a more complete elaboration of a realist philosophical position which makes it possible to speak of the 'reality' of as-yet-unthought-about relationships, and the need of women for such a theory of experience independent of discourse.

PART ONE

THE POLICING OF GIRLS
IN EVERYDAY LIFE

1

Learning to love

Sexual reputation, morality
and the social control of girls

Sue Lees

This chapter suggests that a woman's sexuality is central to the way she is judged and seen in everyday life as well as by the courts and welfare and law enforcement agencies. The denial of what I shall call non-gendered subjectivity, treating women as human beings rather than as sex objects, is the major barrier to women's equality. To speak of a woman's reputation is to invoke her sexual behaviour, but to speak of a man's reputation is to refer to his personality, exploits and his standing in the community. For men sexual reputation is, in the main, separated from the evaluation of moral behaviour and regarded as private and incidental.

The policing of women through sexual reputation starts in adolescence, where, as my research shows, a girl's sexual reputation is a constant source of debate and gossip between boys and girls, and even teachers and social workers. A girl's standing can be destroyed by insinuations about her sexual morality, a boy's reputation in contrast is usually enhanced by his sexual exploits.

When we set out in the early 1980s to talk to 15- and 16-year-old girls from different social classes and ethnic groups about their views of school, friendship, marriage and the future we did not intend to focus particularly on sexuality and gender relations. However, the double standard of sexual morality and the concern that girls expressed about their sexual reputations, which were frequently the target of abuse from boys and other girls, led to a focus on the neglected area of how sexual relations were socially structured. The emphasis in youth culture studies on class has deflected attention away from the power imbalance between boys and girls so that few studies have questioned the taken-for-granted subordination of girls by the structuring of gender relations.

The chapter is based on a three-year research project in three London comprehensive schools carried out in the early 1980s. A research fellow, Celia Cowie, was funded by the Inner London Education Authority and the Nuffield Foundation contributed £2,500 towards the project. A hundred 15- to 16-year-old girls from varied social class and ethnic groups were interviewed singly, in pairs, or in group discussions. The first two schools were mixed: both had women head teachers and were attempting to put into force an equal opportunities programme. The schools differed in their intake. One was predominantly white working class; the other had a high proportion of different ethnic groups. Most of the children had been brought up in the area. The third school was a single-sex school with a mainly middle-class intake. The fieldwork in this school was carried out a year later as the necessity of investigating the significance of social class differences became evident.

The research objective was to explore the subjective world of adolescent girls. I wanted to elicit the terms with which they describe and handle their world and to follow up the meanings through which they relate to the world, meanings both individually held and collectively shared. Such an objective required a qualitative method allowing the research to be sensitive to the girls' experience of the world. All the discussions and interviews were tape-recorded and later transcribed. The design of the research involved analysing the transcriptions according to a schedule developed for the purpose. By focusing on the *terms* girls used to describe five aspects of their lives – schools, friendship, boys, sexuality and their expectations for the future – light was thrown on how those individual experiences are socially structured. The research has now been published (Lees, 1986).

The structure of sexual relations and the concept of reputation

Boys and girls talk about sexuality in quite different ways. It is possible to delineate three main differences. First, while a boy's sexual reputation is enhanced by varied experience, a girl's is negated. Boys will brag to others about how many girls they have 'made', but a girl's reputation is under threat, not merely if she is known to have had sex with anyone other than her steady boyfriend but for a whole range of other behaviour that has little to do with actual sex. Secondly, a boy's reputation and standing in the world is not predominantly determined by his sexual status or conquests. More important is his sporting prowess, his ability to 'take the mickey' or make people laugh. For a girl, the defence of her sexual reputation is crucial to her standing both with boys and girls, certainly around the age of 15 or so. The emphasis on the importance of sex to a girl's reputation is shown by a whole battery of insults which are in everyday use among young people. Finally, for boys sexism appears to be very important in male bonding, in as much as denigration of girls and women is a crucial ingredient of camaraderie in male circles. The masculine tradition of drinking and making coarse jokes usually focuses on the 'dumb sex object', the 'nagging wife' or the 'filthy whore'. This is not the case for girls. As one girl told me:

> One thing I noticed is that there are not many names you can call a boy. But if you call a girl a name, there's a load of them. You might make a dictionary out of the names you can call a girl.

The vocabulary of abuse
This lack of symmetry between the variety of names to call a girl and the lack of names to call boys is the starting-point for an understanding of the role of verbal abuse focusing on sexuality in reproducing, among girls, an orientation towards the existing structures of patriarchal sex-gender relationships. The word which illustrates this asymmetry more clearly than any other term is 'slag'. There is no equivalent to 'slag' in the vocabulary of terms available to be directed at boys. Derogatory words for boys such as 'prick' or 'wally' are much milder than 'slag' in that they do not refer to the boy's social identity. To call a boy a 'poof' is derogatory but this term is not used as a term of abuse by girls of boys. As a term used between boys, it implies a lack of guts or femininity; which of itself connotes, in our culture, weakness, softness and inferiority. There is no derogatory word for active male sexuality. The promiscuous Don Juan or the rake may be rebuffed, as in Mozart's opera, but his reputation is enhanced.

The potency of 'slag' lies in the wide range of circumstances in which it can be used. It is this characteristic that illustrates its functioning as a form of generalized social control, along the lines of gender rather than class, steering girls, in terms of both their actions and their aspirations, into the existing structures of gender relations.

The first thing that is striking about the use of the term 'slag' is the difficulty of getting any clear definition of what it implies from those who use it. This is true both for girls *and* boys. Take this girl's description of what she calls a 'proper slag':

I do know one or two slags. I must admit they're not proper slags.

Can you describe what a proper slag is?

Available aren't they? Just like Jenny, always on the look out for boys, non-stop. You may not know her but you always see her and every time you see her she's got a different fella with her, you get to think she's a slag, don't you. She's got a different fella every minute of the day.

So it is just talking to different boys?

You see them, some of them, they look as innocent as anything, but I know what they're like.

The implication here is that the girl who is called a 'slag' sleeps around but this is by no means clear, and the insult often bears *no relation* at all to a girl's sexual behaviour. Boys are no clearer when it comes to defining what the characteristics used to define a girl as a 'slag' are, which is why they disagree as to who is or is not a slag. In their book about boys, *Knuckle Sandwich*, Dave Robbins and Phil Cohen wrote:

> The boys classified all the girls into two categories: the slags who'd go with anyone and everyone (they were alright for a quick screw, but you'd never get serious about it) and the drags who didn't but whom you might one day think about going steady with. Different cliques of boys put different girls in each of the two categories. (1978: 58)

So whilst everyone apparently knows a slag and stereotypes her as someone who sleeps around, this stereotype bears no relation to the girls to whom the term is applied.

An alternative to asking those who use a term to define it, is to observe carefully the rules whereby the term is used. A look at the actual usage of 'slag' reveals a wide variety of situations or aspects of behaviour to which the term can be applied, many of which are not related to a girl's actual sexual behaviour or to any clearly defined notion of 'sleeping around'. A constant sliding occurs between slag as a term of joking, as bitchy abuse, as a threat and as a label. At one moment a girl can be fanciable and the next 'a bit of a slag' or even – the other side of the coin – written off as 'too tight'. The girls tread a very narrow line. They must not end up being called a slag. But equally they do not want to be thought unapproachable, sexually cold – a 'tight bitch'.

How 'slag' is used This constant sliding means that any girl is always available to the designation 'slag' in any number of ways. Appearance is crucial: by wearing too much make-up; by having your slit skirt too slit; by not combing your hair; by wearing jeans to dances or high heels to school; by having your trousers too tight or your tops too low. As one girl said, 'sexual clothes' designate. Is it any wonder when girls have to learn to make fine discriminations about appearances that they spend so much time deciding what to wear? Who you mix with also counts:

> I prefer to hang around with someone who's a bit decent, 'cos I mean if you walk down the street with someone who dresses weird you get a bad reputation yourself. Also if you looked a right state, you'd get a bad reputation. Look at her y'know.

Looking weird often means dressing differently from your own group.

Behaviour towards boys is, of course, the riskiest terrain. You must not hang around too much waiting for boys to come out (but all girls must hang around sufficiently); must not talk or be friendly with too many boys or too many boys too quickly, or even more than one boy in a group; you must not just find yourself ditched.

Almost everything plays a part in the constant assessment of reputation, including the way you speak:

> If we got a loud mouth, when we do the same they (the boys) do, they call us a slag, or 'got a mouth like the Blackwall tunnel'. But the boys don't get called that, when they go and talk. They think they're cool and hard and all the rest of it 'cos they can slag a teacher off.

Who would be calling you a slag then?

> The boys. They think, oh you got a mouth like an oar, you're all right down the fish market . . . They think you've come from a slum sort of area.

Thus 'slag' can just as easily be applied to a girl who dresses or talks in a certain way, or is seen talking to two boys or with someone else's boyfriend. The point is that irrespective of whether, in a particular case, the use of the term 'slag' is applied explicitly to sexual behaviour, since a girl's reputation is defined in terms of her sexuality, all kinds of social behaviour by girls have a potent sexual significance.

Exercising control

Perhaps the key to an understanding of 'slag' is its functioning as a mechanism which controls the activity and social reputations of girls to the advantage of boys. Girls were preoccupied with what might happen after being dropped by a boy.

> Then the next thing he'll be going around saying 'I've had her, you want to try her, go and ask her out, she's bound to say Yeah'.

or another girl said:

> Some boys are like that, they go round saying, 'I've had her.' And then

they pack you in and their mate will go out with you. And you're thinking that they're going out with you 'cos they like you. But they're not. They're going out to use you. The next you know you're being called names – like writing on the wall, 'I've had it with so and so. I did her in 3 days. And I've done her 12 times in a week.'

It may not be a question of the girl actually having slept with a boy, she may land herself with a reputation as a result of going out with one boy, then being dropped and going out with one of his friends. The consequences for a girl are quite different from those for a boy:

When there're boys talking and you've been out with more than two you're known as the crisp that they're passing around . . . The boy's alright but the girl's a bit of scum.

If a boy takes you out or boasts that he has slept with more than one girl he is more than alright, his reputation is enhanced:

If a boy tells his mates that he's been with three different girls, his mates would all say: 'Oh lucky you' or 'Well done my son, you're a man.'

The pressure is on boys to boast about their sexual conquests. They have to act big in front of their friends. As one girl explained:

They might say, 'Oh I've had her.' Then it starts spreading round. She might be really quiet or something and they'll say, 'Oh she's not quiet when you get outside the school.' Someone else will take it in the wrong way and it'll carry on from there.

No wonder that girls always fear boys going behind their backs and saying, 'Oh you know, had it with her'. It is the girl's morality that is always under the microscope, whereas anything the boy does is alright. A number of girls described girls who had not slept around but had been out with a number of different boys in a short period 'because they were unlucky enough to be dropped by a number of boys'. This led people to start saying, 'Oh God who is she with tonight?'

The crucial point about the label 'slag' is that it is used by both girls and boys as a deterrent to nonconformity. No girl wants to be labelled bad and 'slag' is something to frighten any girl with. The effect of the term is to force girls to submit voluntarily to a very unfair set of gender relations. A few girls did reject the implications of the label and the double standard implicit within it, but even they said they used the term to abuse other girls. What becomes important is not the identification of certain girls but how the term is used. A useful way to understand how terms like slag are used is provided by Colin Sumner in a study of the functioning of *categories of deviance*.

Their general function is to denounce and control not to explain . . .
They mark off the deviant, the pathological, the dangerous and the
criminal from the normal and the good . . . (they) are not just labels
. . . (but) . . . They are loaded with implied interpretations of real
phenomena, models of human nature and the weight of political self
interest. (Sumner, 1983)

To call a girl a slag is to use a term that, as we have seen, appears
at first sight to be a label describing an actual form of behaviour but
into which no girl incontrovertibly fits. It is even difficult to identify
what actual behaviour is specified. Take Helen's description of how
appearance can define girls, not in terms of their attributes as
human beings, but in terms of sexual reputation:

I mean they might not mean any harm. I mean they might not be as bad
as they look. But their appearance makes them stand out and that's what
makes them look weird and you think, 'God I can imagine her y'know?'
. . . She straight way gets a bad reputation even though the girl might
be decent inside. She might be good. She might still be living at home.
She might just want to look different but might still act normal.

You cannot imagine a boy's appearance being described in this way.
How she dresses determines how a girl is viewed and she is viewed
in terms of her assumed sexual behaviour. Whether she is 'good' or
not is determined by how she is assumed to conduct her sexual life;
that sexuality is relative to male sexual needs.

Rather than attempt to specify what particular behaviour differ-
entiates a slag it is more useful to see slag as what Sumner (1983)
terms a category of 'moral censure': as part of a discourse about
behaviour as a departure, or potential departure from, in this case,
male conceptions of female sexuality which run deep in the culture.
They run so deep that the majority of men and women cannot
formulate them except by reference to these terms of censure that
signal a threatened violation. Girls, when faced with sexual abuse,
react by denying the accusation rather than by objecting to the use
of the category. It is important to prove that you are not a slag. So
Wendy when asked what she'd do if someone called her a slag
replies, 'I'd turn round and say "Why? tell me why?"' The term
'slag' therefore applies less to any clearly defined notion of sleeping
around than to any form of social behaviour by girls that would
define them as autonomous from the attachment to and domination
by boys. An important facet of 'slag' is its uncontested status as a
category.

A second important facet of the term is that, although it connotes
promiscuity, its actual usage is such that any unattached girl is
vulnerable to being categorized as a slag. In this way the term

functions as a form of control by boys over girls, a form of control that steers girls into 'acceptable' forms of sexual and social behaviour. The term is uncontestable. All the girls agreed that there was only one defence, one way for a girl to redeem herself from the reputation of 'slag': *to get a steady boyfriend.*

> Then that way you seem to be more respectable like you're married or something.

'Going steady' establishes the location of a sexuality appropriate for 'nice girls', and that sexuality is distinguished from the essentially dirty/promiscuous sexuality of the slag by the presence of *love*:

> The fundamental rule governing sexual behaviour was the existence of affection in the form of romantic love before any sexual commitment. For most of the girls, love existed before sex and it was never a consequence of sexual involvement. (Wilson, 1978: 71)

Deirdre Wilson who studied a group of 13- to 16-year-old girls commented:

> . . . given this threat of rejection (for sex without love) it was difficult to discover just how many girls *actually* believed in the primacy of love, and how many simply paid lip service to the ideal. Nevertheless the fact that the girls found it necessary to support this convention, whether they believed in it or not, was an important fact in itself. (1978: 71)

Nice girls cannot have sexual desire outside love, for them sexuality is something that just happens if you are in love, or if you are unlucky, when you are drunk:

> You might be at a party and someone just dragged you upstairs or something and then the next thing you know you don't know what's happening to you.

If this happens the general consensus of opinion is that it is the girl's fault:

> It happens a lot. But then it's the girl's fault for getting silly drunk in the first place that she can't she doesn't know what's going on or anything.

Few girls were clear about what being in love meant, though invariably love was given as the only legitimate reason for sleeping with a boy. The importance of love seemed to be therefore in permitting sexual excitement while offering some protection from sluttishness. This failure to recognize sexual desire meant that girls often changed their minds about whom they loved:

> You think you're in love and then when it finishes you find someone else you like more and then you think the last time it couldn't have been

love so it must be this time. But you're never sure, are you, 'cos each time it either gets better or it gets worse so you never know.

You think you're in love loads of times and you go through life thinking 'God I'm in love' and you don't do anything. You want to be with this person all the time. Then you realize you weren't in love, you just thought you were . . . I thought I was in love and then I went away and when I came back I realized I wasn't. It wasn't love at all. So I finished it and I was much happier.

The girls here could just as easily be describing the way they felt attracted to a boy and then lost interest. Some girls said they had 'been in love loads of times' whereas others said they 'had never really experienced it':

It takes a while to happen. I mean it sort of dawns on you that you finally love this person. Don't think it happens straight away. I mean you might say, 'Oh look at him I love him', 'I think he's really nice' but you can't really say that until you know him really well.

Given the ambiguity about what love involved it could well be that love is used as a rationalization for sleeping with someone after the event rather than, as Deirdre Wilson suggests, as always existing before sex could occur. The confusion that girls experience over whether or not they are in love arises from the confusion of using the word 'love' to express what is really sexual desire. Love is supposed to last for ever or at least for a long time, and is the main reason that girls give for getting married. The distortion of what is really sexual desire into 'love' means that girls must find it difficult to separate their sexual feelings from decisions about marriage and long-term commitment. As Jacky said:

Girls have got to keep quiet about sex and think it's something to be ashamed of.

However, it is quite legitimate to talk of love. The 'legitimacy' of love is precisely its role in steering female sexuality into the only 'safe' place for its expression: marriage. The result is that a girl either suppresses her sexual desire or channels it into a steady relationship that is based on an unwritten contract of inequality – that she will be the one to make compromises over where she works, lives and spends her leisure. She will bear the main burden of domesticity and child care without pay and adjust herself, and indeed contribute, to her husband's work, life-style and demands.

The importance of the threat of being regarded as a slag in pushing girls to channel their sexuality into the 'legitimate' channels of love which results in marriage is illustrated by the realistic, as opposed to romantic, view of marriage which most of the girls had. Almost all the girls took it for granted that they would get married, yet they were remarkably clear about the grimmer aspects of woman's lot in marriage. As one girl put it:

> The wife has to stay at home and do the shopping and things. She has got more responsibility in life and they haven't got much to look forward to . . . We've got to work at home and look after the children till they grow up, you've got to go out shopping, do the housework and try to have a career. The man comes in and says, 'Where's my dinner?' when we've been to work. They say, 'You don't work.' It's because boys are brought up expecting girls to do all the work. They expect their mums to do it and when they get married they expect their wives to do it. They're just lazy.

The realism about marriage was based on the observation of their parents:

> My dad won't do anything, he won't make a cup of tea, he says he does the work for the money and the rest is up to my mum – she does part-time work too.

The most important reason that girls put forward for getting married was that they saw *no alternative*. Life as an independent, unattached woman is always open to risks:

> If you don't want to get married and want to live a free life and you go out with one bloke one week and another the next, everyone will call you a tart, like you've got to go out with a bloke for a really long time and then marry him.

Besides the constant fear of being regarded as a tart or slag, living alone is seen as too frightening. The need for protection emerged in a number of the interviews. Charlotte describes how her brother is treated differently from her:

> Boys are a totally different physique. I could go out and be raped whereas he couldn't. He'd have more chance of protecting himself. I think that comes up the whole time. It's not that a boy is more trusted. It's that he's freer.

The harsh reality existing in a male-dominated world was that women needed protection from sexual harassment. Girls could never go out on their own, or even with girlfriends, without fear:

> Say you have a boy protecting you. It's as if no one can hurt you or nothing. You're protected and everything. If someone does something to you, then there's him there too and it just makes you feel secure.

The threat of male physical violence takes its place alongside the verbal violence associated with labelling a girl a slag to steer girls into the acceptability of marriage. But it is not just the constraints on an independent sex life that lead girls to marriage but that the family is seen as the only hope we appear to have for the fulfilment of needs for warmth and intimacy and love. Lesbian relationships can of course offer these, but only if the girl manages to resist the pressure towards conformity and, of course, if she is attracted to other girls.

In the face of these strong pressures the girls inevitably subscribed to the idea that they wanted to marry. Nevertheless, their realism about marriage, based on their observation of their parents, led them to devise ways of rationalizing or cushioning its inevitable impact. Almost all the girls wanted to put marriage off for some time. By delaying marriage many girls thought that they would be able to have some fun; they often fantasized about travel and seeing the world. Marriage was something you ended up with after you had lived:

> I don't really want to get married 'cos I want to go round the world first like me dad did . . . they got married when they were thirty years old, they just sort of *had their life first* and then they got married and had us but when you're an air hostess you don't start the job until you're twenty so I want to work until I'm thirty-five.

Girls who did want a career often realized that relationships with boys might upset their intentions and therefore steered clear of them:

> If a boy does ask us out we say 'no' don't want to know, because we want a career and go round the world and all that lot. So we just leave them alone . . .

or Janey put it more strongly:

> I don't really bother about boys now – just get on with my homework. I was brought up not to like boys really 'cos I've heard so much about what they do, robberies, rapes and all that so I keep away from them!

When asked what she meant by being brought up not to like them she replied:

> Well my mum told me never to go with them because they're bad and they damage your health and things like that, don't know.

Boyfriends and marriage could easily interfere with career intentions: the girls could see what had happened to their mums and how little autonomy they had.

Another way of attempting to avoid the predicament of marriage was to attribute the unhappiness they saw in marriages around them to the wrong choice of partner. The subordinate position that many women found themselves in was often attributed to the lack of good sense in choosing the right husband rather than to the general structural constraints on women at home with young children.

Alice, looking at the 'mistake' her mother had made in choosing the wrong man, believed:

> But not all marriages are like that though are they? Like if your mum's goes bad, yours might go good, it's *what husband you pick*.

Alice is right in one respect. Some men allow women more autonomy than others. She does not however criticize the unfairness of the marriage deal itself, particularly if children are involved. Although having children was something that most girls wanted, again, the way in which this inevitably constrained freedom was recognized:

> I think that once you decide to have kids then you've got to accept the fact that you are gonna be tied down for a while. That's why it's important not to get married too early – until you're twenty-eight or so.

In short, the girls were not aware of positive attractions attaching to the married life yet; as far as they saw it, there was just no alternative. Romanticism about choosing the 'right man' can be seen as a way of attributing personal responsibility for structural oppression, but the fact of structural oppression is realistically understood. Nevertheless, despite the unattractiveness of marriage the question is, as a girl from Diana Leonard's study (1980) in Cardiff put it, not of *choosing* to get married or not but whether you *fail* to get married. My argument has been that what forces this closure on all alternatives to married life is above all the power of the 'slag' categorization for the unattached woman who is sexually active. Once we understand the way in which female sexuality is constructed and constrained by the categorization of slag, how a woman's femininity and sexuality is only rendered 'safe' when confined to the bonds of marriage, we understand why there is just no alternative, as the girls see it, to married life.

Sex, class and subculture

As I have noted, most studies of male youth culture have been conducted from a subcultural standpoint in which youth culture is seen as resistance to, and temporary escape from, the pressures and demands of society. Yet the experiences of the girls portrayed here can hardly be seen as resistance or escape. On the contrary, the processes which have been illustrated are very far from resistance; they are the processes of constraint and the channelling of aspirations and behaviour along the well-established paths of sex and gender relations exemplified by the institution of marriage and the role of women in the domestic sphere. To see the rehearsal for entry into a major social institution such as marriage and the domestic sphere as a form of 'subculture' or resistance is, in effect, to deny the reality of the domestic sphere as a social institution akin, say, to economic life and social class relations and to see it purely as a cultural phenomenon. In this way the questions of subculture and the debate over sex and class relations are crucially linked. If the main structural forces or forms of stratification in our society are seen as economic class structures then, of course, rehearsal for domestic life, when seen from the stand-point of those structures, will be seen as a form of cultural behaviour unrelated to class, or possibly as a form of resistance to the consequences of class-determined life chances – in the way in which, for example, Paul Willis (1977) describes the process whereby working-class *boys* reconcile themselves to working-class jobs. But if gender divisions are seen to be of equal significance to economic class in the constitution of social structure and social institutions then it is less easy to view girls' behaviour as 'subcultural'.

It is important to analyse the constraints that the structuring of gender relations and the double standard of sexual morality places on girls. This final section will draw out some of the implications of this.

Morality and sexual behaviour: slags

My research into the language of sexual reputation amongst adolescent girls revealed three things. First, that names like 'slag' function as terms of abuse, to control single girls and steer them towards marriage as the only legitimate expression of sexuality. Secondly, what became clear was the interdependence of male 'non-gendered subjectivity' and female sexuality. This manifested itself in the way girls continually take on responsibility for male actions – especially violence or other behaviour that is irrational or sexually motivated. Girls also bear the moral responsibility for the consequences of sexual relations by taking steps to ensure contraception. Thirdly, the repression of sexuality to the conventional pattern of marriage means that female sexuality has little autonomous expression but is constrained by social station and its duties. The woman becomes the housewife and her virtue comes to consist of the correct performance of the 'duties' of the marital relationship, being a 'good wife', in which sexual expression is allowed only to the extent of meeting her husband's 'legitimate' sexual needs. When women are charged with petty criminal offences social workers and law enforcement agencies have been shown to give weight to sexual reputation and the performance of domestic duties in sentencing. There is also some evidence that girls are sent to institutions on grounds of sexual conduct rather than the nature of the offence.

If in the private sphere it is woman's duty to keep quiet and be a good wife, in the public sphere her inability to achieve non-gendered subjectivity closely follows from her having to take on the responsibility for male sexuality. Because the male 'rational man' is only possible where his sexual and irrational behaviour can be attributed to 'woman trouble' or other feminine influence it is obviously impossible, under present circumstances, for men and women to co-exist as non-gendered subjects. Women's escape from sexual stereotyping in the public sphere would require men to take on responsibility for, and integrate their sexuality into their public behaviour.

For women, this situation limits the possible forms of behaviour in the public world. One can of course 'latch on to' a man and go places but, conversely, a woman who does achieve in terms of skills and capacities other than 'sex' stands in danger of either having her achievements attributed to her sex (that she 'slept her way to the top') or being regarded as sexless (one of the boys and therefore undesirable). To be an honorary man is to be so masculine and 'unattractive' that men and other women will come to dissociate her completely from any concept of sexuality. Thus a type of false non-gendered subjectivity is achieved but only as a residue: a woman is evaluated in terms of her achievements only because no men find her sexually interesting.

For men, on the other hand, virtue is achieved irrespective of sexuality: in public life sexual reputation is largely excluded from the moral evaluation of conduct. In private life too men's sexual conduct does not define moral standing. A man can still be a 'good father' or a 'good husband' and have illicit sexual relationships outside marriage.

Consequences for the education of girls

What implications does this analysis have for the way that social relations and sex education are handled in school? Teachers in the UK who are aware of class differences are much less sympathetic to equal opportunity policies for girls. At a conference sponsored by the Equal Opportunities Commission the director of a research project, Margaret Spear, reported that the majority of teachers surveyed in her research appeared to be in favour of equal opportunities in principle but were far less committed in practice. Some teachers claimed that equal opportunities were irrelevant to their work and some argued that discrimination was necessary. One said, 'Schools have to prepare pupils for work in society as it is. Some boys need restricted workspace more than girls' (Spear, 1985). Acker (1988) in explaining the limited impact of equal opportunity initiatives also points to the ideology of gender that sets limits to what appears acceptable change. There are three main areas where discrimination needs to be challenged: social relations, sex education and sexual harassment.

Social relations and sex education The whole issue of social relations, and gender relations in particular, should be given far more attention in schools than at present. There is evidence that boys monopolize two-thirds of class teachers' time and that teachers pay less attention to girls and even find it more difficult to remember their names.[1] The way that boys and girls integrate in school should be a focus for debate and more attempts should be made by teachers to counteract any indication that boys are either receiving more attention or depriving girls of the use of any school facilities.[2]

Sex education not only needs to be given far greater attention but needs to be approached with reference to the powerful and taken-for-granted assumptions about sexuality which, rather than being natural and biologically given, are social and reflect and reinforce the subordinate position of girls and women in our society. It is only by approaching the question of sex eduation in this context with a knowledge of how sexual relations are structured by the norms and constraints outlined in this chapter that progress can be made. This leads to the other two areas that I would like to discuss from this standpoint.

Sex education in the traditional sense usually focuses on different methods of contraception and descriptions of the biological make-up and the mechanics of the sex act. Even at this level, according to Brenda Spencer, little has changed since 1965 when research indicated that adolescents received little guidance about sex education, virtually none about contraception and sexually trans-mitted diseases and that unwanted pregnancy was a major problem (Spencer, 1984). Although in the UK birth control is now free and available to all teenagers without their parents' consent, in practice only a third of all sexually active teenagers regularly use contracep-tion. This has been explained by girls' hesitancy about approaching doctors and birth control clinics but what may be more significant is the operation of the double standard that condemns her as irresponsible if she does not use contraception and condemns her as unrespectable if she does use it. It appears that using contracep-tives runs particular risks in relation to a girl's reputation. If she uses contraception on a casual date this involves laying herself open to the charge that sex is premeditated and that she is therefore consciously choosing to anticipate that sex might occur with someone she is not 'in love' with or in a steady relationship with, she is therefore a 'slag'. On the other hand, if she has sex without contraception this can be explained by something which 'happens' without previous intent. In fact, it is interesting how often girls describe their sexual encounters not as something that they consciously choose to embark on but as something that 'happens' to them. As Hannah said in an earlier quote:

> You might be at a party and someone just dragged you upstairs . . . and the next thing you know you don't know what's happening to you.

Of course, what is happening is rape. But it is too simple to regard the boys as totally blameworthy and 'potential rapists'. They too are locked in to regarding girls in a contradictory way: on the one hand, there are pressures on them to regard girls as conquests and to 'make' as many girls as they can; on the other, there are pressures on them as individuals to treat girls well and as friends and to care for them. It is almost as though there are two kinds of sexuality: one that is without emotional feeling and treats women as dirty and provocative and the other that involves strong feelings of desire and compassion. These two concepts of sexuality are inextricably linked to the concepts of the virgin and the whore. This may be why even raping a virgin or a respectable married woman, as in 'The Rape of Lucretia', is still regarded as, if not the woman's fault, at least a taint on her character. The transition between the two types of sexuality has been crossed and the raped woman has crossed irretrievably into the 'slag' category. This is one reason why so few women report rape. In her research on sex education in schools, Carol Lee describes how, whenever rape was discussed, at least a couple of boys said:

> But women really want it Miss. You have to knock them about a bit for them to enjoy it. (Lee, 1983)

The difficulty with these statements is that it is easy to reject them out of hand and regard rape as uncontrolled inhuman aggression of one human being to another – which it is – and stop the analysis there. What must be questioned is why these views are so prevalent, and what exactly is at stake. The girl has to deny her sexual desire to remain respectable but should she in any way indicate that she is open to advances she is regarded as fair game and the implication is that rape is not the violent assault that it in reality is but is 'only what women really want'. It may be true that women do want to express their sexuality, they do want active sexual lives but this choice is denied them. Any indication of attractiveness whether in the form of the way a woman dresses, speaks, looks or flirts is taken as grounds for the man to assault a woman. A slippage has occurred whereby the man's desire has been projected onto the woman, turning her from the 'good' virgin into the 'rapacious' whore who will go with anyone anywhere. 'You have to knock them about a bit for them to enjoy it' and knocked about women are, night after night, month after month, as is shown by the studies of family violence that are emerging out of a wall of silence that has surrounded the cruelty that many women suffer within the privacy of the 'domestic haven'. Such issues need to be brought up and questioned in sex education classes, though it is unreasonable to expect teachers to take on such a task without preparation and further training. Rape and violence cannot be explained as the behaviour of psychopathic sex maniacs but rather as actions which are the extension of the normal oppressive structure of sexual relations. It is by challenging the terms on which girls participate in social life that boys and girls can be encouraged to see their relationships not in sexist stereotypical ways but to see each other as human beings irrespective of their sex.

Sex education, in the traditional sense, is also important as there is evidence that girls particularly have little knowledge of their sexual organs and responses, let alone the freedom to express themselves. Jane in this study graphically described her sister's fears about her pending wedding:

> *Jane*: She's frightened of the night. She hasn't been to bed with boys or anything so she's frightened. She's getting married this Saturday.
>
> *Sandra*: Wonder woman she won't be.
>
> *Jane*: What's she gonna do when he jumps on top of her?

Their description of sex as 'jumping on top of her' and as a searing experience is hardly a romantic or informed depiction of sexual love.

Tracy, when asked whether anyone talked about sex to her replied:

> My mum does talk about it. When mum explains it she talks like she's carrying a heavy load.

Sexual experience is for many women just like that – carrying a heavy load rather than an experience that lightens their load and lifts them out of themselves.

Likewise, Stevi Jackson in *Learning to Lose* (1980) describes how the girls she interviewed equated sex with coition and had acquired little information about their own sexual responses or their sexuality. Given the focus on intercourse and reproduction in the knowledge available to adolescents, boys cannot but identify the penis as their chief sexual organ. Most girls, on the other hand, did not even know of the existence of the clitoris. Investigation of the genitals is so heavily tabooed that few girls do so, as is implied by what the two girls, Sandra and Jane in this study, say.

Sexual harassment   The denigration of girls and pervasiveness of verbal sexual abuse needs to be challenged rather than 'swept under the carpet'. Sexual harassment in schools should be recognized and taken seriously. As Helen put it:

> My school work reflects how the rest of my life is going. If I am being sworn at at school or have trouble at home, my work suffers.

The sexual abuse that is often a taken-for-granted aspect of everyday life in comprehensive schools amounts to a form of sexual harassment. Speech is a form of action and even if it is a reflection of the inequality between men and women which will change only when that inequality is overturned, sexist language can also be seen as a way of reinforcing the subordination of girls and women. The elimination of sexist language is a necessary condition for eliminating sexism in our society. The use of racist and sexist language, as Robin Lakoff (1975) suggests, is connected with the inferior social roles of blacks and women and needs to be continually challenged. A disciplinary code should be drawn up in all schools where such terms are outlawed, and deemed to be quite unacceptable. Sexual harassment and sexual abuse need to be taken as seriously as racial abuse. Teachers who turn a blind eye to them or even actively collude in denigrating girls should be rebuked. One difficulty is that many teachers are either not aware of the double standard or accept it uncritically. A good sample of this lack of concern is given by Chris Griffin who reported this conversation with a fifth form teacher, Mr Yates, about girls who reported they had been attacked:

> *Mr Yates*: Some of the girls have been saying they've been attacked coming to school.
>
> *Chris*: Yes, some did mention that to me.
>
> *Mr Yates*: Yes, well you don't believe them do you when they say that?
>
> *Chris*: But if they're worried about it . . .
>
> *Mr Yates*: Yes, but some of them wouldn't know what it means. They're just having you on. These attacks are just nothing. They're not serious you know. (1985)

There is therefore a need to educate teachers and make them aware of the discrimination against girls, not simply in terms of option choices and career opportunities but also in terms of the unfair structure of social relations. Nonetheless, sociologists have been more blinded to the effect of gender than teachers, so it is hardly surprising that such attitudes persist.

Notes

1 Margaret Spear's study (1985) was based on samples of secondary school teachers in mixed comprehensives in southern England (Institute of Educational Technology, Open University).

2 For evidence of this see my article, 'The structure of sexual relations in school', in M. Arnot and G. Weiner (eds), *Gender and the Politics of Schooling* (Oxford: Oxford University Press, 1987), p. 181. Pat Mahoney in *Schools for the Boys* (London: Hutchinson, 1987) described how boys monopolize 'physical space', 'linguistic space' and teacher attention.

2

Boys, girls and the discourse of identity

Growing up in Madrid

Virginia Maquieira

This chapter is an elaboration of the results of an investigation into the urban youth of Madrid carried out by an interdisciplinary team during the years 1981, 1982 and 1983.[1]

The general framework for the study was the question of changes in values and morality and the reasons why and how new forms of morality are emerging in Spanish society. The analysis of forms of morality and value systems as they emerge and are revealed in the process of constructing practical meanings by groups of young people[2] corresponded with a desire to examine new and emerging elements in their value systems and social practices. Without delving exhaustively into the problems of who are the true agents of cultural and moral change, it seemed to us that one undeniable element in that change is the phenomenon of juvenile subcultures, within which alternatives are proposed and established.

This was why we emphasized the moment of *innovation*, the coming into being of new values and practices, which are not institutionalized and which presuppose a break with received wisdom and thus the construction of a *new identity* in the process of everyday life.

The idea of innovation has two dimensions: the demystification of the inherited forms which are present in adult institutions, within which young people also live their lives and without which their life would not be possible (family, work, education); and the construction of ideals which serve to regulate their conduct.

We therefore paid special attention to the processes of interaction in everyday life as being the area where the break, the differentiation, the novelty, or alternatively, the reproduction of the adult world was revealed to us in all its complexities.

To fulfil this task we chose a qualitative methodology which took as its point of departure the young people themselves and not the usual questions that adults ask them. We decided to work through

---

This chapter was translated from the Spanish by D.E. Hanson.

the kinds of discourse that usually circulate among young people. We adopted an ethnomethodological hypothesis according to which the discourse of a linguistic community reflects the practices whereby the world is appropriated, and the type of social interaction in force in the said community.

We were interested in analysing the discourse employed by young people in the conditions of their everyday life. The method of collection of the material, therefore, had to be appropriate for those conditions. This made it necessary for us to depart from the typical precoded replies or enquiries that we thought to be more artificial.

We took into account the character of complex unity exhibited by the discourse, which meant that it was not possible to extract isolated statements, but rather that it was necessary to pay attention to the context and structural organization within a complex system (which is precisely what is meant by discourse) of what was stated.

Recorded encounters and discussion groups were complemented by in-depth interviews with individuals and by participant observation, in contexts ranging from the most institutionalized to the least, which young people define as 'their own' because it is here that encounters and spontaneous interaction between them occur.

We began work with fifteen groups, selected as being representative of different positions in the social structure. Within these there were young people selected according to their:

1　socio-economic status;
2　academic level;
3　the urban zone from which they came;
4　sex;
5　political and ideological allegiance.

We worked an average of three hours a week in group discussions, which were recorded and transcribed for later analysis and discussion by the investigative team. Following the views expressed by the young men and women themselves, the sample was enlarged in order to gain information from those young people who formed part of their discourse, but who were under-represented in our sample. Thus the size of the groups increased to twenty-five, and the work was completed with interviews with those young people whom it was difficult to investigate in groups: militants of the extreme right, and those who were on the margins of society (taking hard drugs).

For the final report we isolated: discourse on the self; discourse on images of the world as the young people would wish it to be; and discourse on the family, sexuality, female/male roles, the education system, work, drugs, and politics. Those aspects most relevant to considerations of gender and deviance are developed in this chapter. I use the following schema:

1   the *we/they* dimension, which demonstrates the emergence of a collective identity as teenagers, demarcating their sense of difference and the borderline that separates them from the adult world;

2   *the critical vision of the adult world* which penetrates the most relevant aspects of what the young people reject of present day social organization;

3   the strategies of the *teenage role*, which attempts to provide an honest picture of the conduct of young people in their hostile interactions with the adult world;

4   the analysis of *affirmative discourse* which has as its purpose the putting forth of those ideal images of life and society that give meaning to the lives of the young people, and provides a counterpoint to their negative and critical discourse on present day society;

5   *'the fragmentation of the we'*, which exhibits gender conflict existing within the collective 'we' of youth identity and demonstrates the difficulty young people experience in escaping from and overcoming institutional inertia.

We/they

In the speech of young people it is not long before reality is simplified into a we/they opposition. The 'they' includes the whole adult world or society which, according to the context, takes on more specific forms: parents, teachers, the authorities of the academic, business, or political worlds. The generic 'we' is used to refer to what is *distinctively their own*.

In the language used by the young people of Madrid we detect a double process in the emergence or construction of an identity as teenagers which they apply to each other without reservation. This sense of identity is developed through a two-dimensional process: negative and positive, interacting simultaneously. The negative refers to the refusal and inner conflict that young people feel when they are defined and categorized by non-peers who tell them *who* they are and *how* they *should be*. That is to say the negative aspect is the stereotyped images that adults maintain concerning young people. As we shall see in more detail later on, these ideas are evident in such statements as:

Youth is the divine treasure.

If *I* were 20 years old . . .

Young people don't appreciate what they have.

The positive dimension refers to the sense of belonging to a group which lives in its own world and where one feels 'different' from adults. This context consists of friendly encounters between both sexes, free from the negatively valued features of the adult world, such as self-interest, utilitarianism and lies. There are also moments when they are free to kick over the traces of established custom, and young people ritually appropriate these actions and these moments as signs of their identity.

In these contexts teenagers feel that they have a collective identity and a 'we' endowed with values and personal meanings which adults can neither experience nor understand. Teenagers refer to or speak of these contexts using the word *atmosphere* and, as we shall see, this becomes very important in the perception that they have of themselves and of their activities, to judge by the frequency with which it appears in their conversation and by the relevance that it has in its various uses. Without these 'atmospheres' there is no such thing as teenage conduct.

With regard to the first element, the definition imposed from outside, the first conflict exhibited is that adults have constructed certain stereotypes and meanings on the basis of which they constitute and classify teenagers, thus organizing their own expectations as far as teenagers are concerned. Teenagers do not recognize themselves in this description provided by 'others'. It seems to them that 'youth' with the specific meaning which adults give to this term is no more than an 'invention' of adults for their own purposes.

Expressions like those which follow, among other very similar ones which we have collected, show how teenagers have clearly distanced themselves from the stereotypes which are current in the adult world:

> . . . to be a rebel is something that's imposed on you as a task at the same time as they seek to forbid it . . .

> They want to convince us that our expectations are shared by them, and I tell them, 'Your expectations are your own; I wish you would recognize mine as my own,' but they aren't capable of understanding us . . .

> What adults would like us to do is to think a great deal about the future. We are expected to be the generation of the future, but what about our present? They don't understand our present and in addition they don't allow us to have it . . .

> They expect you to have things and attitudes that they imagine should characterize young people, but these things don't interest us . . .

These stereotypes rejected by young people originate equally in the context of family life and in the world outside the family and they mutually reinforce each other. 'At your age I . . .', 'If I had had what you have . . .', 'You think that . . . but we who have experience . . .' are everyday phrases from family life. Other expressions originate in institutions and social and political organizations and are mainly transmitted by advertising and the communication media. Symbolizing vitality, dynamism, sport, happiness, they project both the optimistic image contained in the Spanish phrase for 'youth, divine treasure!', and also the contrary idea: youth synonymous with 'danger', 'damnation', 'delinquency'.

These young people of Madrid considered that the public sector of the state administration takes advantage of these images to pursue a concrete policy *for* young people, but not *with* them, a policy which in short serves only to justify their own existence as an administrative body. Thus, the word 'youth' imposed from outside or expressed by other people, is experienced by them as impersonal, manipulating and even remote. This rejection is manifest not only as a rejection of the concepts or images, but also of the concrete situations that arise in interaction with the adult world. In these the young person finds that she or he belongs to a distinct group, whose desires tend to be frustrated or limited as a result of the positions imposed by adults.

From this fact springs the idea that many desires entertained by young people are contrary to the organization and practice of the adult world and, taking the matter a step further, the notion that adults as a group think in a different way from young people as a group.

When we spoke with them about themselves we found that the young people steered clear of definitions and concepts, believing that to start using them would be to fall into the snare of an adult mode of speaking. For them, there are no such things as stereotyped definitions, fixed concepts, essential characteristics which might describe them as a *unified* collectivity. On the contrary, what we discovered (and what they experienced) was a reality which was *plural* and *not monolithic*. This point is linked with the concept of 'atmosphere' we referred to above. 'Atmosphere' is something of their own, constructed by themselves, characterized by self-expression. They participate in a variety of these atmospheres, which are simultaneous, complementary, opposed and/or contradictory. In these they find and realize for themselves figures and images of what it means to be a young person. In this sense, it is possible to speak of a contextual and malleable identity which will do anything to avoid a finished and institutionalized definition.

The clearest distinction between the we/they, which is manifest in the speech of these young people face-to-face with the adult world, can be summarized as a different manner of experiencing space and time. The young people distinguish their own experience from 'adult time', a counterpart of which is a series of fixed and concrete spaces. The time of the adult world is characterized by repetition, routine, by what cannot be changed. It is the time dictated by imperatives and obligations external to the individual. Within this temporal/spatial form of adult life, they stress that there is a distinction to be made between the experience of women as opposed to that of men. Woman's time is cyclic, beginning and ending in the organization of the home, characterized by her being dependent upon her father, from which state she can only escape by entering upon a new form of dependence, in relation to her husband.

In contrast, 'the time of youth' appears as one of authenticity (in contrast with alienation), liberty (in contrast with the slavery of obligation), of creativity and spontaneity (in contrast with monotony, inertia, and the repetition of work). In its turn, the time of youth flows through a variety of spaces, which are neither enclosed nor specialized but are constructed from within, from outside the realm of institutions, with the fundamental characteristic of *malleability* which appears as a characteristic value of the generation.

Critical vision of the adult world

The young generation's critical view of the social order is very much conditioned by their experience in their immediate family. We first noted that here they moved away from a more abstract discussion to a more detailed description of their own lives in the environment of their family. Secondly, we gained an insight into the manner in which young men and women arrive at their own way of thinking, by absorbing or rejecting various aspects of the values and practices which have been transmitted to them, which always originate with reference to and membership of some family circle. It is in the family circle that, in the course of everyday life, they first come up against the imperatives, roles and practices of the adult world, which, in their turn, imply a definite social order.

The great majority of young people in our sample see in their family a world in which *appearance* takes precedence over *real content*. That is to say, there is an effort to maintain and proclaim, both to the outside world and within the family itself, an appearance of unity and dignity, of conjugal harmony, of love for one's children, of economic stability, and of general satisfaction. These conceptions which are transformed into an ideology of the value and importance of the family and of the values agreed upon by society, are transmitted to the children. The latter see that their parents are transmitting these values because they claim that they are the bulwark of a life led in common with the auto-justification of their own families. The young people realize that this is no more than an ideological grid which attempts to mask a reality which is very different.

They criticize the life of adults for being guided by vacuous principles which they support and defend, without putting them into practice in their own lives. This distinction between *principles* and *reality* is experienced by young men and women as an absence of *authenticity* which characterizes the adult world in general. Arising from this experience they judge authority, power and the law as empty and completely without prestige. The authority and law with which they daily come into contact is, of course, that of their parents, but also, that of the schools and of the workplace, depending upon the social position of the young person. Through this prism of disrespect for authority and the law, they extend their judgments to other institutionalized instances of power, particularly by judging people according to the extent to which they accept or submit to authority. Those who submit to the imperatives of power and authority, in whatever guise they appear, are seen by the young people as weak, servile and inane. In this judgment they include not only their fathers and mothers, but also their companions and teachers. For example, they might pejoratively classify the latter as 'un-young'. On the other hand, teachers who manage to ignore the norms of the academic institution receive their profound admiration, being transformed into possible candidates for the 'we' of youth.

This same critical attitude appears when they are talking about politics. Generally, Spanish young people, including those we focused on in our work, who lived in Madrid (and with the exception of a militant minority in the left-wing parties), are at present quite unconcerned with what is usually called political life. 'Politics' seems to them to be one more aspect of that adult world that lives in a state of contradiction between *principles* and real *practice*. Today, more than ever before, they believe that 'politics' is the area in which the struggle for power takes place, the sphere of advertising images and of a marketing practice which constructs images and products that will 'sell' to the public. It is, moreover, the place where manipulation and negotiation occurs, behind the backs of citizens who are attracted by empty and hollow programmes. Young people consider that there is no place for them in politics, since they are not allowed to act in the way that the promises made during the electoral campaigns would have them believe: 'Politicians look after themselves', 'They are people of no importance'.

This critical view of the adult world is even more apparent when we turn to a consideration of the world at *work*. Here the young people distinguish two aspects: on the one hand, the present day form of work organization, and on the other, the attitude of adults towards it. Recently the image that they have of their fathers and mothers has gained new importance. There is less harsh criticism from those young people belonging to upper-middle-class families whose fathers are members of the liberal professions and who are totally dedicated to their work, which has rewarded them with social and economic success. Most of our sample of Madrid youth criticized the *slavery* which they described as their fathers' relation to their work, men who were seen as orientated 'for', 'by', and 'in' their work. Their fathers identify life with work and evaluate their own existence, their self-esteem, in terms of sacrifice and dedication to work which is measured by the money they are able to bring back to their families.

This fact is decisive, according to these young people, in the kind of relationship established between father and mother. The mothers have had to construct their lives on the basis of a state of dependence, through marriage which is 'a life security', but which prevents them from having their own life and produces all kinds of frustrations and injustices. This criticism is more intense and more profound coming from the mouths of young women than of young men. It is important to remember, in this context, that these young people belong to a generation which grew up in very specific economic and political circumstances. In the Spain of the 1960s most workers had more than one job or did overtime in order to be able to pay for their own house, buy a car and attain the external symbols of an improvement in their standard of living.

The young people state with a mixture of pity and scorn that in this pursuit of economic well-being their fathers have lost the capacity for feeling, the ability to be interested in things, and that it has stunted their personal development. They add that they have become remote beings, incapable of carrying on a dialogue with their children and their wives in anything but an authoritarian rhetoric which is intended to sound manly.

In short, the young people criticize a society based on inauthenticity, which maintains in an authoritarian manner principles which in general it fails to practise; a society constructed around rules and authorities lacking in prestige, embroiled in economic activity which enslaves and impoverishes and annihilates its citizens; and finally, a society structured according to male/female relations of hierarchy and domination.

Youth strategies in the face of the adult world

The term strategies is intended to include the means used by young
people to resolve their differences and conflicts with the adult world
which they criticize, and with which they are forced to live. This
analysis reveals the actual conduct of young people in their social
networks and answers the question whether such a thing as youth
culture really exists, a 'unique style', which is quite distinct, of
existing in this world.

In general, the young people of Madrid exhibit a certain
adaptability with regard to the adverse and conflict-ridden circumstances of their lives. Faced with the rigidity and authoritarianism
of their families, workplaces and educational institutions, this
generation does not react by conducting a frontal assault or
engaging in explosive conflicts, but seeks to conduct *transactions*,
to create small openings by means of which it can achieve its
objectives.

This trait distinguishes young people of today from those of ten
to fifteen years ago, for whom power was deemed to have a
monolithic and total quality which invaded everything so that only
its destruction could guarantee a change, and for whom the only
possibility was direct confrontation.

The attitude of our young people today can be described as
'juvenile realism' or 'juvenile pragmatism', and it is a special frame
of mind *quite opposed to idealism*. It avoids heroic and demonstrative
actions which to them seem to be unpleasant, wearisome, ineffectual
and unrealistic. One example can clarify this attitude, expressed
most directly in their own words. The home is the parents' territory
or domain of power, but 'there are always weekends when they go
away and we can do whatever we like, even make love in their bed'.
It could be argued that these or other possibilities have always
existed within families, but what we believe to be novel is the
discontinuous vision of time and space, that is to say, the way of
taking advantage of the space and time given by institutions and
transforming them for one's own purpose.

If we transfer this conduct to the sphere of the education system,
we can say that young people regard the idea of not realizing their
present in order to construct a future in accordance with the wishes
of their parents and society, as something alien. This is a very
generalized view, since there are shades of difference according to
social class.

In the case of young working-class people there is, in spite of this
critical attitude, a certain idealization of university studies for what
they offer in the field of knowledge or opportunities to improve

one's social status. In the upper-middle class, young people have adopted the adult viewpoint which sees success in university studies as providing a means of access to specific levels of the labour market, but this does not undermine their criticism of its real function, which is alien to their world, their expectations and, therefore, a source of frustration.

In general, these young people have in common a way of passing through and establishing themselves in educational institutions while adopting a posture of realism, and yet also distancing themselves from them. The realism comes because they use what is offered them in a utilitarian manner, without any thought that they are going to change what they reject. They are convinced that transformation is not possible and so distance themselves, because they intend to pass through these institutions with the least possible effort, without getting too involved. Their strategy is characterized by a certain pleasure principle, which denotes, in short, an alternative instrumental attitude.

Another strategic resource concerns their mode of assuming and living their identity. They are not interested in choosing and defining a form of existence, but in trying out their own atmospheres and activities, testing the limits and possibilities of the 'self'. They say that one finds oneself by trying and being different things. They oppose this approach to that of adults who are preoccupied with choosing a very definite identity, which obliges them to adopt a rigid system of classification about conventional ways of behaving, on the basis of which they judge both themselves and other people.

This exploratory and fragmentary attempt at achieving self-identity is very apparent when they talk about drugs and explain the reason why they take them. It is well known that the majority of young people in urban areas have tried at one time or another what are known as 'soft drugs' (marijuana, hashish). They point out as a positive aspect the possibility that these offer of trying out new modes of existence, of broadening the limits of the self, limits which adult society would like to keep strictly defined and fixed. Young people prefer to experiment with a range of possible modes of being one's self.

Practically all young people share a common opposition to the ideology about drug taking which they attribute to 'older people'. They think that the latter reject drugs through a 'hypercritical traditionalism'. They underline the hypocrisy of adults who do not make any distinction between different types of drugs and their effects but, nevertheless, without any scruples themselves engage in the use and abuse of alcohol and become dependent on medicines without any discrimination whatsoever.

Adults judge the use of drugs on the basis of what happens with hard drugs – addiction and death. The judgment of young people is formed on the basis of the ceremonial and sporadic experience of soft drugs. The latter is for adults the first step along the path to addiction, but for young people it is not like that. It is a playful experimentation with the self and breaking of the rules by a group or individual as a mode of ordering one's life, which by no means implies that one is going to become addicted to heroin.

For young people, soft drugs provide their very own atmosphere, in which they are able to see many things and above all, themselves, in a clear manner. They use a criterion to define and distinguish between two different kinds of experience: it is one thing to consume drugs in a relatively self-controlled manner and another to be addicted, which involves the loss of one's self in terms of both control and self-awareness, values they establish as ideal forms of self. In this final instance 'one is no longer one's self', and is dependent on external powers which one cannot control.

On the subject of why anyone should go from normal usage to addiction it is almost unanimously agreed that 'the only person who gets addicted is the one who has other problems'. In this they refer not only to personality problems but to fundamental problems of the social environment. They are convinced that a young person would not of his or her own volition wish to destroy the self.

In conclusion, young people in Madrid in the 1980s consider the use and consumption of drugs as a means of living and of exploring to their utmost limits the possibilities of consciousness. They even think that not to take them up is a sign of cowardice, not worthy of free individuals. Nevertheless, they agree that to enter the world of heroin involves a total loss of self-control and liberty, a world where others abuse them, deceive them and manipulate them to the point of being chained and imprisoned and forced to go in daily peril of their own lives.

Once more they point to the hypocrisy of the adult world and they criticize established society which acts as an accomplice in the trade of hard drugs, with mafias which take advantage of young people, who are then bound over to destruction and death and held culpable for what has happened, whereas in reality they are victims.

Returning to our theme, it is quite clear that experimenting with different possible ways of being one's self is one of the conscious or unconscious strategies used by present-day youth to find their way in society. If we unite the activities which flow from this with those which correspond to what we have defined as the *realism of youth* and the *discontinuous* view of social time and space, it is clear that we are faced with a socially critical generation which tends to behave in very versatile and fragmentary ways when it comes into contact with society. This should indicate the extent to which the young generation maintains a constant opposition, although in an oblique way, to those things which it finds unjustified, unjust or absurd.

Affirmative discourse

The critical discourse of youth faced with the society in which they live is, as the material we have collected shows, more forceful, precise, highly elaborated and conceptualized than the positive discourse. By positive discourse we mean the things they wish for and desire, the society they dream about, and in which they would like to live. Young people define more clearly the things that they do not like and reject than those which they seek and desire. Perhaps this is the case for the rest of us too, but it is more obvious in their case because they are more open about it and have not imbibed the positive global view of the possible transformation of society which is current in our culture. They do not believe in the arrival of a brotherly or a sisterly classless society, nor in the realization of the Kingdom of God on earth, nor in the triumph of reason and technology over irrationality and disorder. Nevertheless, it is possible to sift from their conversation a number of selected details which indicate some of the conditions that they would like, or even dream about, for their own lives. The main ones have to do with work, the political framework and relations between the sexes.

The ideal as expressed by our young people, sometimes in constructed formulations, by others using metaphoric images with regard to a world that they conceive as being acceptable for themselves, would have the following characteristics. It would be a world of free and unconventional individuals, without fixed or immobile social positions which militate against change, versatility and continuous experimentation with life. It would be a world of individuals with control over their own destinies, oriented towards enjoyment and the security of the individual, but in no respect concerned to dominate others.

Describing these desired forms of life they consider that a suitable political framework to bring this about is democracy, which some define as 'the possibility of doing things', or 'the possibility, always capable of renewal, of being able to come and go, sing, play . . .' All of them believe that there is no longer any point in becoming active in political parties as was the case in the period of the dictatorship. The extent to which they distance themselves from parties and trade unions is linked with their view that these stand for the adult world of negotiation and manipulation.

When these young people were asked how they would like to change the organization of society as it impinged upon their lives, and how these changes might be brought about, they were in favour of action which was precisely targeted for a specific end. They put their trust in actions arising from the spontaneous solidarity of individuals or groups emerging at the critical moment to deal with specific problems or to defend concrete interests, without finding it necessary to enrol themselves in organizations that they cannot control and whose dynamic is structurally conditioned. This is how they understand democracy and this explains their decision to take part in general elections. Voting for them means safeguarding that framework of liberty which is absolutely necessary for the development of their lives.

Another aspect of the ideal world or representation of the future that young people formulate has to do with their way of understanding work. They are not averse to the ideas of economic well-being, security and consumption, which they consider as absolute requirements if they are to be freely themselves and as a means of maximizing their enjoyment and ensuring a life of novel experiences. All these conditions imply the possibility and necessity of having a job. But they do not desire a world constructed merely around a kind of work which frustrates and alienates them and cuts off all possible development of the personal, emotional and aesthetic life of the worker. They would like to have a job which did not require them to get too involved in it and would allow them to develop their own life outside this work. In this sense, in the group discussions which provided the basis of our study, we scarcely ever encountered opinions advocating the ethic of a job well done; there was no advocacy of the work ethic, the connection between work and self-realization, and no emphasis on the aspect of service to community or activity which was socially useful.

In this respect it is important to emphasize the variation between the sexes. The girls, although critical in their attitude to the world of work, were more inclined to accept certain imperatives in order to secure a job which might finally enable them to be *independent with regard to adult society and the other sex*. However, we noted a discrepancy between the young women who were students and the young women from working-class backgrounds who had already had experience of work. The latter group did not agree with the student girls in their outright defence of work as a means to personal autonomy, or as a way of overcoming sexual discrimination.

When the 'us' is fragmented

In their critique of the adult world and its organization the image that young people have of the man/woman relationship is particularly important. Their experience of family life is still fresh, so the issue is highly charged emotionally. It is not an abstract and generic reference to man/woman, but 'my father', 'my mother'. In a specific and differentiated way they recognize a temporal cycle which is different for each of the two sexes, and which corresponds with the logic of a hierarchical system and exhibits the state of dependence and inequality of mothers in relation to fathers.

Faced with this situation one meets different opinions. The young women inveigh against this state of affairs in a more virulent and emotionally charged way and with greater profundity of analysis. The young women recognize their mothers in a description which sees them as women deprived of personal autonomy for whom only one form of life and self-realization is socially acceptable.

The attitude of the young women towards their mothers is made up equally of affection and a sense of frustration, and they reject them because they are bearers of a conservative ideology, a fatalistic view of destiny and the role of the woman, which they transmit to their daughters. The young men, on the other hand, place more emphasis on affection and do not seem to see them as mothers/women but only as their mothers. In spite of the situation in which they live, they also consider them to be happy and fulfilling themselves in their role.

In the course of the discussions in which this theme appeared, the young men ended by admitting that they could not imagine what the organization of their home would be like without their mothers, since the role that the mothers fulfilled represented the solution of all their everyday problems (clean clothes, food, etc.). In this sense, the regular functioning of the home was maintained with the complicity of their own sons. This different way of seeing is paralleled by modes of behaviour which are distinct for each of the two sexes. The distribution of tasks, the apportioning of roles and stereotypes which holds sway for each of the sexes in the adult world is reproduced and lived out every day inside the family. Carrying out domestic tasks is required of daughters and not sons. Family control and the enforcement of morality is different for each of the two sexes, especially with regard to sex. Parents quite arbitrarily envisage a different future for sons and daughters, which reproduces the unequal relationship through which they themselves have lived.

When these themes are discussed the generic 'us', through which young people feel themselves to be part of a united group, through which their own identity came into being, and which constituted 'their' world in opposition to the 'other' of adults, is fragmented into a female 'us'/masculine 'us', (young women/young men), which has more potential for conflict and is less unified than young people as a whole appear when viewed from outside. The discussions we had with young men and women became more violent and emotional on these matters. It is no longer a critique of 'others' who are distant and far off, but a dialogue which is personalized by being with someone who is opposite to you and with whom you share and live your present. In the discussions young women are the ones who raise their voices and defend, attack, and argue with greatest force.

It is a generally held view of both young men and women that the hierarchy and inequality between the sexes is not due to 'natural' or 'innate' causes, as certain ideologies transmitted by their parents would have it. They see this inequality between the sexes as a further example of the arbitrary order according to which the adult world is organized and upon which it justifies its own existence.

For both young men and young women, this division of roles is overcome in their own spaces, which we have defined using their own word 'atmosphere', which is their own territory, where they are defined according to their own criteria and free from the institutional imperatives of adults. In their 'atmosphere' there are no sexual differences and less inequality between the sexes, neither are there any classificatory stereotypes which constrict the free potentialities of the one or the other.

This way of living, which is unique to them, of encounter and equality, is what makes them believe that a change has occurred, perhaps the only one that they are able to note in society and one which is irreversible. In this field, the discourse of young people takes on an optimistic note. Abandoned to their own fate and with the possibility of constructing their own identity and their own world *they can* and they *are capable* of achieving a new set of relationships between the sexes. They are, in short, in some respects agents of change and can see it through to a finish.

When they speak of change in the relationships between the sexes, they always do so by making a comparison with the adult generation represented by their parents. They are aware that this change was begun by a generation which came between them and their parents, and they often refer to women in general, and the feminist movement in particular. For this reason they do not see themselves as the only innovators, but as a generation which has inherited the fruits of a movement which is still socially relevant.

Nevertheless, one topic comes up in the flux of discussion which is not so idyllic as the one mentioned above, but one which arouses mutual antagonisms, and involves an accusing note which calls to mind a more stark reality: on the one hand, there is the reality which the young people are apparently constructing in their own world, and on the other, there is *complicity* with the imperatives of the institutions in which they live by necessity. The young women hold it against the young men that, despite their criticisms of adult social organization, they have taken advantage of conditions which have been favourable for them and they benefit from a wider range of opportunity in education, work, and freedom of movement, especially within the family unit.

The young women say that the young men do not think twice about making the most of these advantageous conditions. In particular, they carry over into their own lives the same prejudices as the adult generation, demanding, perhaps unconsciously, that young women should occupy the same positions as their mothers. In this way, they undervalue the young women's potential and will to freedom because, in short, they think that women should revolve around them.

For their part, young men consider that both they and young women are victims of a long-term educational process which gives them unequal positions in society, with different duties being imposed upon each sex. They add that, despite the criticisms expressed by the young women, they adapt themselves to the pre-established role which is in fact to their benefit because society has reserved for them, the young men, the toughest life (productive work, competition, the need continually to show their worth); moreover, they say, it is the young women who are the first to demand that the situation should remain so.

This conflict causes us to reflect upon the extent to which these young people have taken on board the values of adult society and to note a characteristic that is omnipresent in their conversation, in all the information gathered and studied: *ambivalence*. This may have been conditioned by the attitude that we have described as 'youthful realism', which indicates a tendency to accept the ground rules which operate in those spheres and institutionalized spaces in which they live.

This ambivalence and contradiction is manifest, on the one hand, in the images of the future which seem to guide their lives and which enable them to take a critical attitude in opposition to society; and on the other in pessimism and fatalism. Expressions such as the ones that follow occur very often in the material collected:

> The generation of '68 attempted to change many things, but what they really showed us was how to be integrated into the system

> Life is a bunch of frustrations and when we are as frustrated as our parents, which will be very soon, we shall think the same as them

> We are saying these things now, but we shall end up jumping through the hoop.

In short, the young people of Madrid see themselves as bearers of a critical discourse, of attitudes and styles which are different from those of the adult world. But they also believe that this will be a short-lived identity, a passing phase, hardly defensible in the future, because inexorably, sooner or later they will take their place in the institutionalized spaces and times which they do not believe they can change.

Notes

1 Studies of 'The Mores and Morality of Youth in Urban Madrid' by R. Aparicio, J. Benavides, V. Maquieira, J.M. Marinas, C. Thiebaut, A. Tornos, financed by the Ministerio de Cultura, Madrid, 1982; and 'Emergent Values of Young People and the Education System', by R. Aparicio, J. Benavides, V. Maquieira, J.M. Marinas, C. Thiebaut, A. Tornos, financed by the Instituto Ciencias de la Educacion de la Universidad Complutense, Madrid, 1983.
2 In Spanish there are special words for boys and girls in their teens.

PART TWO

ROUTES TO ILLEGALITY

3

A typology of the life and work styles of 'heroin-prostitutes'

From a male career model to a feminized career model

Maria Blom and Ton van den Berg

In 1981 and 1982 we carried out an ethnographic research project on the subculture of 'heroin-prostitution'. The study was commissioned by the Mr A. de Graafstichting, a Dutch national institution for documentation, research, information and advice in the field of prostitution. The underlying motive for this research was the question why girls did not participate in treatment programmes as frequently as boys.

Between November 1981 and September 1982 we did fieldwork in the red-light district (the streetwalking areas and heroin markets) of Amsterdam in order to record 'the subculture of heroin-prostitution': the milieu of addicted prostitutes, pimps, dealers, hotel-keepers, etc. Part of the original research plan was to collect a number of life histories in order to obtain material on the process of becoming a prostitute. We also wanted to study the prostitutes' 'subculture'.

Because heroin-prostitution is a delicate subject in relation to the outside 'respectable world', we felt we would have to be very careful in building up research relationships in the field. We did not go into the field from an institutional base first of all because the question we were asking was why so many girls, relatively speaking, were invisible as far as institutions and treatment programmes are concerned. Moreover, heroin-prostitutes who do contact institutions do not always report that they are 'working', as they themselves call it. We preferred to make contacts in the street with girls who were visibly 'working and using'. One of the researchers had access to the heroin-and-prostitution world via his contact with a key figure, a former pimp and dealer high up in the street-life hierarchy, but now a heroin user in an ever-declining position in this world. This person proved to be very useful in making contacts with other key figures in the business. These key figures, or sponsors – a hotel-keeper, an ex-hotel-keeper, and the owner of a black bar close to the heroin market – gave us passive protection. We were able to work as researchers from then on. The combination of a male and a female researcher worked well: we were seen as 'the couple who want to know everything', a non-threatening label. As long as we were not police or journalists, it seemed to be alright.

The interviews were carried out in a room (our 'field station') close to the streetwalking areas. In the course of the fieldwork it gradually appeared that most respondents were willing to tell us their personal histories. In excess of our original expectations, the number of respondents grew to 59, each giving interviews lasting from one to three hours.

This unanticipated quantity of material encouraged a shift in our theoretical perspective: from an ethnographic towards a biographical (developmental) design. Moreover, as we went along the 'subculture' hypothesis had to be dropped: it could not account for the diversity we discovered. Instead the scene appeared to be a 'wild' prostitution *market* in which the street is the lowest level of a larger prostitution structure with specific market mechanisms. In large part the street market takes its character from non-professional prostitutes (heroin users). This finding was confirmed by two-and-a-half months field observations in Rotterdam.

Problems with applying a male career model to prostitution

The different life and work styles which we observed and which the girls reported are connected with different 'routes' leading to the same street-market. An examination of these routes reveals a major distinction between these life and work styles, depending on whether the girls appear at the street level either as prostitutes who use heroin or as heroin users who prostitute themselves. We will return to this distinction later on.

The original theoretical basis of our career model was borrowed from a Dutch research project (Janssen and Swierstra, 1982) on 80 male heroin users. This model is based on the assumption that people have valid reasons for using heroin; reasons that are derived from participation in 'youth subcultures'. The model suggests that at first heroin use is a typical activity of peer groups which can themselves be seen as exemplifying social-class-related youth cultures. The predominant pattern in this model involves a career from a starting position (class and family background) to a transitory position (adolescence) to a present position and perspective within the heroin structure (differentiated into items like structural relations outside the heroin world, present competences, self-image, social vision and future perspective). Janssen and Swierstra (1982) presented their data as a descriptive typology of heroin users, followed by prototypical case histories.

Our female respondents, however, cannot be fitted into this male career model and in many respects they deviate from the predominant pattern. First, females are not as class-loyal in their participation in youth cultures as males are. Some girls in our sample had made a dramatic descent in class through romantic relations. In most cases the girls' parents were separated, so the social class of their fathers (the usual mode of reckoning in sociology) was of little relevance. Furthermore, a number of respondents can be seen as having made a 'false start', a term used by us for youngsters from all social classes whose family situation has not allowed a balanced development of emotional and caring relationships, because of alcoholism, violence, incestuous approaches and so on.

For most of the girls, beginning to take heroin seemed rather to be a natural step in a romantic relationship with a heroin user who was probably from a different youth subculture. The girls' 'opportunity structures' were personified by their lovers.

On the subcultural level, females more or less disappear in masculine subcultures; most participate in male-dominated subcultures only indirectly, through their partners. They derive their positions and perspectives from their partners in male-constructed subcultural discourses. Consequently a break-up with a partner results in an erosion of their former identification with the partner's subculture and its discourse.

Faced by our inability to classify female biographies into a male career model, we had to make a second shift in theoretical perspective. The male model had to be feminized. First, it had to be adjusted to take into account specifically female career transitions. Secondly, it had to take into account the implications of sex-role performance in youth cultures (McRobbie and Garber, 1976) especially those of ethnic minorities.

A major characteristic of female biographies and careers is that most career transitions are made because of personal relationships with lovers and 'best friends'. For girls, personal relations are a catalyst for a change in both position and perspective on the surrounding world, while subcultural experiences play a more or less subordinate role. This came out very strongly in our interviews.

In order to bring some order into our data about the quality of the relationships with their boyfriends which the girls reported, we established a typology of sex-role performance. There appeared to be two dimensions along which the relationships varied: self-determination/subordination and instrumental/romantic associations of sexuality (see also Davis, 1937).

Three variables – family of origin, personal affiliation, and style of sex-role adopted – enabled us to construct a typology of heroin-prostitutes which explains their differing routes into heroin-prostitution and their responses to different kinds of treatment programme. Our more complex alternative model is thus based on the girls' positions and orientations as well as their life experiences. This model explains the differing views of the girls towards treatment programmes, and also why many heroin-prostitutes steer clear of them. It is not surprising that when male career models are used to 'explain' these young women their responses to treatment appear totally arbitrary!

We constructed five different types of heroin-prostitutes to fit the 59 girls and women whom we interviewed in the course of our fieldwork. These types and the number interviewed were:

- the professional prostitute (13);
- the occasional prostitute (5);
- the romantic heroin user (14);
- the loyal heroin user (whose career was affected by a 'best friend' rather than a lover) (7);
- the enlightened romantic heroin user (17).

Three interviews could not be used, in one case because of doubts about validity, and in two cases because of bad tape quality.

The professional prostitute: heroin as a downfall

Girls in this category typically come from lower-class backgrounds where the female style is that of *extreme subordination* to men. Their starting position in life is in marginal social milieux. Often these girls had been given contradictory information and messages by their parents about what constituted a desirable sex-role performance. In most cases the affective ties between the girls and their families were disturbed because of divorce or alcoholism; in a few cases incest was reported. Some parents had apparently been too rigid, others too lax in their discipline. The girls reported that they saw valid reasons for running away from their home situation. They did so at an early age (12–14 years old) and consequently most of the girls had not received the minimum required schooling.

The runaways concerned their parents not least because they were so young and typically became involved in sexual relationships through which they arrived at their inevitable destination as a 'man's woman' prematurely (too soon, that is, according to prevalent standards of female behaviour). Typically again for these girls, their parents (or the law) had sought professional aid to take over the task of education. The girls were taken into care, where education was arranged strictly in accordance with a traditional female role model; but while they were there they built up a history of running away. In their minds these girls had already made the transition from a position as girl and daughter into that of a 'man's woman' – the only social space available to them. Once they had tasted the (relative) freedom of being treated as a woman and not as a child, they said they were not controllable any more. The subcultural discourse inside the child-care institutions, a true 'bedroom-culture' which concentrated on subjects like romance and running away, reinforced the validity of their reasons for running away. 'Safe' addresses of places to go to were exchanged inside. These girls eventually completed their career transition via romantic relationships with older boyfriends, in many cases from ethnic minorities, and landed up in extremely masculine, deviant sub-cultures.

Through subcultural connections the boyfriends of these girls had an entrée to the world of prostitution. Depending on the position of their boyfriend in the milieu the girls started either on a high or a middle level in the prostitution structure. The main reason for prostitution was a financial one; but another aspect of the career transition into prostitution was, paradoxically, a romantic one. The girls started to work as prostitutes in the context of a discourse of extreme subordination to their man, and they did so out of love for him. They said that by using their femininity as a commodity they pleased their lover. In this way they were able to re-translate their behaviour into a romantic perspective (Brake, 1980). Prostitution was the price of their relationship. Their men could be seen as pimps, able to handle the situation and to direct the romance into prostitution without losing their girlfriends (James, 1978). Gradually the girls learned from other people and from experiences in their work environment to see prostitution as a profession, with rules which were necessary to protect the trade.

Heroin entered the lives of these girls via the structural overlap between the world of heroin use and the world of prostitution. Heroin was either part of the girls' working environment or part of the subculture in which they were temporarily included via their man.

The time the girls started to use heroin usually coincided with the 'bankruptcy' of their romantic relationship. In most cases the man did not accept heroin use by his woman, even if he himself was using it. Sometimes new relationships followed, with men in lower status positions in the street culture. However, the longer the girl was using, the less she could afford to be dependent. Because of their heroin use, these prostitutes were eventually driven out of their professional working environment and had to retreat to the street-market. This was the situation of the girls when we interviewed them, but these *professional prostitutes* still held on to their professionalism in their work style and had a strong dislike for the non-professionals who damage their trade by working cut-price on the same street-market.

In general, the perspective of the 'professional prostitute' about heroin is that heroin is a weakness. She finds it hard to accept her addiction, whereas she has accepted without difficulty her life-style as a prostitute.

The occasional prostitute: heroin as a trap

The starting position of the girls of this type whom we interviewed was in the (lower) middle classes. Their female style was one of *relative self-determination*. Although broken homes were reported, this type of girl did not refer to them as an important factor in her career towards heroin-prostitution.

The parents of these girls too did not, or were not able to, make their discipline very effective. Some of them thought there was nothing wrong with a certain degree of freedom for their daughters. It fitted their image of a female style of self-determination. In this ambience the girls had enough space for experimental behaviour without being questioned. They developed a life-style of going out as an everyday activity which pushed school or work into the background. Fashionable clothes, hashish, and sometimes cocaine, were part of this subcultural life-style, to which they were linked both through girlfriends and through flirtations with boys. Romance was not yet a very serious subject for these girls. Their friendships with their best friends were still intimate and protective. The 'swinging' life-style they were involved in was, however, too expensive, given the money they actually had. Extra money had to be earned somehow.

Prostitution, first seriously considered as a possibility by a best friend, provided the solution. Typically the use of sexuality for non-sexual aims (Davis, 1937) was regarded as legitimate by these best friends, and so moral inhibitions could be set aside without too much difficulty. In the discourse between these girlfriends prostitution was typically regarded as an occasional and short-term affair about which nobody else in their personal environment needed to know anything. The girls started to work in the street because they could go there relatively unnoticed. They did not want to identify themselves with professional prostitution and did not see themselves as prostitutes. Their market value was high: they were new and young. The money earned with prostitution enabled them to develop an independent material status which in the context of their overall life-style fitted well with the female style of self-determination to which their families had predisposed them. This contrasts with the subordination experienced by the professional group at the same age and career stage.

Once again, however, the structural overlap of the prostitution and heroin worlds brought the girls into contact with heroin. In some cases together with, in others introduced by, the best friend, they first tried heroin after work as a prostitute. Soon heroin became connected with 'working': it made 'working' a lot easier. The spiral of 'working and using' brought them into full-time prostitution. In this phase of their career, girls of this 'occasional' type of heroin-prostitute got into steady relationships with boyfriends they had met in places where their subcultural life-style flourished: mainly in coffee shops and discos. The boyfriends were from varied ethnic groups, white as well as black, and roughly from the same class background as the girls. Their attitudes towards females were moderately traditional. In this situation romance sometimes worked the other way around: most of these boyfriends started their own heroin use via their girlfriend.

At the time of interview, when they were already heroin-prostitutes, these girls typically were trying to retain their female style of self-determination and economic independence, at least to a limited extent. They wanted to hold on to a separate economic identity; when the boyfriend was unable to earn enough money for his own habit they would support him, but they did not want to be a permanent breadwinner for two.

As long as prostitution provided them with enough money, these girls did not see working as a problem and could survive relatively comfortably in the heroin-prostitution milieu. When the girls in our study did kick their habit for a while, the danger of recidivism was hidden by working from time to time in order to get some money. For these girls 'working' has become so entwined with using that it is hard to stay away from heroin at the place of work.

The way the occasional prostitute sees prostitution and heroin is ambivalent. Her work-style has become semi-professional but she does not want to identify herself with the world of prostitution nor does she want to see herself as a real junkie who goes to extremes in the use of drugs.

The romantic heroin user: prostitution in a caring perspective

This type of heroin-prostitute can also be characterized by her female style of *subordination*. Traditional sex-role aspirations are a matter of course in the lower and lower-middle classes into which these girls were born.

The homes from which these girls came were characterized by alcoholism, violence and neglect. Being female, a structural change of position could only be attained by these girls if they searched for and found 'the right man' with whom a family of their own could be started. Their schooling and their jobs were attuned to this sole end.

A lot of girls of this type also ran away from home when their first serious romance began. These first boyfriends were typically oriented to a subcultural life-style in which the use of drugs was a central activity. Most of the boyfriends were heroin users before they met the girls, but (with a few exceptions) these boys as yet had no links with the world of prostitution. The kind of romantic relations that the girls developed can best be described as 'harmonious inequality': the position of subordination suited the girls as a clear and familiar one.

As in the case of those who became professional prostitutes, running away from home led to a doomed attempt at rehabilitation on the part of the authorities by subjecting the girls to care orders. The girls, of course, ran straight back to their boyfriends again. But unlike those who became professionals they did not get involved in the opportunity structure of prostitution, since they did not have to use their sexuality to secure 'a safe place' to spend the night. For these girls sexuality is connected only with romance and, in the back of their minds, with the stability of their position as a 'man's woman'.

For the romantic heroin user the heroin opportunity structure is personified by her lover: she derives valid reasons for heroin use from her romantic relationship. Heroin will unite her more than before with her boyfriend. Sometimes a process of isolation from the respectable world because of her romance with a heroin user has preceded and facilitated this step; sometimes, however, heroin was tried without premeditation.

At first the boyfriends paid for the heroin. In a few cases the girls co-operated with them (albeit from a subordinate position) in illegal activities, but most of the girls whom we classified in this way said they stayed in the background rather passively. However, when times got hard, when their joint income decreased while more heroin was needed, new strategies had to be developed to enable the couple to survive as heroin users.

Again, as in almost every case, prostitution was thought of because of the structural overlap of the heroin and the prostitution worlds. The girls knew the possibilities from what they saw in their daily environment and from contacts with other girls on the heroin market. After having gone through several economic crises, prostitution eventually became an acceptable alternative for these girls. Most of them started without any knowledge of the work, whether they began on their own initiative or at the instigation of their boyfriend. Discursively and psychologically the girls had been able to build prostitution into their relationships by shifting from a romantic to a caring perspective. The money, they say, keeps their boyfriend from dangerous activities and enables them to bind him closer to them.

In the course of their career as heroin-prostitutes some girls have experienced a 'bankruptcy' of the romantic relationship for a variety of reasons: the pressure of the life-style; rejection by the boyfriend because of her very action in starting work as a prostitute; or because they discovered that they were being pimped after all. Most girls do not regard their boyfriends as pimps, however, particularly when they themselves have taken the initiative in taking up prostitution. They see their present situation as a logical consequence of heroin use which leaves them no other alternative. Besides, their boyfriends do not behave like pimps.

In the course of her career as a heroin-prostitute the typical romantic heroin user comes to see prostitution as a means of survival. Over time, her work-style develops from an amateur to a semi-professional style. With support in their immediate environment (boyfriends) and a still more or less romantic perspective on heroin use, these girls have not lost their self-respect because of being heroin-prostitutes. As they see it, to use heroin is no shame and to work as a prostitute is the only way to sustain the habit. Then again, prostitution does not cause any harm to the outside world, so why is everybody so concerned?

A best-friend route towards heroin use: heroin and prostitution as a downfall

Typically these heroin-prostitutes started life in the (lower) middle class. Their female style is one of *relative self-determination*. The girls we classified in this way interpreted their family situations variously in ways ranging from problematic to normal; in most cases the situation had not led to these girls running away from home.

In conversation all these girls described an intimate relationship with a 'best friend' during adolescence. In some cases, this girlfriend was regarded as the only person worthy of their affection. These best friends were often older, more experienced, and had a wider range of social contacts. The best friends of the girls in our sample had all become involved in a drug subculture themselves as a result of a romantic relationship, and had started to use heroin. They invited their girlfriends to try heroin as well. The girls accepted the invitation, sometimes out of curiosity, sometimes, as they expressed it, because they had nothing to lose except their girlfriend. Looking back at that moment of entry into the heroin world this type of heroin-prostitute often says she was more or less talked into heroin use by her girlfriend. In that respect she differs from the (enlightened) romantic heroin user who defends her connection – her boyfriend.

Once inside the heroin world these girls have not managed to settle into a position that they experience as relatively safe, that is in a romantic relationship with a male heroin user. It seems as if from the moment these girls realized the consequences of heroin use, they felt they had chosen the wrong path; but by then they were unable to turn back. This ambivalence towards heroin use is visible all through their careers.

Heroin-prostitutes who had begun their careers in this way also had a romantic view of sexuality. However, they tended to concentrate their romantic feelings on men they met outside the heroin world. Without a settled position inside the heroin world, an image of the road out of it was kept open, via a romantic relationship with a non-user. Some of the girls had managed to stay away from heroin that way for a considerable period, but went back to heroin use after a collapse of the relationship.

These girl heroin users have always thought of prostitution as the lowest they could possibly sink and have tried to delay this step as long as possible. Their middle-class backgrounds have enabled them to develop alternative competences: some girls were able to stick to their (legal) job for a while; others had learned illegal trades as a result of short-term alliances with other heroin users. At a certain point in their career, however, these girls turned to prostitution: circumstances slowly broke down their resistance to using their sexuality as a commodity. The entry into prostitution was often facilitated through a girlfriend, who was already 'ahead' of them in that respect. Prostitution led them quickly into a vicious circle of 'using and working': heroin is unbuyable without prostitution and prostitution is unbearable without heroin.

This interconnection between heroin and prostitution applied to all the heroin-prostitutes we interviewed, and especially so to those who had not been able to accept the use of their sexuality for non-sexual aims. This type of girl gets no approval from any significant person in her environment. Since in her case heroin does not have a symbolic reference to romance, she has more difficulty in developing a personal theory which can justify her life-style as a heroin-prostitute. Her continuous ambivalence towards heroin makes it difficult to find an excuse for the addiction itself. Some of the girls in this category did have affairs with heroin users in the course of their careers as heroin-prostitutes. If possible, they stopped working; if not, they hardly ever shared their incomes with their partners. In their present situation and with this ambivalent orientation these girls are unable to cope with the fact of their prostitution: their work-style is still non-professional.

This kind of heroin-prostitute is a frequent user of treatment programmes, 'high barrier' programmes included, but after having tried and failed several times such a girl may feel she is a failure on all fronts; these girls feel this more than any other type of heroin-prostitute.

The enlightened romantic heroin user: prostitution as a downfall

The heroin-prostitutes that we classified this way were typically *emancipated and self-determining*, having had an emancipatory middle-class education. Although their families could have supported them during higher education most of the girls did not finish school: a premature break with their home environment prevented this. They reported parental separation or situations of serious conflict, which they themselves saw as part of the reason for their leaving home. Besides these 'push factors', rebellion against the total social order as represented by their parents was for them a valid enough reason for a break from the family. This 'rebellion' was personified in the choice of a boyfriend who participated in the youth subculture. With two exceptions, none of these girls was sent into care. Evidently such institutions do not cater for those from the middle classes.

In tune with the spirit of the times, the girls got acquainted with different subcultures, derived from middle-class discourses (hippies, punks) mixed with lower-class elements. The sex-role performance in these subcultures can be characterized as moderately masculine. The girls got acquainted with the discourse and settled into the subculture because of their romantic attachments, and were able to adapt to the subculture as females presenting themselves as relatively self-determining. But this career transition via a romantic relationship did not mean that now they had reached their destination. Other options stayed open at this stage apart from simply 'being a woman'. However, their relations with men did involve a total way of life: the girls made a total commitment to romance within a total subcultural life-style. In many cases their first big love was a man from a different social economic background from their own.

Typically these girls' partners were either beginners as heroin users, not yet entangled in the problems that are consequent upon addiction, or they went hand in hand with their girlfriend over the threshold towards first heroin use as a result of the man's subcultural connections with the heroin world, which became their joint 'heroin opportunity structure'. The period of starting to use heroin was experienced as a double honeymoon: the euphoria of love combined with the euphoria of heroin. For the romantic heroin users the romantic relation with their lover was an encouragement to set aside emerging doubts about the danger of heroin.

The use of their basic identity, their femininity, for money, was the very last possibility to which these girls resorted in order to get heroin. Before that crucial change in position most girls had learned quite a lot of survival strategies. They made the career transition into prostitution only when all other possibilities such as dealing, burglary and fencing, which they had learned either from their boyfriend or by now through their own subcultural contacts, had failed and neither they nor their boyfriends were able any longer to provide the necessary money for a growing addiction. This type of heroin-prostitute began her trade directly at street-market level, without any prior knowledge of the business.

The career transition into prostitution was a downfall in the eyes of both the girls and their boyfriends. The girl had to adjust her romantic perspective on love and learn to use her sexuality for non-sexual aims; the man, if he knew, had to accept his status as a prostitute's boyfriend. Both had difficulty in coping with it. Prostitution was used to balance the budget; as soon as other possibilities were available, prostitution was stopped. For most of these girls at a certain point in their career as heroin-prostitutes, the romantic relationship ended or became empty due either to circumstances related to drug use (especially cocaine) or to the experienced inequality between the partners because of their differences in social background (the girls were usually the ones who broke up relations because of this). Afterwards the girls chose to operate as prostitutes independently and when they were independent, as at the time of interview, they dealt with love on a part-time basis or put it aside for a drugless future.

Given their present position and self-image, the work-style of this type of heroin-prostitute is non-professional. These girls have not managed adequately to translate their femininity into prostitution. In their work they undercut the market price and use sexual techniques in a way that belongs in a romantic setting rather than in a professional one. In the meantime they keep looking for an alternative.

As prostitutes these girls do not accept themselves: as heroin users they still see valid reasons for drug use in the societal context they live in, which has worsened because of the spiral of 'using and working'.

The success and failure of treatment programmes

These five types of young women, with different approaches to themselves, to prostitution and to drug use, not surprisingly also have quite different views about drug treatment programmes, and use them to a varying extent.

For professional prostitutes, participation in drug rehabilitation programmes is minimal, paradoxically because they see drug use as a weakness. Drug rehabilitation programmes are meant for 'junkies', they say, whereas these young heroin-prostitutes see themselves first and foremost as prostitutes and not as 'junkies'. So long as their professional competence is adequate to sustain their habit, they do not feel the need for help. A kind of pride is involved. Moreover, it will be remembered that this group of women had experience of being in care as children, and this past contact with official institutions has made them reluctant to repeat the experience. To emphasize this reluctance further, most of these girls said they were afraid of a double addiction if they used methadone as a substitute for heroin. They derived this point of view from their association with men from ethnic minorities. Finally, they saw no point since, as professionals, they would continue to work anyway.

The distance which the occasional prostitutes maintained from drug rehabilitation programmes was more remarkable. They no more wanted to be identified as 'real junkies' than as 'real prostitutes'. From time to time one of them might kick her habit, but she would appear in the street again to make some 'occasional' extra money and again find out that for her this had become impossible without heroin. For these self-determining young women, admitting addiction involved a loss of valued independence, and going on a treatment programme involved admission of addiction.

Romantic heroin users were, in some cases, willing to give drug-rehabilitation programmes a try, provided they offered unconditional help. They were willing to use methadone maintenance programmes to ease the burden of their life-style, working full time as a prostitute every single day. Such programmes enabled them to hoard black market methadone for the heroin supply crises which inevitably occur from time to time. They are better able to care for the needs of their menfolk, in this way. But of course, 'high barrier' programmes are ineffective with these girls for whom heroin use is not seen as shameful, the only problem being to finance it.

'Loyal' users, for whom prostitution was a personal downfall and shame, were the least adjusted to their lives as heroin-prostitutes and oriented to a dream of a male saviour beyond the confines of the world of the prostitute–user. So these girls were frequent users of treatment programmes, including high barrier ones. Plainly, those for whom the programmes worked would not have been in our sample; but for the girls we spoke to who had tried and failed several times to kick the heroin habit the experience of failure on the programme left them with no identity props. Such girls could feel that they were failures on all fronts; certainly they felt this more than any other type of heroin-prostitute.

Finally, the enlightened romantics saw no need either to kick their habit or to change their life-style so long as they were living with a partner. Even afterwards when they are operating independently heroin retains a symbolic value related to their romantic period in a user subculture. Heroin is still thought of as a pleasurable drug: only the consequences are terrible. The symbolic meaning of heroin wears off slowly, but traces remained in the girls we spoke to. In any case, they say, it is society which creates the problems that make people want to use drugs.

Like the 'pure romantics', enlightened romantics use rehabilitation centres and methadone programmes not to kick but mainly to sustain the drug habit. In the main these girls do not want to change their life-styles; therefore they do not want to make use of high barrier programmes. Furthermore, they say, social workers are prejudiced and treat all junkies alike: for these girls, their individuality is at stake.

This analysis shows very clearly why the available treatment programmes largely fail especially at the beginnings of the girls' careers as heroin-prostitutes. These programmes are not geared in any precise way to the girls' life experiences or to their specific needs as they understand them. Treatment programmes should take into account the specific reasons for drug use among girls and young women, the specific relationships that sustain their habit, or the specific (and very limited) alternative life-style opportunities open to them.

We have tried to reveal the specific rationalities of the heroin-prostitutes we spoke to, and also the *contingence* of their life chances. Two of the five groups of girls came into their present situation primarily because of particular girlfriends (the occasional and loyal groups). For two other groups (the professionals and the romantics) it can truly be said that they got into their present situation because of their relationships with men. For the last group there was no clear pattern about first use: what was clear, however, was that the enlightened romantics were looking to men as their only chance of a way out.

4

Young women prostitutes in Bilbao

A description and an interpretation

Rosa Andrieu-Sanz and Karmele Vasquez-Anton

Whenever prostitution is discussed in everyday situations the stereotype of sleazy night-life is evoked, as if prostitutes spent all their time slinking along walls wearing mini-skirts and cloying perfume. The discussions themselves, in Spain at least, tend to be moralistic or to offer morbid accounts of the way of life of these women, supporting the moralizing theme by 'demonstrating' that the wages of sin are death.

All this is far removed from the legal and political discussions of prostitution in Spain, from liberal attempts to abolish repressive legislation dating from the Franco era to some feminist led demands that prostitutes should receive the full range of social rights such as retirement pensions, unemployment and sickness benefits, and the right to form trade unions (Andrieu-Sanz and Vasquez-Anton, 1987).[1]

None the less, the mythologies and the moralizings persist; not by chance, in our view, but because they are integral to the phenomenon of prostitution itself. For prostitution, in its social meaning and function, is not a job like any other. Prostitutes, we argue, exist precisely and essentially as the counter-face of the good woman. The normalization of prostitution would undermine this essential social function. Put another way, prostitutes are constitutive of the good woman, and the good woman is constitutive of prostitution. Prostitution exists as a permanent but changing shadow or mirror image of the ideal. Thus if prostitution were normalized it would not, qua prostitution, exist. Before we explore these theoretical points further we would like to present the results of our own sociological study of the reality of the prostitute's world. At least in this way some of the mythologies can be undermined. For our observations reveal that, in Bilbao at least, there is not one world of prostitution but three or four, and that prostitution itself

---

This chapter was translated from the Spanish by D.E. Hanson.

may have quite a different place in the lives and identities of the various women who practise it. Although our study was not longitudinal, the biographies of the women we interviewed suggest that economic and cultural changes have affected both women's attitudes and women's opportunity structures giving rise to new ways of being a prostitute and to changes in the structure of prostitution itself.

The Bilbao study

In 1984 and 1985 we carried out a study of prostitution in Bilbao which was financed by the Instituto de la Mujer (Institute for Women, Ministry of Culture). We wanted to interpret the phenomenon of prostitution as it exists in Spain, a society in transition from a traditional world to a new consumer society. We wanted information both about the daily lives of prostitutes and about the systems of ideas which give meaning to their lived experiences as women and as prostitutes. Plainly a qualitative methodology was called for, and the techniques we chose were observation and interviews in depth. The observations were carried out first, and the interviews later after we had identified the women.

Observation was carried out in three areas which we felt would exemplify the range of social, economic and cultural conditions which provide the frameworks for prostitution. The areas were as follows.

1 The ghetto or 'Chinatown', an area which is clearly demarcated and very impoverished; here prostitution takes place in the street.
2 A working-class area on the fringes of Chinatown, which has specific sites for prostitution such as clubs and massage parlours. There are, in fact, several areas like this, characterized by low income levels, in peripheral parts of the city.
3 The prosperous central area where, we discovered, prostitution is carried out discreetly in clubs and discothèques.

In our observations we tried to be both systematic and flexible. We constructed a careful timetable so that we would be sure to collect for each zone a full description of a working day and a holiday. The timetable was:

mornings	9 a.m.–10 a.m.	12 noon–1 p.m.
afternoons	4 p.m.–5 p.m.	7 p.m.–8 p.m.
nights	10 p.m.–1 a.m.	1 a.m.–4 a.m.

Each spell of observation took place on a different day, so there were enough variations for us to feel confident in our generalizations. In all, we observed for a total of 80 hours.

In our field diaries we tried to record everything in the sequence in which it occurred since we were interested in constructing records of the situations which define the act of prostitution. Thus we recorded both very concrete behavioural data (which were much easier to manage when it came to the analysis) and our own subjective impressions of the general atmosphere, to help us situate the events we observed in a more general context. We have records of our impressions of the area; of the sex, age, and general appearance of the people in the area and of the kinds of things they did which are not (at the level of observation) connected with prostitution; and, finally, of the elements which together define an act as prostitution in a concrete setting.

We cannot report these observations in detail here, although they underpin the analysis. We have tried to put them together in a generalized way, based on our interview material, to give English-speaking readers an overview of our results (Vasquez and Andrieu, 1986).

We used our in-depth interviews with fifteen prostitutes to give us a more complete picture of their everyday lives, having chosen women on the basis of our observations of the different forms of activity. Six of the women we interviewed were under 21 years old, and the others gave us information about their experiences as girls and teenagers, so our data are relevant to this book.

The themes and questions which we wished to cover in the interview were not dealt with in a prearranged order but rather followed the natural rhythm of the conversation so that the interviewer could pass freely from one topic to another. Furthermore, we asked open-ended questions. By using this method we not only collected the women's views on the topics of interest to us, in order to relate their experiences to our own conceptual classifications, but also the flow of the conversation itself. The substantive matters that the women wanted to discuss also gave us information about their cognitive schemas and conceptual systems, as well as some idea as to how much knowledge they actually had of the themes we wanted to deal with. In telling us their life stories the women also gave us information about their implicit models of prostitution and woman-hood. In addition, of course, we collected more objective data about their age, civil status, place of origin and residence, income, level of education and so on, and also about the structure, content and context of the women's everyday lives. The interviews were recorded, since we considered the women's choice of language to be so important.

Modes of prostitution of young women

The three areas we worked in more or less corresponded to the distinct cultural modes of prostitution which we identified, although two different styles of prostitution could be observed in Chinatown. Younger women, with whom this chapter is particularly concerned, were found in each of the areas.

The traditional 'red-light district' for Bilbao is Chinatown, an extremely impoverished area where prostitution appears to be the axis around which the entire everyday life of the community revolves. Here soliciting takes place publicly in the street, and it is easy for the external observer to identify both the prostitute and the client by their appearance and behaviour. It is clear that the women are offering sex for sale, and the transaction is open and businesslike. The street is treated as a private place for this purpose, and there is no personal relationship whatever between the prostitute and her client.

The poverty of the area and of the women epitomizes the isolation and marginalization of both prostitutes and prostitution in traditional society and, indeed, many of the older women participating in this traditional form of prostitution became prostitutes because of just such a rejection by their families and the traditional world, possibly after bearing an illegitimate child. The life of these women revolves around the fact of prostitution: their world of relationships as they described it to us is restricted to people connected with the act of prostitution such as pimp, client and female companions.

This restricted life-style is also found among the girls and younger women of this subtype. It must be said that younger women are a minority among these traditional prostitutes. Most of them are daughters of prostitutes or young gypsies from families that are themselves marginal. They have grown up in Chinatown and adopted ways of thinking about prostitution which are usual there. Being a prostitute affects every aspect of the lives of these younger women, as of the older ones; it is the essence of their self-identity. Even here, however, in this deeply embedded traditional culture, the younger women now have a varied range of attitudes to motherhood, sexuality, salaried work and the family, despite the fact that they routinely associate sexuality with money. Now that the influence of religion has declined, maybe they are able to see new possibilities for women.

This same 'twilight zone' of Chinatown has other elements in its infrastructure which are associated with the second subtype of prostitution to be found there. A new reality now firmly established there is the cycle of drugs–prostitution–delinquency. Younger prostitutes in this area are usually part of this cycle, rather than traditional prostitutes in the sense described above. They are young heroin addicts and their world is principally one of drugs. It is around drugs, rather than prostitution, that they structure their everyday lives and their personal relationships; it is on the basis of drug use that they construct their self-identity. Prostitution is of secondary importance to them, being no more than a source of income which is necessary if they are to continue their drug use. They take to prostitution when their need for heroin increases beyond what their meagre wages allow, their jobs always being those which require little or no qualifications. Typically, the girls are from immigrant working-class families.

These girls, as they presented themselves to us in conversation, are characterized by a total rejection of the traditional way of life, and by a wish to escape from the future society offers an immigrant, unqualified, working-class girl. Their individual escape route is heroin. Any means which leads to this end, including prostitution, is deemed to be good.

Concealed prostitution occurs in the clubs in working-class and peripheral areas, and in American bars and massage parlours in the centre of the city. Not only is prostitution of this type less conspicuous since it happens only at specific times and places but it is also carried on in an environment which is noticeably better. Prostitution of this type is not only peripheral in the life of these areas; it is also peripheral in the lives of some of its practitioners. Once again two ways of relating to prostitution can be distinguished among the women who practise it, although the overlap is considerable.

On the one hand, there are prostitutes working in these clubs and bars who do indeed structure their daily lives in accordance with their work, and in particular with the informal work-based relationships that they maintain with the owner of the establishment they work in. They regard prostitution as their job, which they keep rigidly separate from their private lives, but like the traditional prostitutes they base their personal identity on their prostitution. Typically these women too come from working-class homes, and they may have had a string of low-paid jobs, from which they have been dismissed, before taking up prostitution. Because they regard prostitution as just another job they reject any moralistic world view, they resent the difficulties placed in the way of women who wish to live independently, and regard prostitution as a way of improving their standard of living. They also – and this is what unites them with the other women working the clubs and bars –

consider that their earnings from prostitution will help them to fulfil better their traditional female roles of wife and mother, roles which they could not fill to their own satisfaction without an adequate income.

The other women working the clubs and bars are occasional prostitutes. Their prostitution does not impinge on their daily lives nor does it have any effect on their self-identity; rather prostitution itself is integrated into a completely separate way of life, to the definition of which it contributes nothing. It is a quick and easy way of making money to satisfy transient consumer needs. The part-timers are usually middle-class young women, usually students living away from home while still economically dependent on the family. Often they do other occasional work as well, such as child-minding or private tuition. Prostitution for them has no more and no less significance than these other activities. Their vision of the world is free from moral preconceptions and they seem less angry about traditional moralism and constraints than the other women we have discussed. What they advocate is a change in all affective relationships, which would also have an impact on family life and the status of motherhood.

Other clubs, pubs and discos coexist with the clubs, bars and massage parlours of this second type situated in the city centre. Here something very like the normal prostitution that is therefore not prostitution, which we discussed at the outset, routinely occurs. The behaviour is not defined as prostitution and is integrated into the everyday life of the area. There is a high degree of personal involvement between the prostitute and the client, in which the economic element predominates. Women receiving money for sex in this context do not regard themselves as prostitutes. Rather their personal identity is based upon their other role as student, secretary, dependant or whatever. They see their prostitution as a leisure activity which provides them with access to a world of people and consumption which their normal living standard would not enable them to enjoy. They are oriented towards the idea of a modern and independent woman who realizes herself through both her family and her profession: economic well-being is fundamental to the achievement of this.

Prostitution: from the margins of society to integration

The nature of prostitution in Bilbao is now clear. What is immediately striking is the variety that exists. This is reflected in the differences, not only of the specific ways in which it is carried out, but also in the ways of life and thinking of the prostitutes themselves; which in turn are related to the differing degrees of marginalization to which they are subjected.

The co-existence of these realities can only be explained if we take into account the process of transition of a traditional society to a consumer society based on an ideology that does not destroy the basic fundamentals of the former, but provides them with a different meaning. In this way, the traditional role of the woman, sexuality, and interpersonal and social relationships are being redefined, giving the fact of prostitution a different meaning, which results in its taking place in new contexts and for different reasons. The key to the interpretation of this phenomenon is to be found in the expanded definitions of the terms 'prostitution' and 'woman'. The meaning of prostitution in traditional society is quite different from that which it has in consumer society.

In traditional society the social order is interpreted and founded on Catholic morality, where everything is deemed to be good or evil in a single and fixed way so that reality is dichotomized. As far as women are concerned, the prostitute provides a negative definition which, based as it is on a definition of sexuality as something sinful, transgresses the moral law to such an extent that the only possibility that is open is for the prostitute to be removed to the periphery of society. Prostitution in this type of society is also closely related to the class structure, since it is not by chance that the women who become prostitutes originate in the lowest strata. The same is true with regard to the punishment (of eviction from home) which is meted out for failure to comply with the fixed moral standards which are established for women. It is a necessary but not sufficient cause for her being initiated into this kind of work since, although the same punishment may be applied to higher-class women, the latter have sufficient resources to disguise their transgressions, thus preventing themselves from ending up as prostitutes.

Prostitutes in traditional patriarchal societies transgress the fundamental associations: those between female sexuality, affectivity and maternity. They replace these with the association female sexuality–commerce. Patriarchal ideology, of course, sustains both sets of associations and provides their common basis, that is, the definition of the woman in terms of her sexual function. So far from contradicting this ideology by flouting the rules, prostitution helps to maintain the traditional sexual morality which is in force: by limiting the definition of sex to the relation of penetration between a man and a woman; by confirming that the sexuality of men is different, not restricted to affective relations and paternity, but an instinct which it is necessary to satisfy; and also by providing the woman with a negative model which is not to be imitated.

Precisely because women in traditional patriarchal societies are defined by their sexual function all the other characteristics required of them are deemed to be related to sexuality, and are governed by sexual morality. Passivity, fidelity and internalized dependency are seen as the appropriate virtues for women for whom structural dependence is a permanent characteristic, first in relation to parents, then to husbands, and finally to sons. Passivity affects the way women may participate in public as well as private life, and fidelity goes well beyond the sphere of matrimony, reaching out to all the individuals that make up the circle of relations of the marriage – a political as well as a kin-based family. Women live restricted lives in the private sphere, in relations of such acute dependence that they are not even mistresses of their own sexuality. This is the traditional view of women as it has been in Spain.

The maintenance of this morality requires a negative definition which embraces all types of behaviour deemed to transgress the morality, and thus the abusive term 'prostitute' is applied to all those women who in one way or another fail to live up to the norm, even though they do not use their sex as an object of commerce. This is clearly seen in the use of the term 'whore' applied to women who are unfaithful to their husbands; or who go out at night; or who decide not to get married while maintaining sexual relations with one or many men; or who enjoy sex without having children; or even to those who are too independent (see also Lees, this volume). Prostitution is that which must not be, the 'other' which incorporates all transgressions.

For prostitution to carry this moral load the prostitute as other must be visible. Thus in some sense it is the marginalized, impoverished women of Chinatown who police the morality of traditional society, as symbolic outlaws who can never be readmitted to society. Their spatial isolation epitomizes their social otherness; their believed-in poverty the more instrumental price of sin.

But Chinatown is in crisis. Other prostitution markets now flourish and in spite of the determination of the older (and a few younger) women to cling to their life-style, the traditional mode would disappear were it not that this area has now become the main centre for the distribution of drugs in Bilbao. None the less, more prosperous clients tend less and less to use this market for sex.

A large part of the reason for this is the current Spanish transition to a secular and consumer society. Now a broader spectrum of reality and meaning is allowed: a continuum replaces a duality. And on the face of it there is a greater diversity of potential roles for women, and a consequent reduction in the stigma attached to prostitution. But while prostitution no longer entails total margin-alization, it does still have negative connotations. Why is this?

The newer concept of womanhood involves the principle of equality with men. It no longer rests solely on woman's role in the private sphere: now her participation in public life, and in particular in the workplace, is accepted. In various contradictory ways, a greater equality in the domestic sphere is advocated. Women's sexuality is now recognized, but its legitimate realization is restricted to affective and stable relationships, and sex itself is still defined heterosexually and in terms of penetration. Maternity may no longer be compulsory, but coupling still is. Prostitution thus retains a negative connotation because it breaks the association between female sexuality and affectivity and repudiates the intimacy which is its concomitant in order to transform sex into a public as well as a commercial object. Women who live by prostitution come to symbolize an incapacity for living a well-ordered life in congenial circumstances: they represent disorder, coldness and irresponsibility.

This negative connotation of prostitution, which none the less falls short of total stigmatization, is symbolized by the new form of partial segregation of the prostitute which we found in the American bars, the clubs and the massage parlours. Prostitution is professionalized; it is a job of work. As such, it is separate from real femininity and prostitutes remain readily recognizable. The specialized times at and places in which they operate serve to emphasize these distinctions. The sexual market place is not in a continuous relationship with normal sex, but in a discontinuous, separated one which professionalization makes possible. None the less, sex itself is now closer to being a legitimate commodity like any other. Professionalization achieves the legitimation of the commodity while allowing the negative evaluation and signification of its purveyor to persist.

Although this model is coming to be the dominant one in Bilbao, there is a third way of seeing the matter which has come into being more recently. This involves an absolute equality of social power between men and women, the predominance of women's public life, the maintenance of balance in private life, and a recognition that female sexuality too is physical and instinctual (well, almost).

This third view corresponds with the third type of prostitute-like behaviour we identified. The idea that sex is interchangeable means that prostitution no longer has the same social stigma, although there is still a residue of this since the sale of sex as a consumer object has not met with approval. And there is still a disequilibrium in that participation in a lively circle of public relations devoted to leisure confers prestige on a man, whereas the woman's gains are primarily economic ones.

Conclusion

The girls and women whose behaviour constitutes the reality of prostitution no longer belong only to the lowest classes; they are now also middle class. The decision to become a prostitute no longer results from prior moral stigma and social exclusion, but is instead taken on economic grounds. Since the current economic crisis which affects women in particular, prostitution is sometimes the only job available to supply the necessities of life. In other cases, prostitution provides additional consumer items – drugs, clothes, leisure and goods for the home. With the exception of the very small minority of already marginalized younger women and girls among the traditional prostitutes, young women taking up prostitution today do so for economic reasons. But usually they keep their prostitution separate from the rest of their lives because of the negative connotations of this job which is still not simply a job.

From all this it will be clear that, faced with the need to interpret and develop a policy for the phenomenon of prostitution, it is necessary to pay attention not only to the various forms that it might adopt at a particular time but, more fundamentally, also to consider the economic and cultural changes which underlie these manifestations, and the significance attached to the different ideological elements by society.

As we have seen, the explanation of the phenomenon of prostitution is to be sought in the varying definitions of woman, in terms of her sexual function, provided by patriarchal ideology (and resistances to it). The concrete forms that this ideology take are directly related, as it seems to us on the basis of our observations, to the social structure of the environing society, and change along with it, as do the forms and manifestations of prostitution itself, forever the dark side of ideal woman.

For this reason, to abolish prostitution requires not legislative reform but a definitive and radical change in the very *basis* of the definition of woman. Such a change would need to occur throughout society, both on the level of structure and on the level of everyday life. In this sense the abolition of prostitution involves also the abolition of patriarchy.

Note

1   A full bibliography of works in Spanish on the subject of prostitution is available in Andrieu-Sanz and Vasquez-Anton (1987). We decided not to include it in this edition of our essay which has been prepared for English-speaking readers.

5

Girls in street gangs in the suburbs of Paris

Jean-Charles Lagrée and Paula Lew Fai

Whether they are boys or girls, the population of juvenile delinquents constitutes a special population, constructed or preconstructed by the action of a judicial and penal apparatus which punishes their breaches of the codes and rules commonly accepted in society (Merton, 1983) – their transgression of law.

Our concerns are with what comes prior to that action: in that vague and shadowy zone, with ill-defined outlines, known, though the precise content of the term cannot always be specified, as marginality (Lagrée and Lew Fai, 1985). This chapter is devoted to those who are the object of the policies of social regulation, those engaged in behaviour that exposes them to persecution by others in their environment, and who thus proceed gradually, from one social response to another (Selosse, 1976–7), towards committing reprehensible acts subject to penal sanctions or to some custodial measure.

From this point of view the final transition to the delinquent act itself takes on a secondary character. It is simply the termination, recorded in the civil history of social actors, of these youngsters' special, unique way of locating themselves in their environment and playing with the rules for integration into a collectivity. It is the outcome of a never inevitable process generated in the informal interactions and relationships that shape and cleave their social worlds.

The study was intended as a contribution to the elucidation of the process which leads social actors, in this case young people from working-class backgrounds, to break the law and become exposed to the risk of prison.

Method of research

Following a preliminary look at access to jobs by different categories of young people, we selected our survey population by the sole criterion of the risks of socio-economic exclusion that they ran. Four indicators were therefore adopted: age, sex, ethnicity and social class.

This chapter was translated from the French by Iain L. Fraser.

1   Age was chosen since confronting the labour market under the age of nineteen means increasing one's risk of becoming and remaining insecure, alternating between unemployment, unstable unskilled work, and unemployment again.
2   Sex is important since unemployment and job insecurity hit females harder than males, and the process of socio-economic insertion remains chancier and more problematic for them.
3   Ethnicity constitutes an additional handicap that considerably reduces the 'social capacity' of young people of non-indigenous origin to find a job.
4   Lastly, social class cuts across the effectiveness of all the other characteristics of the actors as regards their chances of securing a place in the labour market and the risks they run of being marginalized.

Our sample was thus selected within the population of boys and girls who run the greatest risks of social exclusion because they are between 16 and 18, from working-class backgrounds, and in some cases, also of non-indigenous origin.

These selection criteria thus define a population in social-structural terms. However, they say nothing, and allow nothing to be predicted, about possible marginality; in other words, about the details of the relationship that these young people from working-class backgrounds have with social norms. The procedure of empirical investigation we adopted, by going to see the young people, by going to question them at length and in depth, thus had the aim of identifying the referents that guide their practices and their social careers. These referents are in fact only implicitly contained in what those questioned say. They emerge from what is not said, from what is, perhaps, unsayable. For they belong to the culture that the subjects have reappropriated and shaped for themselves, to their own ways of being and acting, to their own knowledge and know-how, which are so much a matter of course for them and for those around them that it is impossible for them to be made explicit (Lalive d'Epinay and Kellerhals, 1985). Elucidating these referents therefore involved a two-fold task.

First, the discourse had to be produced. The investigator had the task of inviting the people questioned to define themselves, present themselves, depict their present situation, recount their practices and circumscribe, through an association of ideas, their way of life. But the past, and the adumbration of the future, shapes the present. In order to understand what was said the interviewer also invited the interviewees to 'tell their own story', to specify the future goals they were pursuing and the prospects they could foresee. The interviews were analysed using two distinct though complementary methods. For each young person we established a socio-biographical summary aimed at bringing out the three referential axes of our investigative framework:

1   the young person's social career (pathway or route);
2   their prospects for the future;
3   their practices and modes of relationship with each other and other people.

Secondly, the interviews were subjected to exhaustive content analysis, aimed both at systematically picking up items brought up by each individual interviewed according to frequency of appearance and at verifying and, where necessary, reassessing the validity of the socio-biographical summaries previously established.

Some results

The research was done in 1984 in two boroughs in the southern suburbs of Paris. The two places have contrasting profiles in respect of:

1   duration of structuring of the residential space – one of the localities is a new town, the other one of the 'traditional' suburbs;
2   the social homogeneity and/or heterogeneity of the population.

The researchers worked in the two areas for a period of six months, observing how people used public space – streets, squares and bars – and meeting workers in the institutions more specifically responsible for assimilating young people into the residential collectivity (neighbourhood centres, youth assimilation programmes, and semi-municipal bodies). In this way the researchers were able to form regular, lasting contacts enabling them to get in touch with the population covered by the study.

Thirty-eight young people were interviewed, selected according to the criterion of risks of social exclusion set out above, independently of any possible 'deviance' or any 'informal' or 'institutional' stigmatization that might have been attached to them.

Furthermore it became apparent to us during our individual interviews that life in a group, the actual confrontation with peers, not only constituted a key factor in the youngsters' identity, but was an essential determinant of their location within the relationships which structured their residential collectivity. Thus we decided, when the occasion arose, to hold group interviews, bringing five to seven young people together. Ten such group interviews were done, supplementing the individual ones.

In some of the group interviews, once the *terms* of the discussion had been negotiated, the handling and the course of discussion became primarily a group matter. This was the case for our discussions with the street groups or 'gangs'. The various events in a gang's life (trouble with the authorities for theft, quarrels in the neighbourhood, impromptu outings and invitations to us to join them, etc.) thereby became the components of renegotiation of the interviews themselves.

What mattered to us in choosing this approach was to relocate the young people in the system of relationships which linked with each other and with the other people in their daily environment. For this purpose, in one particularly heterogeneous and newly established neighbourhood we interviewed fifteen adults. These people were selected chiefly with an eye to their residential status as owner or tenant, a criterion repeatedly mentioned by the young people in the neighbourhood. In fact, the adults were largely homogeneous in age, but relatively heterogeneous in respect of social and professional position. As in our dealings with the young people, the interviews were handled in as free a way as possible.

The analysis of all these data yields the following observation: within this fringe of working-class youth, which is particularly insecure and defenceless as regards getting work, the young people belonging to local gangs, involved with peer groups, participating in their activities, hanging about in groups in stairwells or public places, exposed to vituperation and complaints from people in the neighbourhood, are also those in our sample whose situation is the most precarious.

A number of ecological factors help to explain the participation of these young people in street gangs, such as how old they were when they moved into the area, and the age and consequent density of collective relations within the area itself – we have dealt with these elsewhere (Lagrée and Lew Fai, 1985). But participation in gangs results above all from the precariousness of their situations. In fact, almost all the gang members we met come from families in the lowest segment of the working class, with the head of household frequently doing one of the least-skilled and lowest-paid jobs, such as labouring or working as service staff. Moreover, half of them live in families with one parent either ill or an invalid or with the stability threatened by clashes between the children and the (step) father or (step) mother.

Today, for the majority of these young people, the street group operates full time. It is first and foremost the means of filling up the absence of work. By contrast, school, however little attention these young people may pay to it, has the effect of giving youngsters a 'conventional' social status, locating them in the social world as schoolboy or schoolgirl and enabling them to benefit from the relative permissiveness bound up with that status in working-class areas. For being a school-pupil means having a place to be, and at the same time being able to go out, have friends and still enjoy life. In contrast, the local gangs tend to bring together young people who are unemployed, some of whom have never worked or have had only brief casual jobs.

Without in any way prejudging the other functions the street group may perform in other ways, nor the other characteristics it may have had in different contexts or at other times, these observations tend to indicate that in the suburbs of Paris *this form of socializing has less to do with the customary practices of working-class youth than with their position of social and economic exclusion* and the slender possibilities that they have of being integrated into the working class, except on its most precarious and most underprivileged fringes.

The street groups' practice thus corresponds to the risks of social declassing run by these young people. Conversely, we find that none of the young people on more privileged routes to 'social success' take part in these forms of group. Thus, those who are moving upwards socially and have prospects of 'emerging' from the working class have, without changing their place of residence, loosened the bonds linking them to their neighbourhood and their old friends. Family and friends are thus sacrificed to their project for advancement and social success.

Of the thirty-eight young people in our sample, seventeen mentioned participation in local gangs. For our present purposes, however, it should be noted that girls' participation tended to be rather less. Out of fifteen girls we met between the ages of 16 and 18 only five mentioned involvement in these groups.

	Number in sample	Participation in a gang
Boys	23	12
Girls	15	5
Total	38	17

This finding suggests that in this respect there have been few changes since the 1960s. It was then agreed that in France as elsewhere street gangs were primarily single sex,[1] that girls are in a minority and have a status of 'girl as object' (Pouget, 1977: 107)

and that one may rightly regard the gang as chiefly a male activity
(Robert, 1966: 96).

This still seems to be the position today. Girls in gangs are just
as much in the minority, and are devalued both by their fellows and
by their environment, as this girl aged 17 points out:

> Yes, yes, even if the girl didn't want to go out with a guy, she was still
> a whore. To show you the mentality there was there, you had to go out
> with them and do what they wanted, otherwise you were a whore. Well,
> there were some of them, you had to ride with them . . . and you were
> a good girl, except they went off and boasted, 'That one there, I've had
> her.'

For the girls too, gang membership has a meaning as a reaction
to their family and to their perception of the future facing them.
We called the five gang-girls we spoke to Catherine, Alix,
Véronique, Julie and Irene. The life stories of Catherine, Alix, and
Véronique are similar.

Catherine's mother is French and her father Algerian. Rejected
by young French people of her age, she spends her days with the
'Arab' gang of her neighbourhood. The parents of Alix are divorced
and her mother has remarried. She does not get on with her
stepfather and evades his supervision by going to see her friends.
She started by associating with 'French people', in fact her old
schoolmates. Rejected by this group because she had left school
and therefore no longer had anything in common with them, she
met up with the 'junkies', a group of drug addicts who spend most
of their time and talk on finding their drugs, on preparing their fix
and on 'dealing'. She left them and started mixing with a group
called the 'crouches', but people started talking about her so she
went off to join the rival gang of the 'Moroccans', which marked
the nadir of a pathway of declassing even inside the world of young
people in working-class areas. Véronique's pathway likewise started
with her parents' divorce. Shortly after, she left school and joined
a gang of young people 'who had done time'. In the stigmatization
and downgrading she felt herself victim of, she found reasons for
accusing society as a whole, for slandering 'young people with no
problems', that is, the 'bourgeoisie'.

These three stories reveal the slenderness of the resources of the
girls' families, and a tension attributable either to bi-culturalism
(Bourricaud, 1968: 871) or to parental divorce; or, as in the case of
Alix, to both. But in this small-scale and in-depth study we are not
looking so much for the 'causes' of gang membership: rather we are
trying to disclose the meaning these young people give to this form
of grouping in a 'gang'. In this respect, the two other girls who in
the same way spend the major part of their free time in the

restrictive circle of the gang, thereby exposing themselves to the reproach of the neighbours, also supply a line for investigation.

Julie and Irene are similar in their attempt to achieve autonomy and distance from their families, and more especially their parents. But this is the only characteristic that these two young people have in common. Irene is the daughter of a Spanish worker. Brought up according to the most traditional pattern of working-class populations in Mediterranean countries, on leaving school she aspired to more independence and freedom, to living like her friends in the neighbourhood. Unemployment, the 'objective' impossibility of quickly finding a job and thus earning her own money, soon put a damper on these wishes and hopes; still more so did her status as a young, 'not-yet-married' girl, her parents' responsibility until marriage, and bound by both necessity and duty to spend her days in the family home. Her friends in the neighbourhood were thus an escape route, a departure allowing her to mark her opposition to the pattern of socialization imposed by her parents. They also furnished the means of increasingly manifesting her wish for independence, without being able to win it effectively by finding a job and earning her living.

The motivations leading Julie to associate with 'the do-nothings', and 'people who are a bit spaced out on drugs' are apparently of the same nature. However, they operate in a radically different context, since Julie belongs to a socially and culturally more privileged family, is continuing her studies and enjoys the benevolent attention of her parents who watch over her transient escapades. Thus, for a while, she met up with what she herself calls 'the corner loungers', but does not stick to their way of life and is tending gradually to separate herself from it.

In these two cases, the practice of the gang and participation in activities of neighbourhood gangs is explicitly bound up both with the way the girls see their future direction or 'social pathway', and with their image of the stages of life, particularly that of youth and the 'correct' way to grow up.

This is the second finding we have been able to establish during this research: the practice of the gang takes on meaning primarily with regard to *the way the young people define the stages of life*. In this connection, the young people we interviewed show a very broad consensus on their images of the stages and the socio-biographical events that mark the process of growing up and the prescriptive steps to be gone through in order to arrive at 'adulthood'. The age of 16, marked for most of them by leaving school, is the starting-point. For the end of school means the opening up of an era of freedom and of assumption of independence, a period 'where you can enjoy life'. Eighteen, the age of legal majority but also and especially the age of legal responsibility, and the age when you may have a driving licence and thereby be better equipped for jobs, pick-ups and leisure activities, is another staging point. It announces the forthcoming acquisition of adult status and its accompanying prescriptions that have necessarily to be followed unless one is to look like a 'failure', a 'Charlie', a 'bloke who's done nothing with his life' as one boy put it. Subject to the rule of precocity which applies strongly in working-class circles, the end of this period of adjustment is set in an age bracket ranging according to both the girls and the boys in our sample between 21 and 23. Between 16 and 18 there is, according to their chronology, a period of youth where one is allowed to enjoy oneself. After 18, the concern to take one's life in hand gets stronger, a concern to capitalize on social assets regarded as necessary to conform to their image of the 'adult' age. Correspondingly, after 18, since the stakes get higher, you have to give up the 'fooling around' hitherto permitted or tolerated in the social environment. Finally, around 23 or 24, you have, they say, to be financially independent and secure that independence through finding accommodation, 'be like everyone, have a husband or a wife, children, a car', 'be doing all right, like'. *All* the young people agreed on these different reference points on the road to adulthood, and on their value content, whether they were young people in gangs or not, boys or girls. However, there were a number of variations between the different categories of young people. The difference between the sexes is the most readily perceptible, the most obvious, and also the one that is the most meaningful.

For both boys and girls, the definition of the stages leading to the acquisition of adult status takes meaning first and foremost in relation to the priority goal of *joining the ranks of the working class*, of being able to deploy at the right time, that is, at the ages defined as 'normal', the behaviour patterns characterizing integration into that class. For the boys, however, this process of integration, this transition that leads the people they know into the status and role of adulthood within the working class, is intrinsically dependent on their capacity to find a stable job with promotion possibilities, enabling them, at least to some extent, to control their future, found a home and acquire the distinctive signs proving their ability to cope with their environment. It is an adjustment to the mode of behaviour prevalent in that environment. For boys coming from the lower strata of the population, this is primarily if not exclusively conditional on securing a job, on exercising a recognized, worth-while occupation.

For the girls too, the goal pursued is first and foremost to join the ranks of the working class and to behave, like older sisters or friends, according to the cultural models current there. But in our sample, among those young people who lack the minimum education needed to apply for a qualified job, and who are able at best to find only underpaid, precarious positions, the link between placement on the labour market and becoming adult is much looser. Certainly, some of them seek to acquire a qualification, to insert themselves in networks of relationships that facilitate their access to a firm and thereby develop proper occupational strategies. They are, however, a minority. On the contrary, the majority of them have as their goal marriage, or 'living together', and expect eventually to be looking after their children. In this respect, whatever the transformations at work within working-class cultures, the girls tended to be particularly traditionalist. Their plans and desires for social integration translate as the securing of the status of wife and mother, putting in second place paid work, which would in any case be a supplementary activity.

This difference, which comes down to the sexual division of labour in working-class families, constitutes the normative stages and timings of the path to adulthood.

As with the boys, the period of youth starts for the girls on leaving school. For most of the girls in our sample, it therefore starts around 15 or 16. For the same reasons as the boys, the age of 18 is also a turning-point. But here there is an additional dimension. Eighteen is a point of departure in becoming an adult. In the working-class world, it marks the start of the period where you 'can' contemplate leaving your parents and family to take a husband or set up as a couple. It is also the age when you may happen to have a child without departing too far from the environment's rules, without appearing careless or 'irresponsible' in the eyes of the neighbours of either sex. In fact, for these girls from working-class areas who left school at 16, the age of 18 marks the entrance to the marriage market. Its end-point is set at 23 or 24, the age by which one 'should' have settled down and 'made one's life'. For these girls from working-class areas, lacking the essential assets for getting a job, the working out of a conscious, explicit strategy of social placement through marriage or marital cohabitation proceeds from two systems: the cultural referents and traditional models current in their own environment, and the perception of their inability to develop a genuine occupational strategy. It can thus be seen also to be engraved in the feeling of failure they have with regard to the logic of entry into the labour market.

Here the boys and girls in our sample come back together, in the feeling that they have of being lost to their occupational possibilities, in the devaluation they feel about being incapable *at the right time* of locating themselves along a pathway of integration into their class, according to the stages and timings that mark their image of becoming an adult.

On this common base, however, a second distinction has to be drawn, bound up with the modes of reaction of these young people, boys and girls alike, to the assessment they make of their own situation. Thus, of the young people who take part in 'gang' activities, 90 per cent negatively assess their chances of getting out of the situation. Of the others, those who stay isolated, only 10 per cent make the same judgment about themselves. Correspondingly, young people in gangs are much more inclined to be content with their fate, to enjoy life, to wait and see what happens. For, if one group tries to get moving and play the rules of the social game and locate themselves along a pathway that will at the right time allow them to take on the patterns of adulthood, the other group instead allow themselves time to wait, putting off until later the concern for taking their future in hand.

The practice of the gang thus involves a two-fold distancing: from the milestones on the path to adulthood on the one hand; from a pathway valued within the working class on the other. The youngsters see their life-styles as a response to this double distancing; it is the option to play the present against the future. It is an attempt to assert oneself and locate oneself in the local set-up by *reassembling*, on the specific basis they have worked out, the norm and value references of their environment of origin. It is a response to the waiting position that the present economic situation shuts them into, and a reappropriation adapted to their position, of the normative definition of the ages of youth current in their class.

By way of illustration, we shall mention two fields of activity that locally structure gang life, confining ourselves solely to the case of the 'rockers', who are the majority and occupy a prominent position in gang life.

First, there is 'aggro', the value of which is first and foremost symbolic. Almost all the young people we interviewed mentioned brawls, altercations and relationships of physical force. But these statements are less about the history of some physical engagement they themselves or their friends have actually been involved in than about the possibility of such confrontations exploding on one occasion or another, at one meeting or another with rival gangs. The redundancy of the accounts, which from one speaker to the next always mention the same events, shows clearly that the talk about fighting also acts as a myth that primarily affirms their personal involvement in local relationships but also stresses their constantly reaffirmed acceptance of a logic of confrontation and rivalry among gangs, which might bring them as far as actual confrontation. However, physical violence breaks out only rarely, since the rule of the game here consists in showing one's determination to go all the way if necessary, but without proceeding to action.

As Marsh et al. (1978) have been able to show, the protagonists of an altercation have a large gamut of codified verbal defence and defiance which enables them to prolong the engagement and to cause third parties to intervene and break off the argument without losing face. Through the theme of fighting, the young boys interviewed thus stress their personal adhesion to a system of values centred around virility, courage and physical ability. More fundamental, however, it is the way that the group comes into being. For in every conflict, every confrontation, whether physical or merely verbal, values of solidarity and mutual help which are constitutive of the gang are brought into play. Thus, very frequently, the abundance of talk about fighting contradicts and masks its virtual non-existence, just as the mythologized affirmation of solidarity contradicts and masks the absence of solidarity in everyday relationships. The fact remains that through such talk the gang manifests its existence as a collective.

What, then, is the place of the girls in this particular field of activity? They are absent from it. At the very most, they occupy a peripheral position. The fight system, or more exactly the play of evoking past or possible future fights, refers to the values of virility, values of physical strength and courage that traditionally constitute the attributes of men in French popular culture(s). Men and women, boys and girls, accept it: the former symbolically, to be sure, but actively; the latter in an essentially passive manner. The girls in fact take part neither in the fights nor in the verbal altercations among boys. The place assigned to girls in the gang world does not allow them, and even to some extent bars them from, participation in activities involving public risk. The majority submit to this of their own accord, leaving it up to the boys to assert themselves in an escalation which may, from fights to theft to crimes, end them up in jail. A few object and claim a status equal to that of the boys, by taking part in these activities where access to positions of power is played out. Here they are brought back to their status by the very logic of the group's functioning, by its implicit or explicit norms, by its system of internal hierarchization which installs the 'men', as they are according to their image of virility, in the dominant positions and the girls in subordinate positions:

She went out with them. They tell her, go off to bed, because they thought it was time, because they didn't want her to be wandering round the streets. They took her back home. And if she came out again and they saw her . . . they hit her one. Me, I must have been hit something like two or three times in ten months.

There remains scope for the girls to mock or deride this game that they participate in, this mode of structuring the relationships among peers which they nevertheless contribute to generating, if only by accepting the principles that govern the mode of operation of the gangs. It is also possible for them to use this 'game' to provoke fights and rivalries and thus explode this 'formal' ritual, which is based on the position of dominance of boys over girls, dominance of 'men' over 'women'. They can go away, leave the gang, but then they lose their friends, and with them not only the rare chances of leisure activities they offer but also, and perhaps above all, the sole basis that located them within their residential world, that is the world of the gang. Despite the surbordinate, devalued place they occupy there, despite their status as object given them by the mode of operation of interactions among male peers, these five girls found in the 'gangs' a place to stand, a way of gaining a footing through the group's mediation in the world of working-class youth. Accordingly, they also found in them a social identity. If they leave, they lose the support represented by this system of interaction, while retaining the stigmatizing label of 'moll' attached to them by the neighbourhood.

In fact, whether they are boys or girls, members of a gang or temporarily in their orbit, all take particularly close note of rumours and gossip circulating about them in the neighbourhood. The adults, more specifically the mothers and the gossiping *concierge*, constitute a very significant network of supervision and of infor-mation. Subject to this mode of informal social control, boys in gangs thus perceive their environment as a collective actor on which they have scarcely any hold. It constitutes a locus of constraint and domination, liable, perhaps, to reject them by depriving them of social recognition, to stigmatize them, and to refer them to agencies of social control.

Faced with that likelihood, they retain the possibility of submitting to the rules of the social game. They thus have the individual as well as the collective power to cope. Quarrels, vandalism and uproar display their presence to everyone's eyes and remind the local body social of both their existence and their difference. This relationship of forces is most often reflected in a nexus of delinquency. Recourse to municipal power and to the police authorities constitutes a frequent response to their petty thefts that have become larceny, their vandalism that has become pillage, their quarrels that have become riots of physical violence. Having tested the room for manoeuvre allocated to them, boys in gangs thus have the capacity to *negotiate* with their surroundings and try to lay claim to what they want (which in fact amounts to the right to be different) vis-à-vis those who, professionally or by status, are the spokespeople of the residential collectivity.

As for the girls, the margin of tolerance allowed them by the body social is more restricted. Once they are in a local gang, they very rapidly slip from the status of *jeune fille* to that of simply *fille*. It is above all by their own peers that they are disparaged. For in all the practices whereby the gang displays itself as a collective actor claiming a completely separate place vis-à-vis the surrounding social order, the girls are excluded. Thus, they are debarred by their companions from taking part in riots or nocturnal operations. They are also under gang control as far as drug use is concerned. Above all, as regards both the neighbourhood and the regulatory institutions, they are prevented from placing themselves at risk and thus from taking positions of assertion. The protective role that the boys adopt in their regard confines them to a status of passivity.

The interplay of the relationship of forces within the gang, which organizes a traditional model of the sexual division of labour, ensures the passage from 'passivity' to 'discredit'. By taking on board this aspect of the position, adopted by adults, boys in the gangs ensure that the girls experience themselves as lacking in value. As one 18-year-old girl put it:

> If I can get it this evening, I'll buy them a drink and then, when I've gone away, they'll say . . . yes, you're a whore.

The fact is that participation in local gangs *ipso facto* constitutes for a girl a break with admissible modes of behaviour and socialization. If girls persist in the practice beyond a certain age, they find themselves being assigned a status that may, at least locally, bar them from recourse to strategies of positioning and from social recognition via matrimony and coupling. The room for action open to the girls is therefore particularly limited. Stuck with the inability to use the means of pressure traditionally open to their male comrades, unable to make themselves respected by imposing themselves physically in face-to-face relationships, they have to resist the prejudices not only of the adults but also of their male peers. In fact, they have to *negotiate* their presence in the gang in order to derive the benefit of leisure opportunities and diversion without paying the price of social discredit:

> When you come down to it, because they (owners of bars) know that if

they are going to chuck A out, A will get his own back on their window
or their juke-box and I won't do that because I am a girl, when you
come down to it, it's me that's got to take what they have coming to
them. I've often had to take it for them. It's sickening!

Being able to play on sexual identity to assert themselves while at
the same time avoiding the effects of a symbolic representation
centred on that dimension alone, that is the narrow path offered to
girls by the gangs. Their role ultimately proves more complex than
that of passive 'victims' of a relationship of forces acting to their
disfavour.

The second major field of activity that allows the young people
to assert themselves, to find their identity in the world where they
live, is the practice of picking-up (*drague*), which has an essential
position in their talk. This constitutes one of the major activities of
the boys. Through pick-ups, the young men give proof of their
ability to put into action the values of 'virility' which, as we have
just seen, are so prevalent in their world. But as a practice of leisure
and enjoyment, it corresponds also to the general value orientation
that makes youth for the working class into a period where one can
'enjoy life' or where one has to 'experiment'. The behaviour and
manner of the girls in our sample does not depart from this rule.
For them, as for the boys, the stages of life define a moratorium
between 16 and 18, a period during which meetings and keeping
company do not mean lasting commitments. But if the practices of
the pick-up are similar to a 'game', it is a serious game, which has
implicit rules and specific stakes that genuinely and effectively
involve the constitution of the girls' life chances on the marriage
market. In fact, contacts are made principally through the network
of relationships existing among the street group's members.

Young people in the street groups, whether boys or girls, are
confined in their day-to-day universe. The group offers them the
only way of passing the time. In this sense the primary objective of
the gang is the gang itself. The 'game' of picking up, tolerated for
both boys and girls between the ages of 16 and 18 although, as we
have seen, needing to be more skilfully played by the latter,
involves a contradiction. On the one hand it expresses the success
of the collective strategy in terms of the youngsters' own values,
while at the same time expanding the group's all too limited range
of social contacts, and even scoring a symbolic success vis-à-vis their
more or less nominal rivals. On the other hand, however, stable
relationships are not encouraged for the boys: they are experienced
as depleting the entertainment value of the group.

But at the same time there is an articulation between the pick-up
and the search for a partner to settle down with, although in the

lore of the group they are different and carried out at different stages in the chronology of growing up. For the boys there is a disjunction between these stages; for the girls there is a continuity. The subtlety deployed during stage one affects their opportunities during stage two, and ultimately their chance of being valued by other girls, their social identity, and their possibility of establishing themselves in a local community in which they are likely to remain.

Conclusion

The marginality of the young people we talked to stems first and foremost from their position on the fringes of the working class. But we also noticed a double distancing, a second dimension of marginality from working-class culture and standards as well.

Yet the young people themselves spoke to us of what they would have to do to become grown up members of the working class, and described their lives in terms of a discontinuous chronology of approach to that status. These changes underlie the assessment these young people have formed of their own situation, and of their chances and their assets in relation to the goal of joining the adult working class.

Hanging around in the street group, for the boys as well as for the five girls we have described, represents a break in that model of progress to adulthood. It is a life-space not entirely accounted for in their processual chronology, a time when having a good time in the imagined ways is curtailed by a lack of means. None the less, collectively they make a statement which reclaims this teenage space.

As victims of the process of recomposition of the working class, these young people are distanced from the positions and references of the class they belong to, which nevertheless is and remains the class to which they aspire.

In the gang, these young people try to assert themselves and to forge a positive social identity for themselves. As a reaction to the process of declassing that affects them, groupings among peers take up, reinterpret and affirm in a specific and original way the values, rules and principles of their class. In the sexual division of roles, which in the gangs are devolved on to boys and girls, one can thus read, in a caricatured, exacerbated manner, the sexual division of labour that prevails in traditional French working-class culture.

The girls occupy subordinate positions. They are the 'objects' of relationships and interactions among the young men. But they are also 'subjects'. Without any assets that can allow them to develop an occupational strategy, and constrained throughout their youth to spend the major part of their time in the area they live, their route to integration into the working class is through a strategy of matrimonial location played out primarily in the world of the gang, and in response to complex rules by which the boys determine their market value. These rules and the group's modes of operation govern their conduct. But, conversely, the girls are at the heart of and are the stakes of the relationships of rivalry that unfold there. They are in this sense among the reasons for the group's cohesion. The girls exemplify the contradiction that the street group is governed by an original and specific mode of operation, yet nevertheless proceeds from the traditional principles of the working-class culture from which these young people have come, from which they are now in part excluded, and to which they aspire.

Note

1 'La délinquance des jeunes en groupe', *Les Cahiers de Vaucresson*, 1963: 226.

PART THREE

DECISION MAKING ABOUT GIRLS WITHIN THE CRIMINAL JUSTICE SYSTEM

6

Justice or welfare?

A comparison of recent developments in the English and French juvenile justice systems

Barbara Hudson

In both France and England and Wales, as in most other Western countries, the last hundred years has seen the development of a juvenile justice system which has sought to protect young offenders from the full rigours of the criminal law. Although remaining within the criminal justice system, juvenile jurisdictions have evolved which separate young offenders from adult criminals both during court proceedings and in penal or 'corrective' establishments. Children and young people have been seen as 'in trouble' rather than 'in crime', and the emphasis of juvenile justice systems has been on meeting their needs rather than meting out punishments. At all stages, juvenile proceedings seek to have regard for the welfare of the child, and this provision of welfare has, throughout the history of the development of juvenile courts, come to have equality with, if not primacy over, goals of protection of the public from the activities of wrongdoers, and the application of penalties appropriate to the offence.

This commitment to welfare has come under question in the last few years, and from many quarters in Europe and the USA has come a demand for a 'return to justice'. It has been suggested that juvenile justice systems, through their emphasis on needs rather than crimes, have become over-interventionist in the lives of a larger and larger proportion of young people, whilst at the same time providing an inadequate response to rising juvenile crime rates. The call for an improvement in the protection of children's civil rights – especially their right not to be removed from their homes for any but the most serious of offences – has meshed with a demand for 'sterner and surer punishment', giving rise to the so-called 'justice model' agenda for reform. Under this model, practitioners in all aspects of juvenile justice should become increasingly 'offence based' rather than 'needs based' in their approach to juvenile crime (Morris and McIsaac, 1978). Particularly, practitioners are expected not to use the commission of a delinquent act as the opportunity to intervene with programmes designed to provide welfare but which, because of their ideology of treatment rather than punishment, might give the state control over the juvenile's life for many years. As against this, other criticisms of juvenile justice systems have put precisely the opposite viewpoint, namely, that over-intervention by juvenile courts and social service practitioners has developed because of the retention of the judicial/punitive aspects of criminal law in respect of young people (Thorpe et al., 1980). Such critics would complain that welfare considerations and the apparatus of social provision for need have been half-heartedly added on to the juvenile justice systems, rather than the criminal law having abandoned its jurisdiction over children.

This chapter examines recent trends in juvenile justice, looking in particular at two significant developments which took place in 1982. The Criminal Justice Act introduced in England and Wales in that year incorporated several of the ideas of the 'return to justice' lobby, whilst at the same time in France Robert Badinter, then Minister of Justice, sponsored a reform agenda which would enhance the welfare aspects of French juvenile justice. It is the treatment of girls by contemporary juvenile justice systems which is the major concern here, with attention focused on whether their prospects are likely to be enhanced by reforms in the direction of a more welfare-oriented system or by a return to justice. There is plenty of evidence that focusing on the welfare needs (real or supposed) of girls who come to the notice of the social control agencies has led to large numbers of girls and young women, without having committed any serious acts of criminal delinquency, being removed from home or being placed under the supervision of social workers because of adult disapproval of their sexual activity and general life-style and demeanour. The question is whether a 'justice' approach would lead not to less intervention in their lives, but to the same disapproval being expressed through minor offences being viewed disproportionately seriously in the courts. If concentration on the actual offence committed by a female defendant leads to girls being sentenced to penal establishments rather than being ordered to residential welfare or educational institutions, then the justice approach will have little of advantage to offer to young women.

English and French juvenile justice: some basic comparisons

Juvenile courts as we know them today started to appear in both England and France at around the same time. Although from the mid-nineteenth century onwards certain courts began to specialize in children's cases, the first juvenile court as such was instituted in England in 1908 and in France in 1912. In both countries, this establishment of separate juvenile courts followed public outcries about the presence of children in adult penal institutions, and in both countries the development of juvenile courts went along with the development of reformatories and correctional boarding schools for 'deprived' and 'depraved' children (Covington, 1979; Donzelot, 1979). Although juvenile jurisdiction was separated from that for adults, it retained the same format as that of the adult magistrates courts with merely the formalities being somewhat softened and some of the penalties available to magistrates dealing with adults being either reduced or wholly unavailable for juveniles.

Juvenile justice systems thus represent not only a dilution of the adult criminal law, but also a considerable merging of the judicial and educational systems. Thus, in both countries, juvenile courts hear truancy cases alongside criminal cases; establishments such as Community Homes with Education in England and Wales and remedial boarding schools in France take children who are either not attending school or attending and being disruptive, as well as children who have committed offences. The juvenile justice system thus represents a state takeover of private philanthropy towards children (see Donzelot, 1979; Platt, 1969). This virtual monopoly of concern for children, and the judicial takeover of welfare, is in fact the most important feature of modern juvenile justice systems. This penetration of the assistancial by the judicial, as Donzelot describes the development of juvenile justice, has been much more thorough, but much less remarked, than the entry of welfare concerns and welfare professionals into the juvenile courts. This point will be developed further in relation to current trends.

Following the establishment of the juvenile court, reforms in both countries followed a consistent line of progressively raising the age of criminal responsibility, enhancing the role of social workers and other paediatric 'experts' in the proceedings, and deformalizing the courtroom aspects of juvenile justice. The basic structure of French juvenile justice was codified in the 1940s, and given its legal expression in the Ordonnance of 1945. In England, a series of discussion papers in the post-war years culminated in the Children and Young Persons Act of 1969. While the Badinter reforms are a continuation of the direction of change being followed throughout the century, the 1982 Criminal Justice Act marks a radical turnabout.

The system formally instituted by the Ordonnance of 1945 took France much further towards a system of welfare tribunals than has ever been achieved in England and Wales. In fact, the French system is much closer to the Scottish system of family hearings than to the juvenile court system of England and Wales. This would not, however, be apparent to a visitor to the juvenile courts of either country. In France and in England and Wales, juvenile cases are heard in courtrooms, with a bench of three justices. Whereas in England and Wales these three are all magistrates, however, who may or may not specialize in juvenile cases, in France the *juges des enfants* concentrate exclusively on juveniles, and the three-person bench consists of one judge assisted by two lay assessors. These assessors are expected to be 'persons of good standing in the community who have demonstrated special interest in the problems of children'. In both countries the form of the proceedings is that of a magistrates' court case, with some relaxation of the rules of evidence, but with the usual judicial format and the usual array of lawyers and clerks. Evident differences reflect not so much different approaches to dealing with juveniles, as differences in the overall character of English and French judicial systems. The adversarial system of English judicial processes whereby prosecution and defence teams present different versions of events, cross-examine each other's witnesses, with the judge or magistrate adjudicating as to which of the two versions represents the truth, differs significantly from the inquisitorial system of France and many other European countries. In this system, it is the task of the judge or magistrate to discover the guilt or innocence and, if guilty, the degree of culpability of defendants by setting in train enquiries with relevant officials and witnesses, by questioning such people both in and out of court, and then assessing the evidence thus arrived at. This difference in the basic character of the two judicial systems, not surprisingly, leads to substantial differences in practices and procedures in the two countries.

One such major difference between the two systems is the location of prosecution decisions. In England and Wales, the decision to prosecute rests with the police, who in some parts of the country reserve this right exclusively to themselves, but in other parts have established panels comprising themselves, social workers, teachers and other 'experts'. None the less, magistrates take no part in these early stages of the judicial process. French children's judges, however, receive notification from the police, from statutory

and voluntary agencies or from individuals, that something is
untoward, and order enquiries as to whether or not legal proceedings
are necessary.

Once a case comes to court, in both England and France the
judge has a wide range of measures from which to choose. In both
countries, children may be committed to a community school, to a
penal institution or may be given community alternatives (supervision or probation in England; education or *surveiller en milieu
ouvert* in France). Community corrections may involve participation
in various supervised activities, may involve casework by a social
work agency or psychiatric treatment. However, in England and
Wales, once sentence has been pronounced, the judge or magistrate
concerned hands over responsibility to the social worker or
probation officer involved in the case, whereas in France the judge
retains a close interest in the case and the judge's department can
intervene to supervise progress. In welfare rather than criminal
cases in England and Wales the child would be placed under the
care or supervision of the local authority social services department,
whereas in France an 'endangered' child would be made a ward of
the court. Another difference between the two systems is the age
of criminal responsibility: 10 in England and Wales; 13 in France.
Before that age, children can only be subject to welfare rather than
criminal proceedings.

These differences between the two systems make it easier to
extend the welfare approach in France and to adopt elements of the
justice model in England and Wales. However, the recent establishment of the Crown Prosecution Service does move England and
Wales somewhat closer to the French procedural model, and may,
to some extent, counterbalance the ideological shift towards the
crime-centred, justice approach.

Incarceration, females and the two juvenile justice systems

In both France and England and Wales, recent years have seen rises
in the rates of incarceration of juveniles disproportionate to rises in
juvenile crime rates. The 1970s saw large rises in juvenile crime,
but in both countries, the proportionate use of custodial sentences
rose, with 'welfare' measures of supervision in the community and
residential care or education declining. English statistics are broken
down into social work or 'treatment' measures and custody (see
Table 6.1), whereas French statistics are divided into 'educational'
or custodial measures (see Table 6.2), but the statistics show an
increase in the use of custody in both systems. Perhaps the most
remarkable feature of those statistics for the 1970s is the doubling

Table 6.1 *Sentencing of juveniles in England and Wales from 1970–79, shown by sex and type of sentence and order*

Sex and Year	Conditional discharge '000s	%[1]	Probation in supervision order '000s	%	Fine '000s	%	Attendance centre order '000s	%	Detention centre order '000s	%	Care order '000s	%	Borstal training '000s	%
Males														
1970	8.3	17	10.5	22	18.6	38	3.4	7	2.1	4	3.8	8	1.0	2
1971	8.2	17	9.0	19	19.4	40	3.4	7	2.1	4	3.7	8	1.1	2
1972	8.5	17	8.6	17	20.8	42	3.7	7	2.5	5	3.4	7	1.3	3
1973	9.0	17	9.1	17	21.0	40	4.0	8	3.0	6	3.6	7	1.4	3
1974	11.0	18	10.6	17	24.2	40	5.2	9	3.7	6	3.8	6	1.6	3
1975	11.1	19	9.7	16	23.4	39	5.2	9	4.3	7	3.6	6	1.6	3
1976	11.8	20	9.3	15	22.9	38	5.7	9	4.9	8	3.0	5	1.7	3
1977	11.3	19	9.3	16	22.6	38	6.1	10	5.1	9	2.7	5	1.7	3
1978	10.8	18	8.6	14	23.5	39	6.9	11	5.5	9	2.6	4	1.8	3
1979	9.3	17	9.0	16	20.9	37	7.1	13	5.3	9	2.2	4	1.6	3
Females													less than	less than
1970	1.4	26	1.6	30	1.8	34	N/A		N/A		0.4	8	0.05	0.5
1971	1.4	26	1.4	27	1.8	34	N/A		N/A		0.5	9	0.05	1
1972	1.2	24	1.3	26	1.9	37	N/A		N/A		0.5	10	0.05	1
1973	1.3	24	1.4	27	1.8	34	N/A		N/A		0.6	11	0.05	1
1974	1.7	26	1.7	26	2.4	36	N/A		N/A		0.6	9	0.1	1
1975	2.0	28	1.9	26	2.3	33	N/A		N/A		0.7	10	0.1	1
1976	2.2	29	1.7	23	2.6	35	N/A		N/A		0.7	9	0.1	1
1977	2.2	28	1.8	24	2.8	37	N/A		N/A		0.7	9	0.1	1
1978	2.2	28	1.8	22	3.2	40	N/A		N/A		0.6	8	0.1	1
1979	1.9	26	1.7	25	2.8	39	0.1[2]	1	N/A		0.5	6	0.1	1

[1] Percentage of total number of sentences.
[2] Attendance centres only made available to girls from 1 January 1979.

in England and Wales of the proportionate use of the purely punitive detention centre, a prison department rather than an education or social services department.

Table 6.2 *Disposition of juvenile offenders in France from 1970–79*

Year	Acquittals and discharges		Educational resources		Custodial resources		
	Number	%[1]	Number	%	Number	%	Total
1970	2,053	4.4	32,991	70.5	11,735	25.1	46,779
1971	1,961	4.3	31,142	68.5	12,359	27.2	45,462
1972	2,273	4.5	33,979	67.4	14,168	28.1	50,420
1973	2,497	4.9	33,549	65.9	14,870	29.2	50,916
1974	2,923	5.4	34,152	63.7	16,570	30.9	53,645
1975	3,242	5.5	37,161	63.4	18,222	31.1	58,625
1976	3,116	5.5	36,134	63.94	17,709	31.1	56,969
1977	3,434	5.5	38,329	61.9	20,173	32.6	61,936
1978	N/A	N/A	N/A	N/A	N/A	N/A	N/A
1979	3,714	5.8	40,589	63.5	19,630	30.7	63,933

[1] Percentage of all dispositions.

Source: Institut de Criminologie (1982), *Etudes Statistiques*

In France and in England and Wales, the ratio of girls to boys appearing on criminal charges was about one to six, but the numbers being removed from home and placed in residential educational/social services institutions were approximately equal to the numbers of boys. Clearly, in both countries girls were being removed from home for reasons which would not have the same result for boys. This has also been shown to happen in other countries and has led to the belief that welfare-oriented juvenile justice systems are particularly disastrous for female delinquents.

It has for some time been established, mainly through extensive American research (Chesney-Lind, 1973; Emerson, 1968; Smart, 1976), that girls' offences as such are given scant attention by social workers, magistrates or judges. What is examined is their whole way of life: their moral character, the company they keep and whether or not they are promiscuous. Girls' behaviour is 'sexualized' so that rather than being convicted of offences, they are adjudged as in moral danger; in other words, in need of being removed from their families 'for their own good'. Applications of this research to European data show the sexualization of female delinquency to be apparent in West Germany, Belgium, the Netherlands and elsewhere (Elzinga and Naber, 1987). In fact, the sexualization phenomenon has been found wherever the judicial processing of young women has been studied. Recent reforms, therefore, have to be looked at in the light of whether they are likely to reduce the incarceration of juveniles generally, and whether they are likely to reduce discriminatory treatment of females.

Aims of the reforms

Both the 1982 Criminal Justice Act and the Badinter reforms addressed two sets of concerns: a professional concern over rising rates of juvenile incarceration, and a popular concern over rising rates of juvenile crime. In both countries, dissatisfaction with the workings of existing legislation was being expressed in many quarters and, in response to this, the Conservative government drafted a new criminal justice bill for England and Wales which drew largely upon the already existing report of the House of Commons Public Expenditure Committee Report on the Workings of the 1969 Children and Young Persons Act (Magistrates' Association, 1975), and the Minister of Justice in the in-coming Mitterrand government convened a reform commission to look into the workings of the 1945 Ordonnance, which presented its findings at Vaucresson, the Ministry of Justice research centre for juvenile delinquency, in January 1982. M. Badinter stated quite clearly that the problem of increased juvenile incarceration had outstripped the problem of increased juvenile crime:

> Brutalement, sans que le nombre ou la gravité des infractions commises par des mineurs ait progressé de façon significative, le nombre des incarcerations des mineurs a comme un accroissement foudroyant. (Badinter, 1982)

> [Bluntly, without the number or the seriousness of offences committed by minors having progressed in a significant manner, the number of incarcerations of minors has had an overwhelming increase.]

No such order of priority of concern has been stated in Britain, so that the various interested parties have been left in the position of having to vie with each other for influence in new legislation and policies.

One criticism of juvenile justice legislation in many western countries has been that magistrates feel powerless to pass sentences adequate to deter crime and that they also feel that they have lost power vis-à-vis social workers and other child-care experts (Magistrates' Association, 1975; Syndicat de la Magistrature, 1982). Another strand of criticism has been that juveniles and their parents experience juvenile justice as unfair. They see individualized sentencing not as a well-considered, professional response to their needs but as unfair in that members of a group of friends committing an offence together may all receive different sentences (Donzelot, 1979; Matza, 1964; Parker et al., 1981). A further criticism has been that the 'treatment' approach of juvenile justice has led to an over-interventionist system which has brought far too many children within the orbit of formal social control, and given social workers the right to intervene too much, and for too long, in their lives (see especially Austin and Krisberg, 1981, 1982; Cohen, 1979; Donzelot, 1979; Thorpe et al., 1980). All these concerns are addressed by the 1982 Criminal Justice Act and the Badinter reforms; the differences between them lie in which of the various juvenile justice lobbies emerges as most influential, and how the balances between the various aims of the reforms are struck.

Justice or welfare?

These criticisms of welfare-oriented juvenile justice systems have led to calls for the abandonment of utopian notions of 'curing' delinquency and meeting young people's needs, and for a more pragmatic strategy of doing 'less harm' rather than 'more good'. The view has gained currency over recent years that young people will be better protected from the risk of incarceration by adequate legal representation and by adherence to 'due process' legal conventions in juvenile courts, than by the presence of social workers urging the need for rehabilitative measures. It is suggested that they will be more likely to be lightly sentenced if more consideration is given to the offence committed, and less to their real or supposed 'welfare needs'. (All the works mentioned in the preceding paragraph support the position; a good summary of the 'justice model' for young people is Giller and Morris, 1983).

These arguments are very much in the ascendancy in the UK at the moment. The 1982 Criminal Justice Act acknowledges one of the main tenets of the so-called 'justice model', that indeterminate sentences should be replaced by determinate ones, and it replaces the indeterminate borstal sentence with the determinate youth custody sentence. It also introduces a six-month residential care order which, as well as introducing an element of determinacy, takes power from social workers and gives it back to magistrates in that once the six-month term fixed by the magistrate is over, the child must be returned to court for a further decision about whether he or she must stay in institutional care or may rejoin his or her family. Magistrates are also given powers to specify the content of work with young offenders on supervision orders to social workers by the introduction of 'supervised activity' orders. Almost everything the Magistrates' Association asked for in their submissions to the 1975 report is included in the 1982 Act which definitely enhances the powers of magistrates relative to social workers, and takes the juvenile justice system in England and Wales further towards a system of formal criminal justice and away from the alternative, welfare-tribunal model.

By comparison, the Badinter reforms move even further towards the welfare model. Although acknowledging the confusion of roles involved in children's judges and their assistants aiming to dispense bulk criminal justice and individual educational assistance, and acknowledging the repressive and over-interventionist possibilities of supposedly educational measures, the French commission comes out firmly in favour of maintaining the union of judicial and educational institutions established by the specialism of the *juges des enfants*. The Commission recommends the strengthening of educational measures, and also recommends extending the jurisdiction of the *juges des enfants*.

In England and Wales the aim of reducing incarceration is addressed by extending the range of non-custodial options laying down certain rules such as the requirement that no young offender should receive a custodial sentence without a social enquiry report being presented to the magistrates, and by the directive that non-custodial alternatives should be fully considered before a custodial sentence is passed. That the aim of reducing incarceration is not given clear primacy over the aim of satisfying supposed popular demand for 'sterner and surer punishments' for juvenile crime is, however, evidenced by the introduction in the Criminal Justice Act of the short, 21-day custodial sentence, and by giving magistrates the right to pass custodial sentences of up to six months' duration on young people, whereas under previous legislation they were required to remit to the higher court for sentence. At the same time, a large building programme of custodial institutions is being undertaken.

Badinter has addressed the problem of incarceration of young people by coupling his commission to reform juvenile justice law with a simultaneous commission on incarceration. This approach isolates the kinds of incarceration which have been growing most rapidly and tries severely to circumscribe such forms of imprisonment. Of most concern has been the increase in pre-trial remands in custody (*détention provisoire*), which increased by 57.8 per cent from 1974 to 1981. Furthermore, in 1974 12.9 per cent of those remanded in custody were aged under 16; by 1981 this percentage had risen to 23.2. Consensus appears to have been reached amongst the various interested parties that remand in custody should be impossible for those under 16, and restricted only to those accused of the most heinous of crimes for the 16–18 year olds.

Results of the reforms

The Badinter reforms are still in the process of being enacted, so it is difficult to compare results. However, it is clear that the 1982 Criminal Justice Act has resulted in both a rise in the proportionate use of custodial sentences for young people and a trend towards longer sentences, so that in completing their overhaul of the laws relating to young offenders, the French would be well advised to follow through their apparent commitment to tackle directly the worst features of their system, namely the excessive use of custodial remands. They would be further advised to refrain from adding more alternative sentences, since all available evidence indicates that countries (and states within countries) with the highest rates of incarceration are those with the most sophisticated penal systems in terms of having a myriad of possible dispositions (Cohen, 1985; Hudson, B., 1984; Pratt, 1986a; Rutherford, 1986).

Monitoring of the results of the 1982 Criminal Justice Act by the National Association for the Care and Resettlement of Offenders (NACRO) shows that there has been an overall increase in the use of custody for young people, both absolute and proportionate; and that there has been a shift from the shorter detention centre sentence to the longer youth custody sentence; and that youth custody terms are tending to be longer than the terms served under the borstal sentences which youth custody replaced (NACRO, 1985).

The most alarming increases in custodial sentencing have been in receptions of young females into custody. In the first 12 months of the operation of the new Act, the number of 15- to 20-year-old females received into custody rose by 20 per cent (NACRO, 1985). This increase in custodial sentencing because of criminal offending has not been accompanied by any reduction of numbers of young females received into care or placed under supervision, and numbers in these categories have remained fairly constant.

Justice for girls

At the inception of the recent reforms, England and Wales and France already had high rates of juvenile incarceration in penal establishments (that is, high by international standards). These rates were increasing, whereas the use of care institutions in England and Wales and educational institutions in France was declining. The 'justice model' would appear, therefore, to be theory catching up with practice, rather than theory providing impetus for a new direction in practice. It would also seem from present trends that the French attempts to strengthen the welfare elements of juvenile justice are more necessary and desirable than English moves to a more formal administration of even-handed punishment–justice.

For girls, however, efforts to decide in which direction it would be best to proceed are complicated by the fact that they have been disproportionately committed to institutional care for reasons other than offending (see Table 6.3).

Table 6.3 *Children who came into care under 1969 Children and Young Persons Act Sections 1(2)c; 1(2)d; 1(2)f; or 7(7) during the 12 months ended 31 March (all ages) in England and Wales*

Legal status of child	Boys (%)	Girls (%)	Total number (=100%)
1(2)c – Moral danger			
1978	23	77	240
1979	16.2	83.8	277
1980	20.8	79.2	250
1981	21.8	78.2	224
1982	22	78	222
1(2)d – Beyond control			
1978	50	50	601
1979	46	54	666
1980	52.6	47.4	796
1981	46.5	53.5	769
1982	50.2	49.8	739
1(2)f or 7(7) – Offence			
1978	82	18	4,856
1979	83	17	3,470
1980	83.5	16.5	3,339
1981	84.6	15.4	2,934
1982	85.5	14.5	2,649

Source: DHSS Local Authority Statistics, England and Wales (quoted by Gelsthorpe, 1985: 5)

The statistics show both the overall number of children and young persons received into care for offending decreasing quite dramatically, and within that overall number, the percentage of girls falling. The numbers of young people received into care for the 'beyond control' reason has increased, but not by as much as the increase in offence-condition receptions into care. None the less, there have been such obvious inequities in the institutionalization of girls under welfare proceedings that it is tempting to see in the 'return to justice' movement hopes for some improvement in the way girls are dealt with by juvenile justice systems.

The problem is that if we rescue girls from the rigidities of notions of orthodox femininity embodied in our judgments of girls as 'beyond control', or 'in moral danger', we do not eliminate girls being judged by the double standards we apply to girls' and boys' behaviour; rather we transfer judgment from a set of stereotypes connected with girls' behaviour within the family to another set connected with female delinquency.

Current ideas about girls' delinquency in particular, and female crime in general, are quite different from ideas about male crime. Delinquency and crime is somehow held to be 'normal' for males, even if reprehensible, but 'abnormal' for females. Since male criminals outnumber females by so many, those females who do commit offences are regarded as outraging not only the laws of the land but also the requirements of the female role. There is now a considerable volume of research evidence that shows that female criminals, because of this 'double offence' against legality and against femininity, are punished much more harshly for their transgressions than are males. Women, for instance, are far more likely to go to prison for a first offence than men are, and girls are far more likely than boys to be committed to residential care for a first offence. Girls' delinquent acts are seldom looked at in their own right and judged trivial or serious according to the amount of property involved or injury sustained, but rather are regarded as 'acting out' some deep-seated psycho-social problem (Smart, 1976).

The notion of female offenders as 'abnormal' has a long history, starting with Lombroso who claimed that women are less developed than men, and therefore do not have the intelligence or resourcefulness to commit crimes (Lombroso and Ferrero, 1900). Women who do commit crimes, therefore, are not proper women at all, but are more masculine than they should be. Although Lombroso's precise formulation has long been discredited, the idea of the female criminal as overly masculine, as 'unadjusted' to her femininity and the female role, survives and flourishes. Various studies have purported to show that female criminals are less physically attractive than 'normal' women, and that they are not 'successful' in forming relationships with males. One study which is still very influential today was done in the 1920s by W.I. Thomas, an American sociologist much influenced by Freud, who said that in times of changing social roles and uncertain moral values, with parental controls weakened and community ties loosened, the unattractive or maladjusted girl who could not meet her needs for dependency and affection through satisfactory relationships would seek solace in promiscuity and delinquency (Thomas, 1967). This approach to female crime is still dominant today, and the 'treatment' usually offered in establishments is for female offenders is to become 'pretty, sociable women' (Konopka, 1966).

A good English illustration of this casting of delinquency as the acting out of deeper problems is provided by the recent debates on the future of Bullwood Hall, a girls' custody centre. Advocates of the closure of this establishment have been claiming, not that it is unnecessary because there are not enough girls committing offences serious enough to warrant custody, but that the facilities of Bullwood are inadequate. Smaller units able to offer a more intensely therapeutic experience are called for, with more psychiatric treatment and psychological counselling available. Similarly, there were attempts to turn Holloway Prison into virtually a 'therapeutic community' in the 1970s, undermined by staff shortages rather than any change of attitude towards the causes of female crime.

Assault, criminal damage, burglary, taking and driving away, are all taken more seriously in girls than in boys because they are presumed to be so rare and so role-abnormal. Shoplifting is the only crime that is considered in any way 'normal' for girls, but precisely because it is considered a woman's crime, shoplifting attracts psychiatric explanations in a way that other everyday crimes do not (Campbell, 1981). Our stereotyped images of the shoplifter are all female: the menopausal housewife; the confused foreign tourist; the mother unable to feed her family legitimately; the teenage girl unable to afford make-up; the magpie female of any age tempted by bright jewellery or luxury underwear. Despite the fact that males outnumber females in shoplifting as in every other offence category, it is envisaged as a female offence, and as such attracts stereotyped psychiatric labels such as 'kleptomaniac' which have no equivalent for other types of run-of-the-mill offence.

As it is doing with boys, transferring girls from welfare to justice proceedings would involve reducing the differentiation between them and adults. The explanations referred to above all speak of the 'female' criminal rather than the girl or the woman; already female offenders tend to be looked at without regard to youthfulness or adulthood. Girl offenders are judged by criteria of femininity rather than adolescence; they are seen as 'acting out' their failure to be feminine rather than 'acting silly' because of their youth and immaturity of judgment. This means that the standard explanations of delinquency in young males, such as the delinquent or anti-school subculture and peer group pressures, are never applied to girls.

Which theories are influential is of much more than academic interest, since the dominance of particular theories does much to influence practice. If delinquency is regarded as an adolescent phase (as it is with boys) then the aim of professionals in the field is to try to ensure that no opportunity for going through the normal processes of maturing is lost by removal from the community and gradual increase in responsibilities and bonds to the social order. Thus, there is much talk now of 'maintaining' and 'containing' delinquents in the community until they can grow out of their delinquency. The very notion of adolescence and phases implies that current behaviour can be expected to be left behind as the phase ends and adolescence gives way to adulthood. That this is a realistic expectation is attested by the dramatic fall-off in crimes committed by youths after the age of 17. Where the problem is seen not as an adolescent phase but as a failure to adapt to the female social role and to develop appropriate feminine characteristics, however, any delinquent acts are seen as more serious because they are taken as indications of worsening future trouble. Femininity, after all, is something that girls are supposed to grow into, not out of, so any signs of thwarted feminine development or maladjustment to femininity will be treated very seriously indeed. Intervention, both drastic and prompt, is thought necessary before things get even worse (Hudson, B., 1984b). The justice model approach, with its emphasis on the offence rather than the individual characteristics of the offender, erodes the distinction between juveniles and adults, so will tend to encourage even further this judgment of girls' delinquency against standards of adult femininity rather than juvenile immaturity.

The root of the problems faced by girl offenders would seem to be the comparative rarity of female delinquency. Contrast between the rates of male and female crime has prompted successive generations of criminologists either to ignore female crime altogether because it is regarded as too infrequent to be a social problem of any significance or to discuss female crime only in relation to male crime. If the only question ever asked is 'why do so few females commit crimes compared to males?', then, the question having been posed in terms of male/female differences, the answers arrived at are almost bound to be in those terms too. Hence the feminist critique of traditional criminological attitudes to women as it developed in the 1970s gave rise to numerous research projects designed to demonstrate that girls were committing far more offences than were ever officially recorded and, moreover, that they were committing the same wide range of offences as boys. It was claimed that the differences in statistics between male and female crime were due less to actual differences in behaviour than to differential social processing, that is the diversion from criminal to welfare proceedings mentioned earlier. By asking girls themselves what they did, it was hoped to explode the myth of girls not committing offences, committing only certain offences, or playing only minor roles in boys' delinquent sprees. A crop of 'self-report studies' appeared to show little difference in girls' and boys' delinquent behaviour and, in a vulgarized form, these studies received wide publicity.

These self-report studies coincided with the popular fear that as women's roles in society generally expanded, their participation in crime would also expand. This viewpoint was lent some academic credibility by Freda Adler, who pointed to the appearance of all-girl 'bovver gangs' on the streets of London and New York, and the participation by adult women in spheres of crime traditionally the preserve of men (Adler, 1975). Women, claimed Adler and others, were learning new skills and finding new positions in the world, and so were undertaking new crimes: more females were learning to drive, and you need to be able to drive for taking and driving away and taking without consent; more women were achieving positions of responsibility in employment and you have to be in positions of trust to embezzle; more women were having bank accounts and you need to know how to write cheques and use bank cards for cheque forgery and fraud.

There was, therefore, an expectation that female crime would increase; a 'moral panic' that the new woman would be more criminal than her stay-at-home forebear. Traditional feminine virtues were disappearing, and traditional feminine virtues included abstinence from crime. True to expectations, throughout the 1970s female crime rates rose faster than male crime rates, but it must be remembered that the difference in crime rates between the sexes, though it narrowed somewhat, by no means disappeared. Again, though, it is impossible to know how much of this is due to actual changes in criminal behaviour and how much due to changes in official processing. A long-held explanation of the differences in the way males and females have been treated by the criminal justice system has been that of 'chivalry'. According to the so-called 'chivalry myth', police officers and magistrates are mostly male, and as such are chivalrously unwilling to label females as criminal and disbelieve them when they protest their innocence, and willing to believe them when they say they were 'forced into it' by a male. As the first wave of self-report research passed, more recent studies have linked the rise in female crime rates to there being more women in the police and judiciary, showing that these women do not adopt the same attitudes to female offenders as their male counterparts have done. There is also, it can be argued, a decline in chivalry generally. Certainly few men would now stand and offer a women a seat in buses and trains, and this reduction of special treatment of women in society has also meant the lessening of special treatment for female offenders. (These studies are summarized in Nagel and Hagan, 1983.)

Whatever the reasons, we became attuned in the 1970s to expecting female delinquency to become far more common and are somewhat surprised that this has not happened to anything like the extent that was predicted. The reasons for this are less relevant here than the fact that even when the numbers of females involved in crime was increasing most rapidly, the fate of individual girls and women convicted of crimes did not change. Females are still punished more harshly than men for crimes which go against the traditional female role, and the sentencing of females is still much more heavily influenced than that of males by factors such as homelessness or family ties. The most recent research has shown that the lighter sentences often received by women relate not to chivalry, but to involvement in less serious offences, with fewer previous convictions (Farrington and Morris, 1983). Where males and females have the same degree of criminality, females seem to be punished more harshly than males.

This suggests that the 'return to justice' approach would be anything but beneficial for females. Being processed judicially for offences rather than for welfare needs would lead to the accumulation of more extensive criminal records, and they would still be subject to this double condemnation as offenders and as flouting the values of femininity. The 'return to justice' argument should be seen for what it is – the legitimizing rhetoric of the right-wing law and order lobby – and resisted as such. At the same time, it must be accepted that the substitution of a justice for a welfare orientation is no substitute for reformation of social attitudes towards femininity, the female role and female actions.

Bringing about fundamental change in attitudes towards femininity is an extremely long-term task. What criminologists can do more immediately is to look behind blanket statistics regarding females and take up the issues of what particular groups of females are vulnerable to institutionalization. American studies have shown that for both adults and juveniles, females who do not correspond to white, middle-class standards of femininity are most badly discriminated against. At all stages of the criminal justice system it is black females, females who do not show 'appropriate' feminine responses such as tearfulness, females who wear jeans, leather jackets, etc., who are harshly treated from arrest to sentence (Curran, 1983; Steffensmeir et al., 1982; Visher, 1983). Little research of this kind has as yet been undertaken in England, but in France it has been established that the racial differentiation in sentencing is even more marked for girls than for boys (Institut de Criminologie, 1982).

As with the attempt to end *détention provisoire* for juveniles, the safest way to proceed, for the present – whilst not losing sight of the deeper aims of bringing about change in popular attitudes to youth in general and girls in particular – is to tackle the worst features of current practice directly rather than change direction and ditch our traditions of trying to help rather than punish children and young people. Where 'justice model' reforms have been implemented – notably in California and several other American states – their proponents are already proclaiming themselves dismayed at their 'unintended consequences' (see Greenberg and Humphries, 1980). This is already beginning to happen in England (Davies, 1985). Furthermore, although no country has completely abandoned notions of crime and criminal justice in relation to juveniles and adopted a pure welfare model, there is evidence that those countries which have gone furthest in this direction – the Scandinavian countries, for example – are producing the least repressive sentencing practices, and are generally being less interventionist in their response to juvenile delinquency (Pratt, 1986a). If the French continue their attempts further to increase the welfare component of juvenile justice, whilst providing stronger safeguards against possible abuses of the welfare approach, then developing differences in rates of institutionalization of young people, and especially females, in the two countries, will be extremely instructive. Should trends in institutionalization rates remain as similar in the two countries as they have been up to now, then the importance of fundamental attitudes to youth and femininity relative to changes in legislation and practice guidelines will have been demonstrated.

Note

Material relating to French developments is drawn from information collected during a visit to the Institut de Criminologie, Paris. Grateful appreciation is due to Jacques Leaute, Directeur, for granting unlimited access to statistical and other documentary material held at the Institut and for giving generously of his time in conversation. The visit was made possible by financial assistance from the ESRC.

7

Gypsy girls in an Italian juvenile court

Roberta Cipollini, Franca Faccioli and Tamar Pitch

During the last few years there have been indications, in Italy, of considerable increases in the number of female juveniles arrested and charged. At least in Rome, where our study (Cipollini et al., 1986) was carried out, this tendency seems particularly marked for gypsies. Although in this first phase of our research we did not study trends over time, these developments alerted us particularly to the problems of girls who are also gypsies. This chapter therefore presents the results of an analysis of the records of the Rome Prosecuting Office for 1980 in so far as they relate to girls, and to gypsy girls in particular.

The question of gypsy girls is complex. In part their situation is analogous to that of other ethnic minorities in other countries, but the analogies – social marginality, high visibility, the fact of having always been the object of prejudice and fear – should be interpreted within a context which is in fact special. By contrast with many other ethnic minorities, the gypsies are a *nation* differing in language and culture from the host nation. If integration appears to be on the whole an impossible and unacceptable objective, interaction is always problematic and difficult. The gypsies are a continuous object of civic concern, especially since their settlements are perforce near socially and culturally 'deprived' urban peripheral areas. Thus it should not surprise us that the activities which bring gypsy girls within the ambit of criminal justice are different from the offences of Italian girls. The subsequent treatment of gypsy girls by criminal justice agencies is also different from the treatment of Italian girls, as we will show.

Methodology of the research

The research depends upon two initial choices: first, we decided to study the *penal* aspect of juvenile justice; secondly, we decided to study *girls*. In combination, the choices involve a break with current academic conventions, so that a word of explanation is required.

We do not consider here the vast area of behaviour known as 'irregularities of conduct and character', nor the broad range of phenomena, also falling within the province of juvenile justice, variously defined as 'abandonment' or 'maladjustment'. In a later phase of our study we shall examine the interplay between penal and administrative or welfare measures, but at this stage we wish to argue that the analysis of criminal justice is central to an understanding of the transformations of criminal and social policies which are currently being experienced in Italy (see Cipollini et al., 1986).

Although there has been a great deal of social control talk relating to de-penalization and decarceration, this seems to be contradicted by data for the last ten years. In fact, the official statistics show an increase in juveniles brought to court (in 1976, there were 16,174; in 1980, 19,266), even though they reveal that the majority of these had their charges dropped (in 1976 charges were dropped against 69.5 per cent of juveniles; in 1980, 74 per cent). However, the data also record an increase in juveniles found guilty (13 per cent in 1976; 23 per cent in 1980), an increase which particularly concerns females (see ISTAT, 1982–3). If we read these figures in the light of the reduction in administration orders, of the high number of dropped charges, and the trend to shorten the period of preventive detention, the law seems to have acted steadily less as a means of social control and steadily more as a symbolic system of sanction.

While, in the case of girls, much international research seems to be focused on the non-penal aspects of juvenile justice which emphasize 'irregularities of conduct and character' and the administrative and social work measures relating to them, it seems to us crucial to *start* instead from penal intervention as we would have done in research into male juveniles. Since the criminal law is a fairly sensitive barometer of changes in attitude, perception and politics, exploring how, why and with what outcome girls today come into contact with it should come before exploration of other ways in which the juvenile female condition is disciplined. Since they lie more within the traditional measures of control of the feminine, these ways are less *immediately* reflective of novelty and change.

Regarding our decision to concentrate on girls, of the many reasons, both subjective and objective, the following seem to us to be the decisive ones: the lack of existing research; the feeling that what does exist takes little account of the specific nature of the female condition and hence of its social control; and the emergence of a vague sensation, though not (yet) empirically based, of an increased and above all a qualitative change in 'deviance' and social conflict. Certainly in relation to adults, the objects of social alarm in Italy over the last ten years, terrorism and drug dependence, have offered public opinion a scenario with participants of both sexes.

The data base

The object of the research is action by the Prosecuting Office of the Rome Juvenile Tribunal in relation to offences committed by girls in the course of 1980. The data were culled from Prosecuting Office records.

The recourse to official data has made possible a reconstruction of some aspects of the functioning of a control apparatus and the image that it offers of the deviance with which it deals. We are of course aware of the limits of such data gathering, both because of the dimensions of the data themselves, which do not supply sufficient information for an analytic reconstruction of the problem, and because of the nature of the data and the source used. This type of secondary data gathering can only supply an image of penal intervention and female criminality as it is registered by a control apparatus. But it can inform us accurately about the way different people, in our case gypsy girls and Italian girls, are treated once they have been brought within the penal apparatus.

The enquiry was conducted on all female juveniles subject to penal intervention through the prosecuting office of the Rome Juvenile Tribunal (JT) during 1980. From January to March 1984 data were collected on all penal proceedings recorded for the year under consideration, including proceedings relating to offences committed in years prior to 1980, but placed on the Prosecuting Office records in that year. The choice of the year 1980 was determined by the need to cover the greatest possible number of completed cases, given that juvenile proceedings usually last a long time in Italy. Some 23 per cent of proceedings (78) begun in 1980 and finished by the date of our study had lasted more than two years, while 18.6 per cent (63) were still not completed on the date of the survey.

We analysed 339 cases, comprising *all* the female juveniles appearing as defendants. In other words, we sampled people rather than offences. Accordingly, this analysis refers to the *first* offence recorded by the Prosecutor's Office in 1980 for each female juvenile, although where the charge covers more than one offence only the main offence is taken into account. Female juveniles accused jointly with adults are not included, since, until July 1983, the Ordinary Tribunal was competent for these. They therefore do not appear in the records of the prosecuting office of the Juvenile Tribunal, which we sampled.[1] The girls were all between 14 and 18 years old, inclusive.

The geographical jurisdiction of the Rome JT Prosecuting Office covers the commune and province of Rome and the other provinces of Lazio. The aspects of juvenile deviance analysed in the course of this study therefore have to be understood in the context of a highly differentiated catchment area, ranging from the metropolis to predominantly rural areas. It is useful to stress right now that the majority of the 339 female juveniles reported to the police (80.8 per cent) lived in Rome and its province with only 19.2 per cent living in the other provinces of Lazio.

In coding the data from the files we considered a total of thirty-four variables concerned with the characteristics of the juvenile, the characteristics of the offence and the characteristics of the penal proceedings themselves. Here we analyse only those aspects of our data which throw light on the special situation of gypsy girls.

Gypsy girls in an Italian court

Table 7.1 shows the nationality of the girls in our sample. It can be seen that while the 10 per cent of our sample who were gypsies is far greater than their proportion in the population at large, in absolute terms they were a small minority of those appearing in court. We deduced that these girls were gypsies although there was no record of their nationality (gypsies rarely have identifying documents), but most gypsies come from Yugoslavia and their names spoke clearly of an Eastern European origin. An even smaller minority is that of foreign girls whose nationality *is* recorded. Because both groups are very small in absolute numbers, and it cannot be excluded that some of the girls in the second group are also gypsies, gypsy and other non-Italian girls have been grouped together in our analysis.

Table 7.1 *Nationality of girls in the sample*

	Number	%
Italian	294	86.7
Gypsy	34	10.0
Other non-Italian	11	3.3
Total	339	100

The first major difference between Italian and gypsy girls is in the offence with which they were charged. Most of the gypsy and non-Italian girls were charged with theft (77.8 per cent), the only other offence that they were significantly involved in being 'transgressions vis-à-vis the authorities' (15.6 per cent of charges against them). These offences include in particular breaches of residence permit regulations. Italian girls, in contrast, become

Table 7.2 *Nationality and type of offence*

	Theft		Injury		Breaches of regulations		Driving without a licence		Transgressions against authority		Other		Total	
	Number	%	Number	%	Number	%	Number	%	Number	%	Number	%	Number	%
Italian	53	18.0	51	17.3	22	7.5	104	35.4	30	10.2	34	11.6	294	100
Non-Italian/ gypsy	35	77.8	—	—	1	2.2	1	2.2	7	15.6	1	2.2	45	100
Total	88	25.9	51	15.0	23	6.8	105	31.0	37	10.9	35	10.3	339	100

involved in penal proceedings for driving without a licence (35.4 per cent) and, after that, for theft (18 per cent) and injury (17.3 per cent).

The results are summarized in Table 7.2. Apart from the three most frequent offences – theft in its various forms, driving without a licence, and injury whether culpable or voluntary – we constructed two special groups of offences in terms of their sociological relevance. These were misdemeanours including breaches of administrative rules or regulations and breaches of rules regulating conduct towards public officials and/or legal institutions (transgressions against authority).[2] The distinction between the two types of behaviour enables offences concerned with transgression against structures and agencies of social control (which often do not amount to much) to be isolated from offences involving breaches of often little-known administrative regulations in connection with which either indifference or ignorance may be involved.

The next question on which we examined our data concerned girls who were arrested and those who were summonsed, that is, those who did not have to spend even a few hours in custody. As Table 7.3 shows, two-thirds of the gypsies and non-Italians were arrested or taken into immediate custody, compared with only 6.8 per cent of Italian girls. Moreover, most girls (70 per cent) are released (*libertà provvisoria*) after a week in detention,[3] which suggests that ensuring their later appearance in court cannot be the reason for their detention. Rather, imprisonment seems to be a symbolic punishment for some girls, in the main gypsies, who commit minor offences.

Table 7.3 *Nationality and arrest (immediate custody)*

	Not arrested (summons only)		Arrest (immediate custody)		Total	
	Number	%	Number	%	Number	%
Italian	274	93.2	20	6.8	294	100
Non-Italian/ gypsy	15	33.3	30	66.7	45	100
Total	289	85.3	50	14.7	339	100

$\chi^2 = 111.048$; $p > 0.001$.

Part of the explanation for these differences lies in the different offences allegedly committed by the two groups of girls. Forty-seven per cent (42) of the girls charged with theft were detained, whereas *all* those charged with injury, driving without a licence or breaches of regulations were released, and only 8.1 per cent (3) of those charged with transgressions against the authorities were detained. (Five girls, 14.3 per cent, charged with miscellaneous offences were also detained but, of course, no sense can be made of this result.) However, even when only girls accused of theft are considered, gypsy and non-Italian girls are more likely to be arrested and held in custody, however briefly, than Italian girls. The nature of the offence does not explain away this difference in treatment, as Table 7.4 reveals.

Table 7.4   *Nationality and juridical status (girls charged with theft)*

	Not arrested		Arrested		Total	
	Number	%	Number	%	Number	%
Italian	39	73.6	14	26.4	51	100
Non-Italian/ gypsy	7	20.0	28	80.0	35	100
Total	46	52.3	42	47.7	88	100

$\chi^2 = 24.717$; $p < 0.001$.

Another factor affecting the summons or custody decision was the presence or absence of co-accused, and here again there were differences between the gypsy or non-Italian girls and the Italian girls. The overall figures and the figures by nationality are given in Tables 7.5 and 7.6.

Table 7.5   *Summons/arrest decisions and the presence of joint accused*

	With joint accused		Without joint accused		Total	
	Number	%	Number	%	Number	%
Summonsed	63	21.8	226	78.2	289	100
Arrested	38	76.0	12	24.0	50	100
Total	101	29.8	238	80.2	339	100

$\chi^2 = 59.865$; $p < 0.001$.

It is also apparent from the data that those co-accused with gypsy girls are almost invariably girls, whereas for Italian girls who, it may be remembered, are more often charged with driving without a licence, the less frequent co-accused is as likely to be a boy as a girl.

Table 7.6 *Joint accusation by nationality and sex of jointly accused*

	Alone		Jointly with boys		Jointly with girls		Jointly with boys and girls		Total	
	Number	%	Number	%	Number	%	Number	%	Number	%
Italian	222	75.5	28	9.5	36	12.3	8	2.7	294	100
Non-Italian/ gypsies	16	35.6	4	8.9	25	55.5	—	—	45	100
Total	238		32		61		8		339	

It may be said that belonging to a marginal sector of society (and possibly living from petty theft) involves the risk of falling within the ambit of juvenile justice. The girl 'without fixed abode' who steals is more 'visible' and classifiable as a 'delinquent' than her sister with a permanent home.[4] She will also, partly because of the cultural tradition of the gypsy group she belongs to, almost always be accompanied by other females of the same age. The fact that girls arrested are so frequently jointly accused with other girls does not indicate the existence of bands of juveniles, but refers more to the presence of small groups of two or three girls, mostly gypsies, who rob people on the streets, or commit petty thefts in houses or supermarkets.[5]

For offences committed by small groups, institutional intervention is more immediate and more decisive. Groups are perhaps perceived as more dangerous than individual girls.

In general, consideration of the data shows a fair amount of pre-trial 'decarceration' for offences by girls, but also stresses that prison remains if only as a symbolic measure of punishment. Theft, whether major or petty but especially if by girls in groups and still more so if by gypsies, may well result in a few days in jail on remand.

Sentencing girls in Rome
In writing in English for colleagues presumed to be more familiar with a common law system, some words of explanation of the range of decisions available is necessary before our results can be presented. The relevant categories are 'immaturity', 'pardon', 'amnesty' and 'remittal'. These decisions are made by an examining judge working within a prosecutor's office. If his or her advice is for one or another kind of dismissal (the first three of these categories) the case is decided informally by the four judges of the

Rome Tribunal (including one woman and one man who are 'lay' judges) in the absence of the accused and his or her lawyer.

The 'immaturity' decision results from the fact that minors between 14 and 18 years of age are not automatically deemed to be criminally responsible. It is for the examining judge within the prosecutor's office to decide, on the advice of experts such as psychologists, psychiatrists and social workers, whether or not the minor is responsible or 'immature'.

'Pardon' is a measure existing only for minors (those 14–18 years of age). It means that the minor is recognized as being guilty of the offence, but the judges decide that he or she should be let free without a conviction of any kind being recorded. By law, pardons can be granted only once, the first time a minor is charged with a crime. Actual judicial practice, however, supported by a decision of the Constitutional Court, has extended the use of this measure.

Every few years 'amnesties' are granted by law; they are governmental rather than judicial decisions. They involve the cancellation of all charges falling within the scope of that particular amnesty, and their consequences. Judges have no discretion here, but they can, and often do, prolong proceedings over a case if they want it to fall under an amnesty whose granting has been announced.

The examining judge in the prosecutor's office may also decide that a case should be sent for a formal trial, usually when the offence charged is serious or when the accused pleads 'not guilty'. Legally minors have to be tried 'speedily' (*dirette*) or 'very speedily' (*direttissime*) once an examining judge has decided upon 'remittal'. Remittals, of course, lead to a formal trial at which the young person may or may not be convicted, at which stage one or another of a range of sentences may be deployed.

A first look at the recommendations for sentence put forward by the examining judges in the Rome Prosecutor's office suggests extraordinary leniency. Pardon (33 per cent) and amnesty (26 per cent) are the most frequent requests to the court. There follow the *dirette* and *direttissime*, the speedy bringing of proceedings before the Tribunal (10 per cent), and dismissal for 'immaturity', which accounts for 10.5 per cent of all the cases brought. The type of trial, the sanctions themselves and, indeed, the grounds for sanctions follow the logic of a paternalism which many people denounce not only for the absence of guarantees, but also for the overall effect of 'de-responsibilization', or the infantilization of minors.[6] Because of these very characteristics, the subsequent results of the passage through criminal justice are not all symbolic: pardon and immaturity decisions, even if not accompanied by administrative measures,

Table 7.7 Prosecuting office's request by offence

	Immaturity		Pardon		Amnesty		Remittal		Other disposals		Total	
	Number	%	Number	%	Number	%	Number	%	Number	%	Number	%
Theft	4	5.2	27	35.1	17	22.0	24	31.2	5	6.5	77	100
Injuries	—	—	2	4.1	12	24.5	2	4.1	33	67.3	49	100
Breaches of regulations	2	9.1	3	13.6	10	45.5	—	—	7	31.8	22	100
Driving without a licence	21	20.2	56	53.8	18	17.3	3	2.9	6	5.8	104	100
Transgressions against authority	4	12.9	7	22.6	14	45.2	2	6.4	4	12.9	31	100
Other	2	6.9	8	27.6	10	34.5	5	17.2	4	13.8	29	100
Total	33	10.5	103	33.0	81	26.0	36	10.6	59	18.9	312[1]	100

[1] Excluding 27 cases pending in the prosecutor's office.

nevertheless have weight as signs of the passage of the young person through the legal circuit; suspended sentences may leave the young person's debt to justice in abeyance until the age of majority, with the consequent risks. These 'lenient' measures do not mean that for the young women we studied there are no effects. If the scenario presented by the prosecuting office's requests seems characterized on the whole by the desire for dismissal, this is not a complete and total dismissal. Unconditional discharge is requested in only a very limited number of cases. It is true that there are numerous requests for amnesty and it can therefore be said that, as far as the prosecuting office is concerned, around 45 per cent of cases ought not to come before the court. But in most cases, however, the attitude of the prosecutor's office is closer to what might be called 'cautious de-penalization': the charges are dropped, but in some way the girls remain within the ambit of justice. As Table 7.7 shows, the disposal varies by offence and this, of course, disproportionately affects the gypsy and non-Italian girls.

Pardon, remittal, and amnesty (in order) are the examining judge's preferred and recommended disposals for girls charged with theft; pardon (as much as 53.8 per cent), dismissal for under age and amnesty is the order of preference for driving without a licence; injury tends to end up with dismissal because 'no-one preferred charges'; for breaches of administrative regulations and those against public authorities, the request is usually for amnesty.

The attitude to theft seems to be characterized by some recognition of the intention (and hence responsibility) of the accused girls: the small number of requests for dismissal on the grounds of immaturity might be interpreted in this sense. There is 'pardon' but at the same time the 'ability to know what one is doing' is recognized. Although the evidence in statistical terms is not altogether conclusive, it once again seems that gypsy girls tend to be dealt with more severely: half of them are sent for trial, compared with only 21.6 per cent of Italian girls; very few of them are accorded amnesty (Cipollini et al., 1986) and no gypsy girl is dismissed on the grounds of immaturity.

On the other hand, as Table 7.8 shows, requests for Italian girls charged with theft (apart from remittal and pardon) comprise ten amnesties, eight other and five immaturity. However, dismissals for immaturity are recommended more in relation to driving without a licence (20.2 per cent). The striking thing about this minor offence, which is not commonly the object of social concern and is commonplace among Italian young people, is the negligible number of full discharges, and the high number of requests for dismissal on grounds of immaturity. Such a measure is judged by many

Table 7.8 *Nationality and prosecutor's requests (girls charged with theft)*

	Remittal		Pardon		Amnesty		Immaturity		Other		Total	
	Number	%	Number	%	Number	%	Number	%	Number	%	Number	%
Italian	11	21.6	17	33.3	10	19.6	5	9.8	8	15.7	51	100
Non-Italian/gypsy	13	50.0	10	38.5	3	11.5	—		—		26	100
Total	24		27		13		5		8		77[1]	

$\chi^2 = 10.399$; $p > 0.01$.
[1] Eleven cases which have not yet been decided have been excluded.

commentators to be more ambiguous and risky than a legal pardon, to the extent that it implies non-recognition of the juvenile's ability to know what he or she is doing.

It is of course very hard to draw up an objective scale of the 'seriousness' of the measures, the allocation of which in fact depends on an evaluation based on theoretical and methodological, rather than on empirical criteria. Pardon and dismissal for immaturity are both measures of 'cautious' dismissal. But while pardon assumes the young person's awareness and represents the power of juvenile justice to act with discretion, like a father, by pardoning the offence, dismissal for immaturity looks like the *de facto* finding of a young person's incapacity, which the judge merely recognizes and sanctions. This may then in some sense seem to be a heavier measure and it is paradoxical, if perfectly understandable, that it tends to be more frequently used for the 'minor' offence of driving without a licence than for the more 'serious' one of theft. The surprising fact remains of the considerable severity with which breaches of the highway code are generally treated.

By and large, in all but 44 (16 per cent) cases, these requests for sentence put to the Juvenile Tribunal by the prosecutor were accepted. Prosecutorial requests for pardon tend to be changed by tribunal decisions (33 cases) and one might say in the direction of attenuation of the paternalistic 'discretion' of the judge. In fact, pardon becomes 'immaturity' in 12 cases, while 19 cases are changed to amnesty. In the case of gypsies, there was no discrepancy between the prosecutor's request and the tribunal's decision.

Conclusions

These data suggest that, offence for offence, gypsy girls suffer some discriminatory treatment in the Rome juvenile justice system. But such small numbers preclude the more elaborate statistical analyses that would be necessary to establish this beyond all doubt. However, in a more important sense this does not matter, for what the data do unequivocally reveal is that gypsy girls, for whatever reason, are more likely than Italians to be arrested and briefly detained rather than summonsed, and then to be sent for formal trial. The questions posed, however, are not only about fairness, but also about whether these disposals are appropriate, and about what they are meant to demonstrate or achieve, particularly when there is evidence (Mattioli, 1985) that gypsy girls suffer more than others from the rigours of prison life.

We would also like to make one comment about the other aspect of our study, namely, that it is a study of *girls*; indeed, we are concerned with all young females, the Italian as much as the gypsy and the non-Italian. The general point we wish to make here is this: theft and arrest appear much more frequently for boys and represent a very high percentage of offences for which boys are charged (and arrested); but for boys too driving without a licence is frequent, a point generally neglected not only in official statistics but also in research into *male* juvenile delinquency. Perhaps these researchers are making the implicit assumption that DWL is not what one has in mind in referring, on various levels, to *delinquency*, nor in referring to 'anomie' or 'marginality', nor in evoking the spectre of 'danger' or 'alarm'. It seems significant to us, therefore, that this point emerges with some weight from an analysis of penal practice in connection with *girls*. Driving without a licence is the 'offence' with which girls are most frequently charged, so understanding DWL is revealed as essential to an understanding of the operation of juvenile criminal justice. That much of the activity of the police and juvenile magistracy has to do with DWL, and that many boys and girls find themselves in contact with justice for this 'offence', does not seem to us, any longer, a negligible point.

The present volume emphasizes the criminalization of deviant female sexuality, and we have moved from that to the realization that it is essential also to study the gender aspect in the criminalization of males. We have demonstrated in this chapter once again, but in a different way, that focusing on the behaviour of girls can illuminate an overlooked aspect of criminalized male behaviour. Both boys and girls are in many cases drawn into the net of the criminal justice system as a result of offences such as driving without a licence. Sociologists must therefore transcend the common sense which characterizes such activities as minor in order to grasp the realities of their implications for the young people involved.

Notes

We wish to thank the Rome Juvenile Tribunal for their helpfulness and co-operation. We also thank Maureen Cain for all the work and care that she put into making our paper comprehensible to a non-Italian audience.
1 The constitutional court's ruling of 15 July 1983, no. 222, gave the JCs' penal competence for *all* juveniles charged.
2 Breaches of regulations include the following offences: 111 TULPS, 662 and 663 Penal Code (Publishing, selling, distributing written material without a permit); Law 30.4.1962, no. 283 (Food selling without a permit from the Health Authority); Law 28.1.1977, no. 10 (Building outside regulations). Transgressions against authority include Arts 341 Penal Code (Outraging a Public

Officer); 495, 496 and 651 PC (Giving a false identity to a Public Officer or refusing to give one's identity to a Public Officer); 658 PC (Provoking alarm about non-existent dangers or disasters); 366 and 372 PC (Refusing to bear witness and bearing false witness); 367 PC (Simulation of a crime); 368 PC (Slander); 378 PC (Aiding and abetting); 405 PC (Disturbing a religious function); 15, 17, 142, 144, 162 TULPS (Infractions to Laws governing the status of foreigners).

3 The information on the reason for decarceration was taken from records of entry to Rome Rebibbia Female Prison for 1980. In that year, female juveniles arrested were held in a special section of the Rebibbia Prison for adult females.

4 The prevalence of gypsies among the girls detained is a fact found by other surveys on juvenile justice in Italy. Cf. B. Bertelli (1979) and the reports produced by the Social Service of the Rome Juvenile Court, published annually in the journal, *Esperienze di rieducazione*.

5 Consultation of the entry records to the Rebibbia Female Prison allowed the collection of information on the type of theft committed by the female juveniles arrested. The main type was bag-snatching, but there were also thefts in flats and shop-lifting.

6 See De Leo (1981) and the discussion 'Pena risocializzazione e controllo nel sistema della giustizia minorile', *Dei Delitti e delle Pene*, 1(2) 1983: 315–62.

PART FOUR

HOW NOT TO TREAT GIRLS . . .

8

The institutional control of girls and boys

An attempt at a gender-specific approach

Joachim Kersten

The significance of social deviance/criminality and its control in producing and reproducing structures of domination and power is customarily considered in terms of class, but much more rarely in connection with possible gender-specific differences. Studies of criminal youth relate almost as a matter of course to *male* young people, without the sex of the people under study being given any attention apart from statistical banalities.

Deviant behaviour by young men, male juveniles and young people, was and still is seldom treated from the consideration that it is *male* behaviour, that it might have something to do with *maleness* (or images of maleness). The question of how socialization into maleness is controlled and what meaning deviant behaviour, especially violent or violence symbolizing behaviour, might have for the structuring of male identity has not yet been posed in Germany, far less answered, even cursorily. Although critical approaches have regarded the structure of social control and institutional action as necessary for maintaining domination, the patriarchal nature of domination has very rarely been considered in this connection. The terms 'state', 'capitalism' and 'social control' appear, just like youth, to be gender-free realities. The present call for the intensification of research into the deviance (and abnormality) of girls and women, justified as it is, conceals a misconception. As long as the social sciences, including criminology, and the investigative techniques used in these disciplines, masquerade as neutral in relation to the perception of male/female, separate observations of female life situations, biographies and so forth will not contribute anything more to answering the question of the role that 'maleness' and 'femaleness' play in relation to deviation and social control.

This chapter was translated from the German by Iain L. Fraser.

This chapter looks at the way carceral institutions[1] and their staff handle young people of both sexes according to gender-related differences. Recent German studies of law enforcement (Kersten and von Wolffersdorff, 1980; Ludwig, 1983) and of juvenile recidivists (Lamneck, 1982; Ludwig, 1982) contain numerous references to the connection between institutional socialization and criminalization. While these studies almost exclusively concern boys, the literature on social deviance among girls also contains some relevant material on the connection between institutional socialization and early maternity, drug abuse and prostitution (Conen, 1985; Girtler, 1984; Kersten, 1982; Kieper, 1980). The concepts of juvenile welfare and of juvenile (and societal) protection, as well as the nature of the education that inmates in the institutions can expect, are highlighted by the traditional names for the institutions: 'houses of rescue' and 'compulsory education institutions' (Reicher, 1904). Although this explicit naming has had its day, the idea of reform and the concept of education as legitimate compulsion have in no way disappeared. The more the conspicuous behaviour of the young people (mainly running away and delinquency) leads to problems for the authorities and staff of the institutions, then the more the so-called 'care' for the young people increases. The care is bound up with the need to stop by custodial treatment any further deviance and any further endangering of self or others, at least for a while. Reform and compulsion go hand in hand. The coercive measure of committal to the closed section of an institution appears as the ultimate argument of youth welfare. Under the aegis of a wardship order under paragraph 1631(b) of the German Civil Code or of a previous Care Order, the added evil of loss or restriction of freedom can, clad in the language of treatment or therapy, be presented as doing the young people a favour.[2]

These considerations of gender-related differences in the treatment of detained boys and girls are mainly based on some qualitative research materials collected for another study (Kersten et al., 1987). In reality, of course, these gender-related differences are incomparably richer in shades of meaning and complexity than it has been possible to portray. It should also be noted that a full description of the staff's dealings with the young people (here men/ boys and women/girls) would require a third and fourth level of description.

First, we have not discussed the perceptual level; secondly, the range of alternative approaches between institutions is not considered, although if we had not encountered these alternative approaches in some areas of traditional practice, we would not have become so aware of the rigidities and taboos in other institutions. This chapter therefore presents a schematic and simplified view, which is intended to be suggestive rather than closely documented and definitive.

Traditionally, custody in an institution, whether termed a house of correction, a compulsory education centre, or a care institution was extended to 'poor, neglected' children of the 'lowest proletariat', a considerable proportion of them from families where 'crime, drink and idleness' were prevalent; so says a study of children entering care in corrective educational institutions in 1898–9 (Reicher, 1904; cf. also Schultze, 1910: 18). The young people we studied in closed sections of institutions during the period 1983–4 (741 in total; three-quarters of them male) superficially show similar characteristics to their historical predecessors, as regards the social status, number of children and notoriety to the authorities of their families of origin.

What is striking, however, is that more than one-third of the welfare, as opposed to the penal, institutions are for girls. Furthermore, in comparison with boys' institutions, regulations on going out and on visits are stricter for girls even in 'semi-open' institutions. Legally, therefore, the confinement of girls is 'voluntary' rather than penal (under para. 1631(b) of the German Civil Code, and not paras. 71 and 72 of the Youth Tribunals Act). The regimes, however, belie this.

In quantitative terms there were also differences between the girls and the boys which encouraged my pursuit of gender-specific analysis. A few examples will perhaps be enough. It must be borne in mind that all the children in the study had already been institutionalized before they were committed to the *closed* institutions we were studying.

Roughly half (265) of the male and one-fifth (43) of the female young people had been transferred to a closed institution for a criminal offence. A second major reason for committal to closed accommodation was running away. This was the case for two-thirds of the girls (181) and one-third of the boys (132). However, boys appeared to have run away from their previous institution(s) about as often as girls.

Within the closed institutions, where even closer confinement or 'solitary' was available, girls are more frequently subjected to it (14.6 per cent of girls; 7.8 per cent of boys). For the girls, the reason offered in two-thirds of the cases (20) was 'attacks on staff'. This was the reason for only one-third of the boys' detentions.

The experience of release, after an average period of three months, was also different for the two sexes. Twenty-two per cent (97) of the boys, mainly under paras. 71 and 72 of the Youth

Tribunals Act, and 7 per cent (22) of the girls were released to their families. Over half the boys (250) but over two-thirds (90) of the girls were released to further institutional education.

These statistical results give pause enough for thought. The following look at the qualitative part of the study examines the question on various levels (reforming ideology, staff behaviour, young people's group behaviour) and considers the extent to which gender-related patterns can be identified in the responses of youth welfare authorities to deviant behaviour.

Sections for male juveniles

The politics of reform

If boys are sent to an institution, saving them from the penal system is more or less clearly in the forefront of the reasons given. Especially when an intensifying mechanism in the direction of withdrawal of freedom has already begun, institutional education is regarded and legitimated as the last chance of salvation from a 'criminal career' and therefore the ultimate argument of juvenile welfare. But there is another factor that is decisive for a gender-specific view of how institutions react to deviant behaviour by young people; though seldom articulated it is none the less clear. It is a salvation policy towards conspicuous young people of male sex from the lower classes; the point being to protect them from homosexuality. The concern, however, is not lest they go on the streets or are harassed, as is the case with girls. Many boys from care institutions go on the streets during their escapes or when they are on the run. This is more commonly recorded for boys in institutions than for those still living with their families. If working-class boys end up in institutions, youth care centres or closed sections, then the educators, psychologists and directors distinguish between the occasional prostitution of the youth 'out for a quick quid' (who is supposed to be 'revolted' afterwards) and the one with 'real' homosexual 'tendencies'. The salvationist youth welfare efforts are directed at the risk of the 'infection' of still 'healthy' boys by 'real' homosexuality.[3]

Staff and atmosphere in closed sections for boys

Boys in the age group 12–17 confront the male staff with their youth and puberty. This is a time when the homosexuality taboo mediated by father and mother, by school and peers, is experienced particularly strongly by many boys. Combined with the compulsion to the heterosexual 'notching up' of girls, with simultaneous collective denigration of the female sex, the fear of being effeminate and therefore 'queer' becomes a source from which socialization to maleness, to a practice of familiarity with violence and readiness for violence, draws its negative energy.

If the gamut of roles that men can take on in working with boys is looked at from a gender-specific point of view (given that housework and work to do with relationships are, apparently self-evidently, female territories of operation), the identity problems for male staff and their charges become apparent. Staff carry out, even with enjoyment, many care activities such as cooking and baking during weekend duty. But since these activities take place in the form of special performances or are presented as 'educative' measures (for example, the wholesale cleaning of the section may be carried out as a kind of organized combat on free days), the connection between care and emotional need (for security, for food as a gift), never becomes a matter of course (cf. Ingham, 1985). The provision of food, clothing and so on, which in any case is usually supplied from centralized kitchens and laundries, in the main retains the character of a legal entitlement, met in accordance with principles of administrative logic.

Furthermore, the recognition and sharing of needs expressed through the body raises the danger of touching. Touching and physical tenderness between men must, because of the northern European patriarchal conception of maleness, be rejected as 'effeminate' or 'gay' or 'queer' or transformed in such a way that male physicality can be expressed *legitimately* through work, sport or fights (Connell, 1983; cf. also Foucault, 1977b; Willis, 1977). Work and sport in the setting of an institutional upbringing for lower-class boys take place as aspects of social work or juvenile welfare. Thus emotional needs have to be shifted on to a strictly verbal ground.

As a consequence of recent reforms in the youth welfare sphere, some conditions for boys in institutions have improved. Sometimes the vocational training opportunities are well above the standards that lower-class boys socialized through the family could realistically attain, even allowing for state provision. Workshops, vocational training, sport and leisure opportunities, and also activities such as sailing, riding and adventure holidays, are more accessible to the boys while in the institutions than after leaving them, when they move to a life of unemployment and social welfare. But despite these positive developments, the handling of the boys' emotional needs remains firmly within the old clichés. In their seclusion (their closedness) the external and internal conditions of institutional education often correspond with each other.

To summarize, the environment and staff offer a lot of scope for employment, work and sport, but rather limited scope in relation to emotional care. If the boys' conditions of origin are brought into the picture, it seems that the social and emotional experience of a closed institution will tend rather to consolidate than to compensate for a basic deficit whose roots go back to the experience of childhood.

An involvement with difficult, anti-social boys that aims at positive formation of identity cannot, then, be confined to leaving certificates, welding courses and successful experiences of riding, sailing or whatever (important as these experiences are for a positive atmosphere). If, at the same time, these promote a fossilized image of 'maleness' as the ultimate resource of identity, it makes further criminalization and individual consolidation of social notoriety likely.

The fixation of lower-class boys or declassed male working-class juveniles on such images of maleness, brought about by the socializing influences of family, environment and peer group, and by the need to acquire a positive self-image if only along the lines of criminal male hero/outlaw, cannot be abolished by youth work and welfare. More aware pedagogical handling and cautious counter-activities might nevertheless be possible. There are, however, no approaches or guidelines for this in either the pedagogical or the therapeutic concepts for work with boys in an institution.

Youths in a closed section: 'Boys don't cry'[4]
The taboo on touching mentioned above fixes the range of possible personal relationships between staff and boys in the areas of school, work and sport. Housework and the provision of the necessities of life are, depending on the policy of the institution, treated as an area of learning or of discipline.

Man-to-man talks   During longish stays in a total of five boys' sections we gained the impression that although there is talking (man to man) among the boys, it is usually about the trouble they are in or their emotional disappointments and needs. If boys do talk about their problems this results from compulsory adaptation to the requirements of therapy and a corresponding threat of punishment in a 'therapeutic' context. Talk about problems with a staff member, if voluntarily initiated by a boy, is treated by the other boys as ingratiation or 'sucking up', and is not infrequently experienced by the staff as being 'buttonholed'. Old hands in institutional education often suspect that behind a problem conversation there is a tactic by the boy for gaining an advantage or mitigating a punishment.

Only isolated trainees and beginners on the staff can still be 'taken in' with such strategies. The 'toady' is equally unpopular with the staff and with the other boys.

Boys talk about themselves, about the staff, about conspicuous outsiders in the section, and about their adventures in the 'real world' outside the institution. Talking seldom takes place as an exchange: more frequently it is 'contractual', that is, used to effect specific deals; alternatively, it takes place as a ritual 'put-on' with no fixed theme, in which latent aggression teeters on the brink of actual conflict. Especially in cases of deals concerned with planned escapes or the punishment of hated outsiders, the information involved is kept apart from official communications in the section, and almost clandestine.

Even more taboo than speaking about problems is serious conversation about girls and women, for instance about a girlfriend or a hoped-for sweetheart. If a boy has a girlfriend 'outside', he will beware of telling the others. Women on the staff (a rare thing in boys' sections) are not talked about either, other than in the pejorative way typical of male communication. Just as much as collective denigration of the female sex is an important component of male discourse, so individual fantasies or longings for affection directed at girls, are a strictly avoided topic.

Spaces and symbols The boys' rooms are, depending on their interests, covered with posters of racing cars, big motorbikes, pin-up girls and macho figures from the cinema and rock-music (Arnold Schwarzenegger and heavy metal bands) and with photos of football and ice hockey heroes. The group rooms reveal the staff's interest in 'decent living' more than the boys' conceptions. To a varying extent, and in spite of all those territorial conflicts in which the staff seek to make it into *their* room, the office is the main locus of meeting and communication for the boys as well. All information, regulations and plans, and all gossip too, are made and discussed here.

Fighting and bodies Disputes over honour, whether about sport or about the objects and privileges which are scarce, though highly desired, in institutional life, mostly start verbally without the staff intervening. If it comes to a fight, there is no longer any discussion of the object in dispute; instead the opponent has to be ritually 'finished off' in the conflict, shown up and abused, especially when he has physical or other peculiarities. Staff mostly tend to stand aside in such matters, acting uninvolved or evidently pained. If a staff member takes a stance, this tends to be an assessment of such conflicts as unpleasant, ineffective and ultimately 'boorish'. It has nothing to do with situations or people.

Yet in the fights there is less hitting than tussling. There is a kind of wrestling and grappling with each other that might, in the less serious cases, be regarded as a kind of body-language transformation of an embrace. Excessive violent conduct is a special phenomenon of closed institutions (Kersten and von Wolffersdorff, 1980). This must be understood as an interaction between male and institutional violent tendencies. An important part is played by the humiliation of a victim, plagued and tortured by a collective, since 'maleness' is restored by the staging of a ritual subjugation.

Girls' sections

Where girls are committed for recorded, feared or merely supposed prostitution, the idea of salvation is today no longer primarily oriented towards the classical reformatory ideology that sought to protect the girl, by means of the most extreme repression, from her own 'sexual incontinence', which was seen as culpable. Institutional schooling, particularly in closed sections (in the case of girls often called 'semi-open' to get round various legal restrictions) is nowadays intended rather to serve the purpose of protecting the girl from the street, the customers and the pimp. Education in the institutions for girls, still considerably more closed than boys' institutions whatever they are called, always took the salvation of 'fallen girls' as its legitimation, and aspects of this orientation can be found even in feminist arguments. The mental construct which legitimates the salvation ideology, the way the pimp and the customer or their respective stereotypes are constituted, is however, with a few exceptions, scarcely tenable.

The images of the lecherous customer, the brutal pimp and the zombie rapist lurking in the park are used to shift everyday sexual violence against girls and women to apparently exotic planes and places, located outside social normality. The 'normal' man, Dr Jekyll, comes into being because the zombie Mr Hyde is constructed. Prostitution, prostitutes and pimps become a subcultural problem – a view that social science has always readily shared and supported when the point was to define structural violence away into exotic marginal areas, so distancing its actual relationship to social normality (on this see also Girtler, 1984). Correspondingly, prostitution by girls is reinterpreted as a sexual and moral problem and not as a problem of the learned competence of minors in male-dominated societies. Yet every day the psychic and physical endangering of girls and women, the violent attacks on their identity, proceeds, except in individual cases and in the collective imagination, primarily from the close social sphere of the family, from fathers, uncles or friends of the mother and father.

As far as the social reality of the social threat to girls is concerned, the salvation idea is a fiction. It becomes completely unbelievable when the institutionalization of girls has as its objective not equipping them for an independent life but their integration into that dangerous place, the 'family', whose maintenance by compulsion is sought as the guiding idea of therapy. If 'running away' appears in the girls' records as a major sign of maladjustment, bringing corresponding punishment measures with it, it happens in the first place most frequently as running away from the family (Conen, 1985). Sometimes this is because here the 'best-kept secret' (Rush, 1982) of the sexual abuse of girls plays a far more significant role than has hitherto been assumed. By emptying the running away of its causes and displacing it into the female individual as a pathological structure, this avoids any more intensive investigation of why girls run away from home.

Moreover, the more intensively the hierarchy inside the institution (direction, psychological service, section leadership) is dominated by men, the more intensively does the salvation policy present itself in girls' institutions.

Coupled with the salvation policy of the institutions towards (against) girls is the apparently unshakeable belief that a 'real' friendship with a 'decent' boy could have a stabilizing effect on girls, could protect a 'respectable' girl from temptation and bring a no longer 'respectable' one back to the proper female path. This way towards the proper female path in the firm strong hands of a decent man (a super-highway with no speed limit) is the counterpart of salvation from the blind alley that leads to the abyss of condemnation to prostitution. The paradoxicality of the ideology of salvation from men by men, of a demand for 'real friendship' with boys coupled with protection against 'male importunity', leads at the level of everyday life in the institution to the most remarkable mental somersaults and contradictions.

Staff and atmosphere in girls' sections
By contrast with boys' institutions, in institutions for girls the homosexuality taboo does not seem to count as such a severe problem. In the girls' sections we studied, the taboo on touching and tenderness was nowhere so great, even in sections led by nuns, as in the institutions for boys. To be 'truly female' girls and female staff need neither permanently repress nor transform the need for mutual contact, physical closeness and tenderness

in dealings with each other, as the converse for boys and male staff.

Leaving girls' institutions dominated by men aside for the moment, the largely unshattered concept of having to save girls from prostitution seems to us to rely not so much on making prostitution as such taboo, but in the challenge that non-conformist (McRobbie, 1985), and in some cases even promiscuous, behaviour by girls presents to the staff and to the youthwork-and-welfare ideology. As with male staff, the suspicion arises here that the external appearance, behaviour and 'style' of the girls are acting to highlight the staff members' own socially conforming female sex-roles, and sometimes even to question it.

Open rejection of the conformist female role may emerge in the girls' behaviour or during escapes. Female staff may either let this affect them, or place a taboo on it. In this challenge to those who have 'achieved' a painful conformity lurks the repressive potential, in part characterized by open contempt, that is sometimes expressed in female staff's conduct towards girls in their sections. Precisely because of the lack of success of pedagogic efforts to produce 'decent' (asexual) girls, many a female staff member must ask herself to what extent her own 'respectability' is due to compulsion from outside. If these thoughts are banned as taboo, there follows an inner distancing from the girls, from the work and ultimately from themselves. Here young lay female staff members sometimes show less awareness of the problem than some nuns, whose behaviour towards the non-conforming girls is characterized more by acceptance than by contempt. On reflection one might even arrive at the position that the nuns, because of having adopted an equally non-conforming female identity (and possibly sometimes because of their own personal experiences with men), have more empathy with 'unrespectable' girls than is generally assumed. Moreover, nuns go far beyond what the German Federal Employees' collective agreement permits, as far as their presence and general accessibility to the girls goes. This is no doubt experienced by the girls to some extent not so much as supervision but as personal involvement, which is much less marked in the case of lay women staff, although this is partly because of the high staff turnover frequently found in girls' institutions.

Female staff in the institutions we studied seemed to us to be more sensitive and vulnerable and less 'socially assured' (in a conforming sense) in the world outside the institution than their male colleagues. In cases of conflict, whether in the teams or with the girls, strategies of withdrawal and illness are more readily adopted than is usually the case with the men.

As with the hidden curriculum for boys, girls are exposed to pressure towards a conforming female identity. As with boys, so with girls the emotional need is poured into an available system of channels which is supposed to prevent overflow: the outlets of conformity, illness and longing.

Conformity means, apart from this more-or-less passive fitting into the female role, the active adoption of qualities regarded as 'female work': being understanding; always understanding work as partly also a matter of relationships; always and under all circumstances ensuring a 'nice atmosphere'; always placing one's own interests last and approaching problems through talking about them. It is the tradition of most corrective institutions for girls that they are committed to the ideology of female social behaviour, and thereby make demands on the juveniles' conduct that the girls had already found difficulties meeting in the family or had already failed at there.

Illness is a perpetual theme of 'female discourse', but even more so in an institution, where illness becomes the last recourse of a self-assertion which cannot be directed anywhere else except against one's own body, and in this way compels attention and care. Whether it is a matter of looking after self-inflicted cuts and lacerations,[5] avoiding, fearing or having to deal with pregnancy, or of the unspeakable compulsory internal examination after escapes, the medical model is always an answer to bodily and other needs. The accomplice is not the staff, not even the psychological staff, but the doctor as the person who is above everyone, staff, management and even the Youth Welfare Office. The girls' knowledge of the doctors' omnipotence results from the lack of certainty that is allowed the institution and its staff in dealing with physical problems and their forms of expression. Many medical terms, a cupboard full of pills and a continued 'deadbeat' way of dealing with the physically acted out problems of the girls are frequently the result.

By 'longing' we mean fixation on the concept of the male saviour which, against all empirical evidence, is almost compulsorily kept going, specifically in the institutional education of girls. The longing necessarily conceals behind it the desire for normality, and that means the patriarchal model of the relationship of the couple and the gender-specific division of labour. Combined with conformity, longing acts like a two-component adhesive as far as deviant careers by the girls is concerned.

As regards the spectrum of roles for female staff in girls' sections, we feel (of course with a male bias) that we can see more room for manoeuvre combined with more ambivalence. Women staff can relate to the girls in a multiplicity of 'female' and 'male' roles without immediately coming up against taboos. The ambivalence in this spectrum emerges in the interaction of the *compulsion* to a caring coupling relationship (much less in the case of men and boys) and the simultaneous confrontation with the conduct, the life-style, of street girls which may represent a threatening model for the female staff's own perspectives on life. If this is repressed, for instance through the obligation to maintain a 'nice atmosphere', then resistance and aversion between girls and female staff cannot be expressed through conflict but has to find an outlet in concealed distancing and contempt, messages to which institutional children in particular have very sensitive antennae.

A broadened role spectrum for female staff, however ambivalent, looks like a very narrow offering compared with boys' institutions, in the sector of work, employment, leisure and adventure. The traditional use of institutional girls as free household help in looking after the institution is, to be sure, not the rule in the ones we visited. Apart from schooling (sometimes remedial schooling) and occasional vocational training possibilities (for example, in the apprentice workshops in a neighbouring boys' home), girls in the institutions do not have much made available to them. Nowhere did we meet with girls' apprentice workshops or other forms of vocational training for girls. As far as sport, physical activity, weekend activities or holiday trips are concerned too, what is offered to girls is a reduced, cheapened, narrow-gauge version of what is possible for boys in institutions. Whether the (allegedly more intensive than for boys) psychological and therapeutic treatment makes up for this lack of offered pathways to social and economic independence, or whether this 'advantage' is in danger of appearing as an additional mechanism of control and compulsion for girls, requires longer study and more thorough discussion. The fact that posts for psychologists always automatically have actual effects on the therapeutic possibilities of institutions in the everyday life of the sections has already been doubted in other studies (Büttner, 1982).

In the case of girls, conversely to that for boys, there is a broader scope for relationships in institutions, and a very narrow one for activities.

Girls in the section: 'Girls have more fun'[6]

The pressure to conform to a socially normal female role and the girls' previous biographical experiences determine the main topics of girls' conversation in the institution. Housework and caring activities meet with little enthusiasm or even with decisive rejection as far as the institutions' policy allows this: this is an early manifestation of rejection of the housewife's role.

The good talk   Girls talk more than boys, both about their own problems and about those of others. But in the choice of interlocutor (male or female) girls appear to be cautious and choosy.[7] Talking is neither understood as 'toadying' nor looked down on by the other girls. The excuses for talking are indeed chosen by the girls themselves. Talk can arise, for instance, from a game, around painting a picture, when the atmosphere is good and the occasion appears suitable, or it can 'just happen'. The greater readiness to talk, for the 'good talk' so valued in pedagogy, is counterpoised by the low degree of commitment to the insights and agreements arrived at in such talks. At the very moment that, for instance, a staff member is reporting a 'fantastic talk' with a girl about her alcohol problem to the team meeting, the same girl may well already be sitting in the nearest pub.

Talking is not done in order to deceive or 'suck up' to the staff (in contrast with boys' sections); in the good atmosphere of the talk, girls can make open exchanges about problems. But the perspectives they develop in them last only a very short while after the conversation. Talking for girls is a *relational* activity, not a voicing of some uniquely individual position.

The girls' capacity to portray themselves authentically on certain occasions, for instance in a curriculum planning conversation, to argue skilfully and to win over all the participants, and especially initially sceptical official people such as teachers, is astonishing. Perhaps we felt astonishment partly because such communicative and even linguistic skill is not ascribed to these girls at all. After such an 'important' talk, the future initially looks rosy again to the staff member, and the almost lost belief in the power of education gains renewed force. This mood, however, seldom lasts longer than a couple of days, and sometimes only an hour or two.

Girls often talk about the other sex; in strong contrast with the boys, however, girls do not seem compelled to denigrate the other sex (particularly on the plane of sexuality). In the perspective of longing, the point is more how 'sweet' this or that boy or man really is. In parallel with the 'real' friend, romantic stars from films, television and music also play an important part. With us as men, talk in the sections was, if anything, about the boyfriend and the problems (more than the prospects) that the girl concerned had with him. Every man here quickly becomes an ally, is drawn into the role of helper and confidant, sometimes even as part of a strategy intended to make the boyfriend jealous.

Rooms   The girls' rooms are hung with the sweet stars of the romantic vision gazing faithfully and soppily from the posters. With a few more personal photos on the wall, soft toys and other souvenirs and sometimes bits of furniture of their own, the girls' rooms generally have a friendlier appearance than the boys'. (Sometimes so much concentrated 'niceness' is not much easier to put up with than untidiness and mess.) Again, in the romantic perspective, there may be posters of sunsets, sad autumn days and cuddly kittens in baskets.

Girls party more spontaneously than boys, if the right mood is there. Nevertheless, the common rooms are no more liked or involved in the daily life of the section with girls than they are with boys. For girls, even more than for boys, the office is the centre of communication and the 'waiting room' in which everybody hangs about waiting for something exciting at long last to happen, something new to come in, if only a phone call. If the telephone rings, the girls are often there quicker than the staff, trying to involve the person at the other end of the line in conversation.

Conflict   Conflicts have different causes among the girls. The point is not 'honour' or 'who is stronger', but a missing pullover or the suspicion that a girl is trying to get off with another one's boyfriend. The escalation in aggression takes place rapidly (with the boys it is more latent and ritualistic) because the causes seem more arbitrary, and verbal aggression shifts more often into physical fighting. Once this level has been reached, the point is also to inflict pain on the opponent, to injure her, and not just wrestle about with her on the floor. In other words, it is not disguised 'embracing'. As indicated above, friendship with a boy is a perpetual theme, very frequently in the form of jealousy and corresponding scenes, with which the girls impose their concerns on the everyday life of the section: waiting for the boyfriend, for his phone call, for the weekend . . .

Conclusion

As far as social and economic standards of societal normality are concerned, youth administration services and residential care institutions have very little to offer to their protégés. Lacking other concepts to achieve normality for boys and girls under their auspices, youth services stick to their most traditional domain: the policing of sexual normality and gender role conformity. Girls have been subject to this since the early beginnings of social work; but the fact that this policy also affects boys/male juveniles as inmates of institutions has hitherto been ignored. Boys are coached into prevalent concepts of 'maleness'. Girls experience a strong pressure towards the role of the 'normal wife'. At the end of selective processes to exclude deprived juveniles of both sexes from family and neighbourhood roots, and from access to school or vocational careers, and on the verge of entering long-term institutional careers, these boys and girls have no means at their disposal to meet expectations of normality. There is nothing left to back up a 'normal' transition from adolescence into adulthood. With little support in their social and economic background for gender-role conformity (models which have become obsolete or dysfunctional even for those who do have the background) conventional concepts of maleness and femininity turn into a trap leading into deviance and marginality.

Maleness as the last and only recourse for developing a 'positive' identity means, for boys with an institutional background, that the 'outlaw' as the image of the *negative* male *hero* turns into a perspective of identity. As much as the outlaw is accepted in novels, westerns, and war movies (cf. also the streetfighter as a left-wing hero), control agencies perceive deviance and individual violent behaviour from a less romantic standpoint.

Peer group behaviour of male lower-class juveniles consists of many elements of fossilized 'maleness', and this is exactly where the mechanics of criminalization start to operate (Kersten, 1986).

Girls in institutions have even less elbow-room as far as expectations of gender role conformity are posed. In the event that they obviously 'misbehave', the grasp of control becomes more forceful. A neglect of norms means asking for sanctions of a less criminalizing and more institutionalizing type. 'Femininity' as a last and only recourse is dependent on the appearance of a male 'saviour'. Before the saviour enters the scene, apart from the fact that he may well turn out to be another maltreater, there is only a standby or 'pending' identity for girls. Early pregnancy and single-motherhood proves to be a bad alternative for low-income girls lacking family support for both the mother and the child (cf. McRobbie, 1985; Miller, 1987).

Boys and girls in institutions attempt to achieve conformity in terms of gender role. The result, however, is the production of deviance, or more accurately of *individual* careers of no autonomy and marginal existence.

Institutions also reproduce the average gender-related division of labour. For boys it is physical labour and sports; training for the male body and repression of emotionality. For girls it is housework, relationship-maintenance, auto-aggressive body-politics and a stereo-typical pattern of feminine emotionality which resembles cartoon stories. The societal structure of gender relations has its parody in control policies for agencies and institutions for already marginal young people.

Gender-role conformity and patriarchal concepts of gender identity seem to be necessary for the implementation of power and of relevant control policies. The impact of this silhouetted gender training and the extent to which this affects the reproduction of power structures, the construction of 'normality', and the production of deviance, quite apart from class structure and the distribution of socio-economic resources, is to a growing extent a topic of feminist studies. The connection between deviance and the emergence of gendered identities, and the effects of gender conformity politics on the reproduction of deviance and marginality should become more respected topics within criminology, especially for male scholars. Are not the differences revealed here sufficiently striking?

Notes

The idea for a gender-related perspective on my work was generated at the conference in Florence where the other essays in this volume were presented. Many aspects of this chapter were worked out as a direct or indirect response to the contributions of female colleagues. For their patience and intellectual assistance I should like to thank Carola Schumann, Gerlinda Smaus, Lising Pagenstecher, Lerke Gravenhorst, Franziska Lamott, Maureen Cain, Michael Voss, Reinhard Kreissl and Christian Wolffersdorff.

1   The institutions studied are residential institutions with a closed section. Most of the young people who live there do so because of decisions by the Youth Administration, rather than of the criminal justice system.
2   Para. 1631b of the Code entitles the head of an institution to place a minor into a locked ward for a period of 3–6 months after a court's decision.
3   Against the background of the media and a public worked up about AIDS, this 'danger of infection' of course takes on special urgency, in which the 'need to protect' the 'normal' population also plays a part.
4   Title of a song by The Cure.
5   Girls in institutions tend to cut their arms in parallel horizontal cuts, partly to symbolize suicide, and partly to show their amount of pain and hurt.
6   Title of a song by Cindie Lauper.
7   A more differentiated consideration of girls' sections with mixed sex teams shows that, depending on the problem, girls choose either men or women for more intensive individual talks.

9

Compounded misunderstanding

Relations between staff and girls in an Italian juvenile prison

Gabriella Ferrari-Bravo and Caterina Arcidiacono

This chapter describes an attempt to 'integrate' girls into a penal institution originally containing only boys. This experience is described and analysed as we lived through it, revealing the extent to which integration involved the taken-for-granted subordination of females to such an extent that the girls' attempts to manipulate and eventually to resist this secondary status were themselves accounted for in terms of the discourse which they were seeking to deny.

First, however, a brief history of integration as a policy in Italy is necessary. This is followed by a surface description of the institution and the girl inmates. In the third and final sections begins our analysis of these events and our deconstruction of the discourse in terms of which they were lived.

Italian integration policy

The official attitude to the specific problem of female juvenile delinquency, and consequently of detention, is very lukewarm, even on the part of local authorities. A thorough analysis is needed, on the one hand, of the mechanisms that determine (or do not determine) responses which are institutional rather than directed towards the needs of inmate girls and, on the other hand, of how and when the very existence of the special features of such a group are recognized. Our work as consultant psychologists in the juvenile penal section for both sexes in southern Italy has induced us to reflect on some of the characteristics of the institutional management of juvenile female offenders. Despite the small number of girls among the total number of juveniles detained, there has been a progressive increase over the last ten years both in the absolute number of female detainees and in their proportion of the juvenile

---

This chapter was translated from the Italian by Iain M. Fraser.

total. This has occurred even though, in absolute figures, juvenile detention as a whole has shown a constant downward trend. (See Table A11, p. 230 of this volume.)

This increase has generally been assumed to be connected with the spread and affirmation of the process of emancipation of the female population. Our interpretation, however, is different. An analysis of girls detained at Eboli in 1982 shows that most of their offences, whether against the person or against property, happened within the family circle. Moreover, they usually involved the connivance and participation of other members of the family group. This is a pattern of offending which has been typical of women for a long time. At least in southern Italy there appears to have been no dramatic change as a result of the apparent greater freedom of movement for women outside the family.

What might be assumed to have happened is that control agencies have paid greater attention to women as active subjects, responsible for their own actions. Thus in terms of a strictly institutional logic, both a greater number of charges and more recourse to penal sanctions, including detention, might be justified.

Over the years, the institutional response to female adolescents has taken three different forms: detention together with adults; separate detention within institutions for adults; and detention with only females of the same age in male juvenile institutions.

As far as the district of Campania, Molise and Basilicata is concerned, at first girls were sent to prisons for adult females, with some positive discrimination as regards placement in sections intended for younger women (where these existed). This approach obviously denies any specific character to the juvenile condition: the girl is entirely equated with an adult female detainee; the female role absorbs any other specific feature.

A second solution, adopted in Campania from 1977 to 1981, accommodated female juveniles in an autonomous section within the Pozzuoli Prison for adult females (a prison with a high-security wing). The staff were not generally differentiated from those for the adult women; only in the last two years did a new direction in treatment lead to the provision of specific staff for the female juveniles. For obvious logistical and structural reasons, there was no truly specialized programme for the girls. Moreover, the separate section for juveniles was not well tolerated by the prison management, which was forced to find a balance between security needs and the pressure for openness, to introduce different regulations for the adult and juvenile sectors, and to cope with the conflicts and tensions necessarily bound up with an ambiguous and contradictory practice.

As far as the Italian situation is concerned, there is no juvenile penal institution intended exclusively for girls. There are, by contrast, various separate sections for male juveniles, some with only ten to twelve boys, for which the financial burden involved is evidently thought justified.

From 1981 the need for differentiated treatment for girls was finally made manifest, albeit with great delays in comparison with boys. Female juvenile sections were opened, all attached to existing structures for males. The first of these was the Altavista (the Eboli prison at Salerno).

This chapter presents some critical reflections on the experience of male–female prison integration on the basis of research done in 1981–2 in Eboli (Ferrari-Bravo, 1982–3). Of course, the group of female juvenile detainees involved cannot be regarded as representative of the whole institutionalized female juvenile population, and the duration of our study was short. However, this discussion may contribute to thinking about the practices of penal institutional administration and about the assumptions embodied or even underscored in them, particularly with reference to models of interaction between staff and female juvenile detainees.

The penal administration of girls: a description of a mixed institution

The research was done in 1982–3, a period during which an experiment in integration between girls and boys was in hand. It was based on direct observation and participation in institutional activities and interviews at successive intervals with the staff of Altavista and with the girls detained. The institution was described both spatially and functionally, and the female wing in particular was analysed. A case analysis of all the girls admitted during 1982 was undertaken, with data collected from the register and from psychopedagogical files. The data included notes on the offence, the legal position and records of personal and family case histories.

The structure of the Altavista prison

The prison is a medieval castle, ring-shaped with no breaks. All the sectors, including the services, offices and workshops, and the accommodation on the second floor, face a single central space. This is a strong factor in the organization of work, the relations among the detainees, and the relations between girls and staff. The whole prison is divided into three operational units, each divided into two sections each of ten to fifteen young people. The second operational unit comprises the one female and one male section.

The female section, with a capacity of some twelve beds, consists of large rooms, each occupied by two to three girls, with independent bathrooms, a dining-room, a small kitchen, a sitting-room, and a wide corridor with large windows opening on to the courtyard. There is also a room used as a professional tailoring workshop, intended exclusively for females, plus an isolation room with bathroom, and, on the other side of a gate, a guardroom for the female warders. The female section does not differ in arrangement or equipment from the male one.

This description of the building is important since it largely explains why 'integration' was the authorities' chosen arrangement. Had the sexes been totally separated the building itself would unavoidably have had to be equipped for the female section, with 'duplication' both of spaces and of programmes and activities. This would have meant a considerable burden on the whole organization and on the staff.

Staff and organization of activities

When the female section was opened the staff consisted of a team of one educational officer and an assistant, thirteen to fifteen female warders on eight-hour shifts, and three rotating consultants. Although there were two female educational officers working at Eboli, two males ran the section for the entire period of the integration and the roles have not been changed since. Apart from the institutional staff, others work in the institution, and hence also with the girls. There are professional teachers, male and female (for four hours in the morning), elementary school teachers and teachers of the training courses for the compulsory student-worker training, and free-time organizers of sports activities, painting, music, and so on.

The opening of the section did not change the organization of work, except quantitatively. The girls were incorporated in the institutional routine, in the same activities and at the same times, as the boys. The typical day involved, as it still does, morning training activities in the workshops; after lunch, school work for those who have not finished school, and free-time activities; after supper, boys and girls could use the communal areas of their respective sections.

The girls and their official records

Over the course of 1982, the female juvenile detainees in Eboli numbered 57, three of whom were subject to security measures (Judicial Reformatory). These three, along with other girls accused of serious offences and hence on long terms, were the most stable group. The others, arrested for less serious offences, had short or very short stays. Except for the gypsies with no fixed abode and a few others, they came mainly from Campania and to some extent from other southern regions. The 14–15 age group accounted for 65 per cent, with 35 per cent of the total in the 16–17 age group. The index of recidivism is lower than for boys: this fact, taken along with the non-seriousness of the offences for which the 14- and 15-year-olds were arrested and the fact that almost all the episodes of recidivism concerned gypsy girls, might indicate that it is easier for girls to get out of criminal circles than for boys of the same age. As far as schooling levels are concerned, the figures for illiteracy and semi-literacy were three times higher than for boys. Though this figure was inflated by the presence of the gypsy girls, on the whole the unfavourable situation of women is strongly marked, with considerable consequences for treatment and for job possibilities.

As far as the type of offence is concerned, while the traditional predominance of offences against property, both occasional and professional, remains, the most interesting figure is the high percentage of serious offences against the person: 7 per cent as against 1 per cent for the boys. Among these were one parricide, one homicide of a stepfather, one infanticide, and one attempted murder of a female consultant psychologist. There were, however, no violent offences connected with robbery or other property offences.

We did not take into consideration here the files on the gypsies, even assimilated and now settled ones, since the typical cultural factors in these groups are the basis for a different perception of social and penal norms (Mattioli, 1985; Cipollini et al., 1987 and this volume, Chapter 7). But, among the remaining group of girls guilty of offences against property, in the vast majority of cases accomplices were involved: family members, cohabitants, or boyfriends.

The offences not falling within these two categories again related to family members and spouses. For instance, 17 per cent were cases of perjury, generally in favour of the cohabitant, plus aiding and abetting.[1] These instances support the assumptions on which our conviction is based, namely that female offences are still linked with family situations and with role stereotypes connected with them.

Platitudes of the feminine and the course of the integration

On the arrival of the girls from the Pozzuoli juvenile wing, accompanied by a group of female warders, the institution was hung with banners saying, 'Welcome Women'.

It would take too long to list here all the verdicts about the girls' arrival expressed by the staff in the course of the interviews. They may be summarized by saying that the integration was regarded as having been achieved in the course of a week, without any particular problems!

A conflict between female educational officers and girls that immediately appeared was resolved by accepting the girls' request to have male educational officers in the section. In the same way, the conflict between girls and female warders, which could not be solved by replacing those warders, was attributed to mechanisms of rivalry among women concerning the male teachers present. Instrumental use of sexuality was evident, particularly sexual provocation by the girls. The response strategy of the male teachers was the assumption of a paternal role, in a clearly defensive and authoritarian fashion.

The greater somatic response by women to the discomforts of detention were noted, with the special feature of 'psychological contagion' in the female section, with chain-reactions that were hard to stop. Significantly, the report of 'greater corporeal self-perception' was followed in one of the interviews by an emphasis on the greater 'superstitiousness of women' with their practices of fortune-telling and reading hands, especially before trials. These practices are very common in female prisons.

The staff felt that they were discriminating in favour of the girls; not by choice but almost because they were obliged to do so by the very 'unpredictability and insistence' of the female pressure.

It was finally argued, again in the interviews, that the admission of the girls had vivified the asphyxiating dynamics and atmosphere of the prison. The situation as a whole was defined as 'more natural' with this 'naturalness' of relationships being indicated, for instance, by the fact that some boys, some times, had their best clothes washed by girl friends. This is evidently expected, as being something that girls want and are destined to do.

Revelation of the institutional complexity of the integration

A year and four months after the opening of the Eboli female section, the institution was the scene of a full-scale revolt in which a good proportion of the girls and boys took part. The revolt lasted two days, was characterized by the absence of any type of violence against either persons or things, and was resolved by the intervention of the police, because of the alarm aroused in the magistracy by the 'unusual and anomalous' circumstances in which it had arisen and was taking place. Out of a total of fifty inmates, thirty boys and eight girls took part. The girls in prison that day totalled thirteen; five of them, forewarned by the other girls, declined to take part in any activity during the day, and stayed in their rooms. Girls and boys barricaded themselves in some of the common rooms, refusing to go back to their respective sections after dinner for the night. Subsequently, following the arrival of staff members and the prison director, ten boys disassociated themselves from the movement and were allowed by their companions to leave. The complete agreement between boys and girls in working out and implementing their 'plan' to stay together is shown by the rather striking fact reported by a staff member that all the girls involved were having their menstrual period, with obvious contraceptive intentions regarding the foresee-able sexual relationships. We may imagine the staff's relief when it could be stated that none of the girls was expecting a child following the events of those two days!

All the endeavours by the staff to come to terms with the group were nullified by the position of open, albeit non-violent defiance adopted initially by all the young people, but in the end by the twenty boys, and above all by the eight girls. These seemed in fact not to tolerate any yielding by the boys, particularly as regards their essential request not to be transferred to another prison if they stopped the revolt, on pain of rejecting their role as leaders and consequently breaking all comradely and even sentimental links with them. The group was in fact made up of several couples, or at least of boys and girls between whom a preferential relationship had been set up. The head of the revolt, for the girls, was a 16-year-old from Venice, who came from the juvenile section of Pozzuoli, and was hence part of the original group of female detainees at Eboli. She was a girl with a very marked personality, with characteristics of extreme reactivity and aggressiveness, and she had already accumulated various stays in judicial reformatories and in preventive custody, initially for deviant behaviour, subsequently for specific offences.

We cannot give the girl's life story here; suffice it to point out how her situation as an adopted daughter with parents alive, with many flights from home and experiences of prostitution and association with youth gangs behind her, made her someone who had broken all ties and was engaged in the construction of an identity that was increasingly being defined as a criminal one. The memory of this girl has remained with the staff as that of an extremely vital and intelligent person, with an enormous capacity for affection despite the innumerable problems (from a suicide attempt to the revolt itself) she had caused them. It is indicative and very disturbing to note how at the time we are writing, a legend has formed around this girl: from time to time some remember her phrases, attitudes or acts; others speak about her as if fascinated by the very memory. Some swear she is dead; and even we who write, having known her, cannot bring ourselves to seek exact information on this announced death, which we hope has not happened.

Needless to say, there was no male equivalent of this heroine of the revolt; no boy's name has been handed down in connection with the events. Here too, we can see how the phantasms of the prison's collective imagination had female form. It accorded with the staff's feeling of unease in connection with the whole group of girls, impenetrable, as it were, to any talk of consensus, despite the intensity with which it was pursued by the institution, round its own goals and educational practices.

The reaction of the two male educators in the female wing who had fallen into (or taken refuge in) a comfortable paternal role was to feel themselves as betrayed as they would have in the face of unheard of, upsetting, revelations on unknown aspects of the lives of their own daughters. Indeed, the outbreak of the revolt caught the whole Eboli team by surprise and brought the operational models, especially with regard to integration, into crisis for a period.

In fact the practice of integration has not been resumed, nor is it planned that it should be in future. It is now regarded as too risky for the running of the prison. The unjustified and trivializing criticisms from several sides have concerned exclusively the scandalous aspect of the affair, seeing the 'sexual needs' of a certain number of girls and boys as the main cause of the revolt. Of course, if adolescents are brought into contact in a close situation with no alternative relationships, affectual and sexual needs emerge, are expressed and become known, and cannot remain indefinitely unsatisfied. But beneath this level, as obvious as it is superficial, what should be done is to analyse how all the behaviour and consequent approaches to the boys and girls by the staff were in the direction of constituting an 'artificially natural' group (in which sexuality is clearly a strong relational element). The heightening of personal interaction and awareness, a typical feature of prison, was held to have been overcome precisely as a result of the integration. On the contrary, as it proved, it was that which brought out precisely the conflictual responses typical of total institutions.

As Smart (1976) says, 'Most of the methods applied in female penal institutions are chosen from among those that particularly reinforce the traditional, stereotyped role of women in cultures like ours', and we can now number integration of the sexes too among these methods.

Another thing amply shown by the whole affair, however, is that 'feminine behaviour is encouraged, while simultaneously the expression of sexuality is repressed' (Richardson, 1969). In the type of observation according to which 'those who don't, err, and those who do err even more', there is also the idea that linked the revolt with the tense atmosphere created *among the boys* (our emphasis) by living side-by-side with the opposite sex in close contact within the same structure. No one officicially proposed attributing the revolt to the intention of a few couples to spend the night together, but that does not mean that nobody thought of doing so. It is a rather significant pointer to an ambivalent attitude that many staff members have towards integration: on the one hand they have always seen it as encouraging uncontrollability and hence as too exacting an endeavour; on the other hand, it is a special feature of the Eboli prison which gratifies group pride.[2]

Nevertheless, the assessments of the event, which were careful and accurate, failed to raise the institution's organizational model for discussion. Reflections on the specific style of work of the staff with girls were, in our opinion, marginal. Thinking was concentrated more on minor 'errors' of comportment, than on the fundamental issues of identity and relationship.

An alternative interpretation

Success in living conditions were said to be shown by 'the lack of serious demands or complaints, and the existence of a good relationship (even during the revolt) with the staff.'[3] In our opinion, before the concept of integration as interpreted and applied at Eboli, there had been the mistake of accepting as normal, and of exactly replicating, the conditions of life experienced every day by the girls in their cultural environment and home situation. One indicator of this mistake was precisely the refusal by the female educational staff to take part in running the girls' group, and the corresponding refusal by the female detainees to accept a method of running the section with the female educational officers and other female staff in a management role. Neither of these attitudes was analysed sufficiently at the moment when the 'conflict between women' arose. Instead they were dismissed by most of the staff interviewed, and rejected as not essential to understanding the experiment which was under way. The issue was reduced to a constant element, taken for granted, of typical but unspecified 'female dynamics'.

Placing the girls in their 'natural' subordinate role within a mixed group in which hierarchies were significantly and strictly maintained could be done only through mixing males and females. One cannot in fact speak of integration, since this presupposes a relationship *inter pares*. With the revolt, the tacit ideology guiding the apparent liberalization of this institution which had been 'normalized' through integration came to light. Faced with the category of 'girl detainee', the second word had been deliberately devoided of meaning and instead the femininity implied by the first word was emphasized and understood in an extremely regressive manner.

The path chosen, in good faith and unconsciously but with unanimous conviction, reproduced within the prison the same conditioning that the girls were exposed to outside. However, it was translated into less explicit terms since the whole gamut of relationships was not available to them, but the control was just as violent and compulsive. Indeed, it may be said that 'integration' was used as a valid control factor in the prison, just as, in wider society, the relationship of dominator and dominated between the sexes is a factor of social normalization (and apparently resistant to any type of ideological criticism or reforming practice).

We therefore tried to interpret the revolt, during which the girls had the decisive role of the intransigents, as a breakthrough by the women, an *achievement of equality* with the males of the same age, thus paradoxically bringing about a true 'integration'.

A picture emerges that is both homogeneous and fractured, with marked non-conformities between the programmed plan and the action taken. What is really apparent is the lack of analysis of the feminine role, a topic mentioned by only a few staff members and then only in passing, yet present in a creeping, pervasive manner through common-sense judgments on which were based erroneous approaches to running the female section and to the staff–inmate relationship.

It should further be noted that the choice of the Eboli institution to accommodate the girls from the district of Campania was a result of a positive evaluation of its ordinary administration. The staff and the organization of the institution were regarded as the most suitable among those in the area for taking on the burden of a female section with some chance of success. The integration of males and females in fact involved the whole structural set-up and required considerable organizational effort on the part of management and staff. Considering that running a female group constituted a sort of leap in the dark for the staff of a male juvenile prison, the Altavista institution was chosen because both the civilian and the military staff were deemed more trustworthy, and there was a sound organization.

Over and above this assessment, which may be defined as a common-sense one, no analysis of the inmates was done before the section was opened and the integration option actually taken, nor was any research done to establish operational approaches that might be different from those regarded as valid for the males. Integration was the preferred model for a good approach and successful treatment. It is well known how all institutions, especially total institutions, are modelled on organizational parameters which govern their functioning on the basis of criteria of self-conservation and self-reproduction. However, the paradox at Eboli is that, while 'imitating' originality and a break with traditional schemes (integration), it in fact moves along tracks that are perfectly consistent with its own previously established approach, as well as with the most deep-seatedly conventional social norms.

Gender specificity: needs and management

In a context that places the feminine in a logic of subordination, power figures of the female sex are not given authority by the institution. Recognition of the authority and reliability of female educational staff and warders was therefore not accorded to them by the detainees either.

The female warders and educational assistants themselves colluded with the institution, tending to delegate decision-making power in order not to have to take on responsibility. This reflects a traditional mode of distribution of burdens, responsibility and authority between male and female figures within the social structure of southern Italy. We were not surprised, therefore, at the presence of sexual rivalries, which are an indication of a seduction type of relationship that runs through the relationships between staff and female detainees but also between staff members. This is true even though the use of sex as challenge and aggression was reported only on the part of the girls.

The presence of women in a male total institution allowed the spectre of the feminine to haunt the prison. We call it a spectre, since we are not referring to a relationship between real men and women, but to the image that the men have of the feminine and that the women themselves have of themselves, which tends to be amplified in a closed institution.

At a semantic level, the welcome banner is a sign of this hypothesis. The institution was preparing at an organizational level to welcome the girls, but on the level of fantasy and imagination it was Woman that was being awaited. The actual girls themselves thus stayed hidden and obscured behind the imaginary Woman.

Moreover, if the prison institution relocates girls in a context of institutional subordination, what this induces and elicits is the behaviour characteristics of subordinate groups. The logic of seduction and of sexual challenge is characteristic of someone who is in a position in which there is no other possibility of being seen.

The prison is, in this sense, only an extension of ordinary modes of social interaction. The sociological analysis we propose locates the female juveniles in a closed, traditionalist context. If it is true that the girls were not seen except as stereotypes, yet at the same time the experience of prison was for some a genuine occasion for growth, making them demand as of right their own role as both person and subject. In this sense the revolt may also be interpreted as a sign of the accomplishment of an individuation process, or more simply as the girls testing and verifying their own strength on a territory that officially allowed them nothing other than a subordinate role. After the revolt, because of the spatial limitations and the pervasive common sense, the institution relocated the girls entirely in the marginal role they had clearly occupied in the family circle.

After these consequent restrictions, the girls' life turned to being 'up' (*sopra*, which in dialect indicates being shut up or staying at home). Significantly, this word the girls used is the same one mostly used to answer the question: 'What did you do before you came in here?' The reply, 'I was up', summarily describes their status of 'housewives', shut up in the home, or in the prison. The word here becomes a semantic indicator or recognition of an essential continuity between conditions that formally seem so different.

What suggestions can be made? As far as we are concerned, an initial objective must be liberation from the oppression of the platitude. Through a recognition of differences, the capacity should be acquired to overcome stereotypes. This transcending of an oppressive common sense will make possible more directed interventions.

The process involves, in a more general sense, the man–woman relationship within present gender roles. But there is also the possibility of interpreting and approaching this specific clientèle by highlighting possible difficulties among staff. For these reasons after the revolt we embarked on a systematic study of the offences the girls committed in adolescence and an interpretation of individual histories. In fact, it frequently seems to us that in the case biographies of young deviant females there is a long enumeration of facts whose meaning escapes us. Presently there is no discourse in terms of which they could 'mean'. In this sense our objective is to give a voice to the secret feminine silence, covered up by naturalistic platitudes, which permeates the courts, defences and the observations of experts and specialists.

The overall attitude to the girls of the Eboli staff, whether men or women, can also be explained in terms of perceptions of the 'normality' of the feminine dimension that totalizes the female detainees. There can be a means of access to the interpersonal relationships of girls and staff by recognizing those factors in the life stories of the girls that are the basis for the normal experience of relationships with women (mothers, sisters, wives, daughters), even outside the prison.

The life stories must therefore be mute, since they retell, albeit in more strident tones, status and role stereotypes, which can be communicated but which are embedded in the discourse in which they are told. Their transformation into a project opposing the normality of a human condition impoverished by the schematization of the eternal feminine involves what is presently unspeakable: a new discourse of a new female subjectivity.

The obscenity of the revolt, assessed by legal and administrative circles as an uncontrolled explosion of sexual tensions, for us consists in its banality: the obscene and the banal are closely interwoven, and often equivalent, in the girls' stories. Separating these two concepts and restoring a specific meaning to each of them is a preliminary task for any proposal for transforming social intervention with women, in particular in our field of activity.

The Eboli staff conducted an experiment which has the merit of having revealed a highly problematic area as regards the treatment of female juveniles. They carried it out with passion and essentially in good faith. But lacking specific historical knowledge about both women and Woman, not to mention the dynamics of adolescence, such well-intentioned efforts can only reproduce and conserve existing models. As researchers and fieldworkers our task is constructively to help both them and the girls by finding a language for what cannot yet be spoken and so pointing to alternatives.

Notes

1 For a more detailed analysis, see the annual statistics of the Italian Juvenile Justice Office. The figures for 1982 in the Eboli research are confirmed in those for 1980–1 for the Pozzuoli (Naples) juvenile section gathered by the Campania Social Service Office.
2 From the report approved by the operational group, drawn up by Professor M. Corsale, consultant sociologist of the Eboli prison.
3 Ibid.

10

Intermediate treatment for girls in England and Wales

Anthony E. Bottoms and John Pratt

In this chapter we examine the level and type of provision for 'intermediate treatment' for girls and boys in England and Wales, concentrating on girls. Our argument is that girls have always formed a significant minority of the population receiving intermediate treatment in England and Wales but that, nevertheless, the various types of treatment provision have been such that the dominant discourse in intermediate treatment policy analysis has always been primarily male-oriented. We present data from a recently conducted national survey to show that intermediate treatment for girls differs substantially from that for boys, and we indicate reasons for believing that provision for girls will become proportionately more important in the future. That being the case, some significant and controversial contemporary issues relating to girls and intermediate treatment need to be examined, such as whether this should be provided in gender-specific groups and by women workers only. But before we can reach such issues it is necessary to cover a good deal of background material about intermediate treatment in general.

Intermediate treatment

'Intermediate treatment' is a generic term for a range of provisions in England and Wales for juveniles (under-17s) who have been adjudged delinquent or in need of official care, or are thought to be at risk of delinquency or of being considered appropriate subjects for official care proceedings. It is termed 'intermediate' because it comes between, on the one hand, custodial or long-term residential provision and, on the other hand, ordinary supervision by a social worker of a juvenile and his or her family. As such, 'intermediate treatment' can cover a very wide range of provision: adventure holidays, evening discussions, alternative education on a day-care basis, motor-cycling groups or community service, to give but a few examples.

Intermediate treatment (I.T.) was first established in England and Wales as an adjunct to the Children and Young Persons Act

1969, a welfare-oriented statute on juvenile justice. From the outset, it has been available as a provision which may be officially prescribed by the juvenile court in conjunction with a supervision order.[1] However, it was always also intended that I.T. should be available to social workers on a broader basis than this, and (as we shall see more fully later) substantial proportions of children and young people receiving intermediate treatment participate in the programmes on a technically voluntary basis.

Although it is only twenty years since intermediate treatment was formally established, its development has been extremely varied and complex. For our purposes, however, and at the risk of some over-simplification, I.T. can be seen as having had three main phases of development.

The phase of 'interesting activities'

At the outset in 1969, I.T. was seen as a wide-ranging provision which was to be 'an experiment in liberal education' for those who 'need, either by their own volition or by direction, new experiences in human relationships and in interesting activities' (Cooper, 1970). The Department of Health and Social Security (DHSS) 'Guide' to I.T.,[2] published at the beginning of its practical development in the early 1970s, thus described the mainstream of I.T. as:

> one or more activities of a recreational, educational or cultural nature, or of social value . . . including (but not limited to) the following: physical education, competitive sports or games, adventure training, camping, cycling, walking, climbing, sailing, boating, canoeing, riding, swimming, amateur dramatics, arts, crafts, music, dancing . . . (DHSS, 1972: 26)

The emphasis on physical and 'adventure'-oriented activities at the beginning of this list is probably not accidental, and it certainly reflects much early I.T. in practice.

The phase of activity groups

Early I.T. was strongly criticized by many social workers as being devoid of true social-work purpose; derogatory remarks about 'table-tennis therapy' were made. Particularly influential critics Paley and Thorpe (1974) argued instead for a 'continuum of care', in which social-work-oriented experiences of various kinds would be provided. Style and intensity of intervention were seen as the qualitative and quantitative dimensions of this continuum, and children would be placed at different points in the continuum on the basis of an assessment of their personal and social needs.

In practice, provisions reflecting the continuum of care did not develop fully in all areas, though the concept was often a very important guiding principle. A particular absence was the general lack of more intensive, or 'heavy-end' provision for those otherwise likely to be placed in custody or residential care. I.T. developed in practice as a 'light-end to medium range' strategy in many places in the second half of the 1970s.

A decisive shift occurred, however, in the matter of the service-providers for I.T. Whereas in the early phase I.T. was provided by youth and voluntary organizations, by the late 1970s social workers had taken over. Indeed, in 1979, Jones and Kerslake were able to write that, particularly in local authority social services departments, 'intermediate treatment and groupwork are interchangeable terms', and further that 'groupwork in I.T. automatically means "activity" groups' (Jones and Kerslake, 1979: 16). These 'activity groups' usually consisted of up to a dozen children with two or more social workers or specialist I.T. workers, engaging in certain activities regarded as interesting by the children, but interspersing this with group discussions of an intendedly therapeutic kind.

The Lancaster critique and the development of I.T.
in the 1980s

This second phase in turn came in for strong criticism, linked to wider developments in the juvenile justice system in England and Wales. It was felt that I.T., by concentrating too much upon the light and medium ranges, had missed the opportunity to influence sentencing practice in an era of escalating rates of committal of juveniles to detention centres and borstals; and also that social workers were too often recommending residential care through a misguided belief in its effectiveness. Hence, a move towards 'heavy-end I.T.', or more intensive I.T. provision designed directly as an alternative to custodial or residential sentences, was seen as appropriate. Furthermore, it was argued, with some cogency, that the proliferation of 'preventive', 'light-end' I.T. was having the effect of 'widening the net' of official social control over children (see Cohen, 1979); also early provision of I.T. on a preventive basis for an individual child could mean that he or she would, on the next court appearance, receive a more severe or intensive sentence than otherwise because the I.T. experience already undergone would be seen to have 'failed' ('bumping up the tariff'). Criticisms of this sort emanated especially from social work academics at the University of Lancaster (see Thorpe et al., 1980)[3] and the subsequent developments in I.T. therefore became known in England as the 'Lancaster approach'.

Central tenets of the Lancaster approach to I.T. have been:

1 that the overriding aim of I.T. policy should be to keep children out of custody or residential care;

2 that I.T. provision should be restricted to offenders only, or (in later versions) to offenders and those at direct risk of committal to residential care for non-offending reasons (truancy, 'moral danger', etc.); that offenders should preferably receive I.T. only if they are at risk of custody or residential care; and that at all costs one should avoid 'preventive' I.T. for 'light-end' juveniles at no risk of residential care;

3 that other provision for youth, if made, should not be called 'intermediate treatment'.[4]

It should be noticed that the Lancaster approach stresses the place of I.T. clients in the juvenile justice system rather than personal/social need as the basis of intervention. Furthermore, its primary emphasis is upon the question 'who should be the clients of I.T.?' rather than 'what should be done to or with the clients when they are on I.T.?', though in fact some initiatives have also been made by Lancaster in the area of. programmes for clients, centring round discussion of offending.[5]

The combined effect of the Lancaster approach and a recent insertion of DHSS money for 'heavy-end' I.T. (£15 million) has been powerful at the level of local policy.[6] Preliminary analysis of our national survey of I.T. carried out in 1984–5 suggests that no fewer than 88 per cent of local authority social services departments (the main providers of I.T.: see note 2) subscribed to 'alternatives to residential care and custody' as a main policy aim of their I.T. provision; with the two next highest aims being subscribed to by only a quarter of areas. Some 30 per cent of all areas listed 'alternatives to care/custody' as their only aim; the other 58 per cent mostly mixed this aim with other aims not strongly congruent with the 'Lancaster' approach (Bottoms et al., 1986). The survey also asked all local authority social services departments about changes in their I.T. policy and/or provision over the previous two years; and some two-thirds of all areas had in that period moved to endorse at least one aspect of policy congruent with the Lancaster approach (Bottoms et al., 1986).

Although the movement of policy and practice has therefore been quite strongly in a 'Lancaster' direction in recent years, it would be wrong to give the impression either that this direction of policy has been followed in all local areas, or that ground-level practice is always congruent with stated policy, even where a Lancaster policy has been adopted. On both points, the national survey has shown clearly that there is still much practice owing more to earlier phases of development than to the Lancaster approach and, in some places, some more or less sophisticated attempts consciously to marry the two.

The national survey also asked a question concerning likely developments over the following two years. Surprisingly, 21 social services departments (out of 95 responding to the survey) made responses of the kind 'we're evolving a broader-based approach', 'we'll take a broader definition', 'develop preventive work/community-based provision', etc.; that is, responses apparently moving away from a Lancaster approach (Bottoms et al., 1986). There would seem to be a number of reasons for this development. For example some authorities, having learned the 'net widening' lesson of their earlier I.T. programmes, are seeking to hold on to the policy gains of recent years while providing other facilities for children with needs and problems. On the other hand, the development in some areas may have more to do with managerial pragmatism, taking account of a range of extraneous factors (for example, a declining child population, over-provision of resources for serious offenders), which is now beginning to shift policy towards less 'heavy-end' areas of the youth population. Whatever the reasons, this shift to a broader-based approach seems likely to have important consequences for the level of I.T. provision for girls.

Girls and the history of I.T.

The above account has been written in a deliberately general, non-gender-based way. But how have girls fitted in to these various phases of I.T. development in England and Wales? Harrison (1985) has said:

> Sometimes it seems as if I.T. is inherently sexist – made by men, to be performed by men upon men. From its origins in the outward bound organisation to the present emphasis upon alternatives to custody . . . the role of women has been distinctly limited.

Certainly, if one examines much of the literature on I.T., one could easily imagine either that scarcely any girls have ever received I.T., or that I.T. for girls is an insignificant matter, not worth commenting upon specifically. Thus, for example, the National Youth Bureau bibliography on I.T. for the period 1968–76 lists only 8 out 169 items as being about girls or about mixed groups; in the updated bibliography to 1984 it is 14 out of 122 (National Youth Bureau, 1978; Skinner, 1985).

Nevertheless, it does seem that girls have consistently formed a sizeable proportion of the clientèle of I.T. The few figures available are given in Table 10.1, which, on the face of it, shows a slight

Table 10.1 *Girls and boys in intermediate treatment*

(a)	1978–9 National Youth Bureau survey	
	Estimated number of young people involved in I.T.	20–25,000
	Estimated proportion of girls	20–30%
	Figures include estimated 3,500 children on supervision orders with I.T. conditions, of which only 10 per cent were girls	
(b)	1981 National Youth Bureau survey	
	Estimated number of young people involved in I.T.	20–25,000
	Estimated proportion of girls	20–25%
	Figures include estimated 4,600 children on supervision orders with I.T. conditions, of which only 12 per cent were girls	
(c)	1984–5 National survey: preliminary sample of clients in 200 units of provision	

Males	1,096	(83%)
Females	229	(17%)
Total	1,325	(100%)

Data are from only 179 units of provision as information on sex of clients was not given from 21 units.

Because of the structure of the questionnaire, sex of clients is only given for the first 15 clients of any unit, but few units have more than 15 clients.

Data probably under-sample girls; see note 8 for details.

decline from 1979 to 1984–5. However, not too much should be made of this in view of methodological weaknesses in the earlier surveys and an apparent sampling bias in the preliminary figures for the 1984–5 survey (see note 8 below); it would be safer to assume a constant figure of around 20 per cent of girls among clients of I.T. programmes in the period in question. This figure is not too dissimilar to the proportion of girls among known offenders (convicted or cautioned) in England and Wales, which in 1983 was 19.3 per cent, though of course I.T. covers non-offenders as well as offenders.

If girls have been consistently provided for in I.T. practice, why have they often received so little attention in the proliferation of comments, statements, project reports – in short in *discourse* – about I.T.? The answer to this question, we think, depends upon understanding the nature of the dominant discourse at each of the three main phases of I.T.

In the first phase, the 'outward bound/adventure/physical activity' project components always seemed to take precedence, in practice, over some of the other activities mentioned in the original DHSS list of 1972, such as 'crafts' and 'dancing'. Inevitably, in our culture, these physical and adventure-based activities were strongly male-oriented; the girls, if they came at all, played a secondary role. The DHSS's (1972: App. C) early guidance booklet listed eighteen hypothetical projects by way of example; none of these was for girls only. Fourteen projects were mixed, but this surely represented pious aspiration rather than any serious reality.

Paley and Thorpe's (1974) text contains descriptions of ten projects specifically selected by the authors as moving away from the pure 'activities' model towards one based on relationships. The authors' assumptions about gender are indicated in their view that 'the importance of relationships in intermediate treatment resides particularly in the form of the delinquent's association with his fellows' (Paley and Thorpe, 1974: 18). None of the ten projects was for girls only; seven were for boys only or contained within them some boys-only groups. Activities in some of the projects included judo, football, basketball, cricket, darts, skittles, cards, model-making and 'rough games'.

In the second phase of I.T. (the activity group phase), girls had in principle a more equal chance of participation, since the emphasis shifted from male-oriented activities towards non-gender-specific relationships, discussion, and the gaining of insight; also, the criteria for selection were based simply on personal and social needs, as in the following specific project example:

Criteria for selection
1 Young people with problems in relating to authority, e.g. school or parents.
2 Young people who are members of families with a pattern of delinquent behaviour.
3 Those who are strongly influenced by friends who are either in trouble or on the fringes of trouble with other young people.
4 Those who present relationship difficulties with their peer group.
   (DHSS, 1977: 100–1)

At this time, the DHSS published a booklet with examples of twenty-eight I.T. projects (DHSS, 1977). There are no specific references to girls-only groups in the projects reviewed, but there does appear to be more emphasis on mixed groups than at the earlier phase. Indeed, it could be argued that mixed groups had an important part to play in I.T. at this particular juncture, in view of the primary interest in relationships and family structure, and the fact that mixed groups can be seen as more representative than single-sex groups of relationships at home, school and the workplace. Nevertheless, in practice of course ideals of equality of the sexes were not at all easy to maintain in mixed groups, since the usual wider cultural influences were reinforced by the low proportion of girls among the referrals to I.T.

However, the dominant model of I.T. changed again, towards the Lancaster approach. This inevitably shifted the emphasis once again towards boys, since boys are very much more likely to be dealt with as persistent or serious offenders than girls, and are also much more often found in custodial institutions and residential care – the target groups for the new approach. One woman I.T. worker who accepted aspects of the Lancaster approach drew the logical conclusions so far as I.T. for girls was concerned:

> It is my view that Intermediate Treatment should be concerned with delinquency, in terms of offending, and that it should intervene within the juvenile justice process. Examination of the care and custody systems in this London borough seems to suggest that *Intermediate Treatment has little need to intervene in the juvenile justice process on behalf of girls*. Intermediate Treatment may possibly become involved at the level of advising social workers as to what to recommend in social enquiry reports, or by deterring them from making a custodial recommendation. It may also be feasible that in the future there would be a demand, in terms of numbers, to create an alternative to custody or care project for girls who offend. However, it is more likely that an individual programme will have to be created for the occasional girl. The inclusion of girls into predominantly male-oriented projects should be considered very carefully. (Roach, 1983; emphasis added)

This approach, then, if pursued, would probably lead to a decline of the proportion of girls in I.T., and this may have happened in some local areas.

As a counterbalance, however, there have been at least two new developments which seem likely to increase the proportion of girls in I.T. First, there have been changes in the general range of I.T. provision itself. As we have already hinted, a shift of emphasis away from a strict Lancaster approach towards generic welfare provision is likely to provide I.T. workers in the future with access to a larger number of girls for consideration for I.T. than has recently been the case. Secondly, a growing development among social work professionals of feminist consciousness and general interest in and awareness of issues related to women and justice has sustained the growth of girls' I.T. groups.

During the 1970s, although I.T. *was* being provided for girls (almost wholly in mixed-sex groups) there seems to have been virtually no interest in trying to establish specially-tailored provision for girls or, indeed, any recognition (with some exceptions, see Warren, 1977) that this possibility should be considered as an issue. This is not the case today: in the last few years there has been a steady flow of 'talk' about girls and I.T., even if this is just to complain about the lack of existing provision for them, as in the case of Harrison (1985). For example, at the National Intermediate Treatment Federation conference in 1984, one of the themes was I.T. for girls; in addition some regional I.T. associations have held study days and organized training workshops on sexism and I.T., and there was a special issue of the journal produced by the London I.T. Association on this subject (Eureka, 1983). We realize that this does not even begin to balance the previously and currently prevailing discourse that is slanted towards boys; but it does seem to represent a real growth of interest.

Girls and I.T. in the national survey

So far, because of a lack of data, we have been somewhat speculative. We are now able to provide a little more hard information about girls and I.T. in 1984–5 from our own national survey of intermediate treatment.

We must, however, emphasize two preliminary points. First, the advent of the Lancaster approach has necessarily introduced within the I.T. world a definitional problem in doing research. This is because some areas now continue to do preventive youth work, but no longer call it 'I.T.' owing to (especially) the 'bumping up the tariff' problem; other areas still continue to operate with a much wider definition based on a philosophy of I.T. derived from earlier, more 'welfarist' assumptions. In conducting a national survey of I.T., we adopted the course of taking a very wide definition in order to encompass all traditions, while allowing local authorities, probation services, etc., to make clear to the research team the extent to which the agency was itself operating on narrower criteria. Following these procedures some local service providers had to give us details of projects which they did not themselves regard as I.T. We are checking further on the statistical size of this phenomenon but, on the data we have at present, it is not a major constraint in interpreting our survey data at face value.

The second technical point concerns the status of the data presented in this chapter. Our full data are still being analysed, but for the purposes of preliminary analysis we have used two *provisional* data sources (see also Bottoms et al., 1986). The first of these, already drawn upon earlier in the chapter, was an interview about I.T. policy with a key 'contact person' in each local authority social services department (95 out of 116 social services departments were interviewed).[7] The second source, which is drawn upon in the remainder of this section, is a special random sample of units of I.T. provision in local areas; these have been divided into girls-only units, mixed units and boys-only units.[8]

Table 10.2   *Nature of units of provision*

| | Girls' units (all) | | Mixed units (sample) | | Boys' units (sample) | |
	Number	%	Number	%	Number	%
Diversion from court	16	22	16	28	16	15
Preventive I.T.	50	68	35	60	33	31
Medium-range I.T.	27	36	26	45	58	54
Heavy-end I.T.	12	16	20	34	54	50
Detached community projects	5	7	3	5	3	3
I.T. for assessment	2	3	9	16	14	13
I.T. as after-care	15	20	12	21	16	15
Other	6	8	9	16	7	6
N	74		58		108	

Columns do not add to *N* because multiple answers for one unit are allowed. Percentages are percentages of *N* and therefore do not add to 100 per cent.

Table 10.3   *Type of heavy-end provision*

	Girls' units (all)	Mixed units (sample)	Boys' units (sample)
Alternative to custody	—	5	20
Alternative to care (or care + other)	8	3	5
Alternative to care and custody	3	12	29
Other/not stated	1	—	—
N	12	20	54

Table 10.2 shows the nature of the units of provision, broken down by gender composition, and using such conventional categories relating to I.T. provision as 'preventive' and 'heavy-end'.[9] It can be seen that there are considerable differences between the three gender-composition groups, with, for example, a much higher proportion of girls' and mixed units than boys' units containing a 'preventive' population element. Conversely, half of all boys' units had a 'heavy-end' element, compared with only one-sixth of girls' units.

Table 10.3 shows that where there is 'heavy-end' provision, in the case of boys' and mixed units this usually takes the form of alternatives to custody or alternatives to care *and* custody; but for girls-only units the bulk of heavy-end provision is an alternative to care. This striking difference in part reflects the fact that while boys vastly outnumber girls in committals to custodial institutions, and in receipt of care orders for offence-related reasons, care orders for 10–17-year-olds for non-criminal reasons are roughly evenly divided between the sexes.

Two other points of some interest arose from the analysis of the units of provision. First, almost all girls-only units were provided by the local authority social services departments, either alone or in conjunction with another agency (93 per cent); this is a higher proportion than for boys-only units (80 per cent) or mixed units (78 per cent). Secondly, as Table 10.4 shows, girls-only units are more likely to function in a group-based rather than an individually oriented way. This probably reflects the fact that the rationale of having girls-only provision is precisely so that adolescent girls can gain mutual support and help in a shared group experience.

Table 10.4   *Structure of units of provision*

	Girls' units (all)		Mixed units (sample)		Boys' units (sample)	
	Number	%	Number	%	Number	%
Group provision only	59	80	30	52	62	57
Individual provision only	7	9	16	28	24	22
Mixed group plus individual provision	7	9	7	12	16	15
Other	1	1	5	8	6	6
Total	74	100	58	100	108	100

Table 10.5   *Offender status and gender within types of unit*

	Girls' units (all)		Mixed units (sample)				Boys' units (sample)	
			Girls		Boys			
	Number	%	Number	%	Number	%	Number	%
Offenders	109	23	32	30	192	66	394	80
Non-offenders	364	77	75	70	101	34	100	20
Total	473	100	107	100	293	100	494	100

No information on offender status and/or sex: girls' units (111); mixed units (164); boys' units (246).

All the above data are on a *unit* basis. Turning to *individual* data, Table 10.5 shows the offender status or otherwise of the I.T. clients. There is a very striking boy–girl difference. Among boys, four-fifths of those in boys' units and two-thirds of those in mixed units are offenders; while among girls, only a quarter of those in girls' units and less than a third of those in mixed units are offenders. These data are amplified in Table 10.6, for those in single-sex groups only, by showing the legal basis of the initial contact with the I.T. unit of provision. As many as 69 per cent of those in girls units, but only 22 per cent of those in boys' units, were there on the basis of voluntary contact. By contrast, the boys were much more likely to be on I.T. linked to a supervision order (59 per cent boys; 14 per cent girls). It is quite clear from these data, provisional as they are, that the female population receiving I.T. is quite different from that of males. Further analysis shows that the difference is not attributable to age differences in the two gender groups.

Table 10.6 *Basis of initial contact with I.T. provision in girls-only units and boys-only units (mixed units excluded)*

	Girls		Boys	
	Number	%	Number	%
Care order	72	13	69	10
Supervision order without specific I.T. requirement	37	7	136	20
Supervision order with I.T. requirement	39	7	195	29
Supervision order with supervised activities requirement	—	—	51	8
Deferred sentence	—	—	17	3
Caution	21	4	33	5
After-care licence	3	1	6	1
Voluntary	375	69	142	21
Other	—	—	30	4
N	547	100	679	100

Excludes cases with no information about basis of initial contact.

The strongly voluntary referral base of these modern girls' groups is intriguing. Women workers in I.T. would undoubtedly claim that they are developing a new practice for girls which forms a radical departure from old ideas, but the population composition raises queries as to whether old problems (like net-widening and bumping up the tariff) might re-emerge in a new context. Moreover, since few girls become identified as serious or persistent offenders, and thus at risk of custodial sentencing, is it wise to seek to expand I.T. provision for girls, as there is now pressure to do? Or are all these fears misguided, and a practice being developed which will not fall into the earlier difficulties?

We will now examine some issues of this kind more closely.

Girls' groups and I.T.: some issues for consideration

Girls-only or mixed groups?

The overwhelming majority of recent project reports available on girls and I.T. indicate, from their respective authors, both a strong preference for girls-only groups and for the groups to be staffed and supervised by women workers.[10] The rationale for girls-only groups appears to be usually that they would create an important 'space' for girls in several ways.

First, it is argued that girls can talk and act more 'naturally' in such a setting; by contrast, the structure and activities of mixed groups would inevitably be oriented towards male outlooks and interests, thus imposing a silence or constraint on girls present. As one girl's project report puts it:

Specific objectives
  (a) to give the girls the opportunity to taste a number of activities more 'normally' associated with boys, in a non-threatening atmosphere. This is hoped to encourage the girls to begin to realise their potentials and therefore feel more confident and able to make greater use of existing facilities within a mixed situation;
  (b) to provide a supportive female environment where they have the opportunity to explore, through shared experience, their feelings and fears about their developing sexuality, which is clearly a major issue for these particular girls;
  (c) to provide an experience that is enjoyable in its own right, encouraging the girls to see themselves as capable of enjoying their own leisure without being dependent on boys;
  (d) to allow the space for the girls to discuss their own individual difficulties at home, school and in the wider community, if they wish to. (NYB Pack)[11]

Secondly, there is a belief that adolescent girls face specific problems and issues, particularly on the subject of sexuality, and that participation in a girls-only group would be the only viable setting for rational discussion of such issues. For example:

Only women get pregnant. The girls in our group, we know, are at risk. Through group discussions we have discovered that although they are familiar with the 'biology' of reproduction, the girls are ignorant not only about contraception, but about their own bodies. For instance, they all knew that periods were unfertilised eggs (hardly a helpful description!), but none of them used internal sanitation, and they had no idea about how to cope with pre-menstrual tension or menstrual pain. (NYB Pack)

Following on from these reasons for the establishment of these girls' groups in the first instance, it is generally argued in project reports that the staff should be exclusively female as well. For example:

> In view of the above stated reasoning for forming a girls' group, the workers should be women. Perhaps when the group is cohesive and feels confident, the group might collectively agree for men to be invited on a one-off or irregular basis. It would be interesting for the group to be aware, and note the effect on the whole group, as well as for individuals, of the presence of a man. (NYB Pack)

However, it must also be said that in one of the few exceptions to this view, the presence of a male worker was not perceived as creating any particular difficulties:

> We spent some time discussing the appropriateness of having a man involved as a leader. There were two views – one being that it was totally inappropriate and that an all-girls' group should be run purely by women and on feminist lines. Another that it would be advantageous to have the involvement of a non-sexist male, who was interested in all that the girls did and related well to them.
> In fact, involvement has been completely successful. The girls have accepted him totally, have shown no embarrassment in discussing personal issues with him and have not reacted any differently to him than to (the female workers). (NYB Pack)

The great emphasis in project reports on single-sex groups, in terms of both clients and workers, seems to raise two key issues. First, to what extent were these provisions dictated by the desire of the girl clients themselves to find such 'spaces' or 'havens'? Secondly, how far does single-sex preference reflect the ideology of the professional workers themselves? On the first point, one of the few consumer studies undertaken in I.T. research (Jones, 1979) indicates a preference amongst girls (albeit on a small majority from a very small sample) for participation in *mixed-sex groups*. More generally, it could, no doubt, be argued that single-sex groups are 'unnatural' and that, in terms of socialization, participation in mixed-sex groups would be preferable. The alternative argument, of course, is that precisely because of the predominance of mixed-sex venues in a whole range of aspects of the social life of adolescents, and the way in which male attitudes and perceptions are likely to dominate such arrangements, this specialist type of provision is needed for girls.

Equally, the lack of specific demand from girls for this could be seen as a weak argument, in view of the significance it attaches to the way in which these adolescent girls might be able to articulate their intentions and concerns, and judge what is in their own best interests. Alternatively one might ask why the issue should be raised only for girls and not right across the I.T. field. Where, for example, is the express motivation from boys to participate in motorcycling groups, football teams, outward-bound ventures, and so on?

The second point – whether the ideology of the professional workers determines what their clients 'need' – would seem to be more important. Given that, as things now stand, the majority of girls in I.T. are non-offender voluntary attenders, there is no sure supply of clients. They have to be found from non-criminal justice system sources. One such source may be the non-offender element in the care population and elsewhere. Here, feminist ideology that specifies the significance of work with girls may be seen as potentially tactically allied with a managerial pragmatism concerned with keeping the numbers of the young people involved in I.T. at a respectable level.

It also seems that other sources of referral become apparent once the idea of actually providing a girls' group becomes established, as we see in the following project example:

> Workers have identified the need to work specifically with girls for a variety of reasons:
> 1 There were girls 'hanging around' in the club centre who did not participate in the activities on offer and they wanted 'to do something' with them.
> 2 Not many girls came to the club and they wanted to encourage more to do so. (NYB Pack)

For others, the need for a girls' group was simply taken as being self-evident:

> This group was set up as a response to the obvious need for some form of group experience for teenage girls in the . . . area. The lack of provision for young people in general, and girls in particular, coupled with the increase in self-referrals to the Department of girls in the 16– 18 year age range, confirm our own feelings that a short-term focused group could be a very useful and effective way of working with this age range. (NYB Pack)

Similarly:

> The creation of this girls' group was a recognition of the importance of girls having the opportunity of being together in a caring environment where they can begin to relate to one another and learn from this interaction. The setting up of the group was also a response to the lack of provision for girls in this area, many of whom tend to remain isolated during adolescence and are less likely than boys to participate in the group activities which do exist in the community. (NYB Pack)

As such, criteria for referral appear to be much wider than those for entry into most boys' groups: rather than being specifically offence-related, they have come to include 'isolation during adolescence', school problems and 'problems of unemployment, starting work, as well as the usual range of problems faced by young people'. (NYB Pack)

Net-widening by another route?

It is impossible to read such reports, which problematize features of everyday life and then make these the criteria for admission to I.T., without a sense of *déjà vu*. There seem to be close parallels here with the second phase of I.T.: social workers decide, for whatever reason, that an I.T. group would be 'a good thing'; there is then the matter of introducing clients to it; in this way, criteria based on servicing generic problems can prove to be very useful (see, for example, Pitts, 1974). Hence, it may be that the tendency to 'widen the net' of social work intervention and regulation is to be continued, but by means of another route set out in advance by radical sections of the social work profession sympathetic to feminism. If this should prove to be the case, it will not be the first time that social work in this particular trajectory has had the effect of widening the orbit of social control (see Donzelot, 1979).

The current conceptual confusion about, and sometimes pragmatic categorization of I.T. provision, may exacerbate this problem. However, as we indicated earlier, it is clear that social work professionals have become well aware that 'good intentions' as the dictates of policy are likely to have inflationary consequences. Thus it may be that, in the light of earlier experiences in I.T., local strategies and tactics can be deployed in an attempt to prevent these developments. However this develops, it remains to be said that the history of penal reform suggests that we must expect uncertainty and non-correspondence between intentions and results (see Austin and Krisberg, 1981; Foucault, 1977a).

The sexuality problematic

As will have been evident already, most of the available literature on girls-only I.T. groups indicates that the sexuality problematic – the idea that girls are subjected to a range of discriminatory and unfair assumptions about themselves solely on account of their sex – is a very prominent theme in these groups. The following is a typical programme based round the idea of 'talking through' such issues and raising the girls' consciousness:

The Girls' Group ran for ten weeks with a different theme for each session as follows:

    1   images of girls;
    2   getting through adolescence;
    3   family relationships;
    4–6 sex, sexuality, abortion and related matters (three sessions);
    7   social skills for finding work;
    8   predicaments and assertion;
    9   up against the law;
    10 barbecue/summing-up session (NYB Pack)

Of course, we have already covered some of the reasons for this:
a space for girls to allow them to talk about issues which uniquely
affect them as girls and which, outside of this setting, will be
reduced to silence by predominant male discourses, and so on.
While we recognize the validity of these arguments, we think there
may be some dilemmas arising from them. Could it not be the case
that what begins as an attempt to make problematic perceived ideas
about female sexuality, becomes in practice a focus on the supposed
sexual problems of girls? Just as Smart (1976), Heidensohn (1985)
and other feminist writers have been critical of the way in which
other areas of the criminal justice system operate so as to
pathologize female sexuality, might this also be happening here?
'Sexuality and problems' was the topic in one group session; another
project reports that

> The aim is to . . . offer a befriending service, where girls feel that they
> are able to talk freely, about their worries and problems, which can be
> enormous during puberty . . . (NYB Pack)

The effect may, however, be to turn the issue of female sexuality
into a grid of sexual problems by which deviations from what is
considered to be 'normal behaviour' can be calculated. This
emphasis on normalization was a particularly prominent feature of
one group reported in the NYB information pack. In this group,
deviations from the standard had to be examined and then rectified:

> The emphasis is on developing the 'Image' of that person, correcting
> any unpleasant and unsociable characteristics, e.g. swearing, smoking
> under age, control of temper, poor hygiene, lack of social graces such
> as eating properly, while also bringing out the 'positive' side to that girl,
> thus giving her pride, confidence and a belief in herself. (NYB Pack)

The way to bring out the 'positive side' in this group, to enhance
the 'images' of these girls, included sessions on 'keep-fit'; basic
cookery; beauty and hygiene; hairdressing; etiquette and posture;
and 'care of clothing – including washing and ironing'. This
culminated in a residential weekend preparing for a

> real-life situation, i.e. buying, budgeting and cooking for the weekend;
> preparing a three-course meal before dressing and making-up to go out
> to the theatre. (NYB Pack)

Not all girls' projects, of course, share this group's strong emphasis on producing 'normal' girls; nonetheless, girls' groups often include activities similar to those here regarded as 'positive'. But the question has to be asked, are activities in this mode likely to challenge existing ideas about female sexuality, women and deviance, women in society or will they simply reaffirm them? Whatever the answer to this question, the paradox is that, for all the issues raised by this literature, there is little doubt that participation in these 'positive' activities is highly popular with the girls who are attending.

We have raised these various issues not by way of a critique of the concept of I.T. for girls and the strategy of girls-only groups, but simply to put some new questions on the agenda for discussion.

Notes

The national survey reported in this chapter is part of the Intermediate Treatment Evaluation Project at the University of Cambridge Institute of Criminology, and is financed by the Department of Health and Social Security. We would like to express our appreciation for the help of our colleague Brenda McWilliams in the preparation of data for this paper.

1 However, in the 1969 Act, if a court made an I.T. condition in a supervision order, the supervisor was not obliged to implement it. The Criminal Justice Act 1982 introduced a new kind of requirement (generally known as the 'supervised activities requirement') which the supervisor is obliged to implement; but courts may still also use the old 1969 provisions.

2 The Department of Health and Social Security (DHSS) is the central government department responsible for I.T. However, responsibility for actual I.T. provision in local areas rests with the relevant local authority social work department (the main providers), together with, in many areas, the local probation service and perhaps some voluntary organizations. Thus, the DHSS has no central controlling role, and its main function is to provide advice and some financial incentives for local developments.

3 This is the same David Thorpe who earlier promoted the concept of the 'continuum of care'. Subsequently Thorpe, in a self-criticism, has said that 'Paley and Thorpe (1974) were unable to recognize that the "needology" of which they were evangelical proponents was one of the most important factors in the erosion of justice in the juvenile courts and in the increased use of penal dispositions' (Thorpe, 1983: 78).

4 Another important aspect of the Lancaster approach has been *diversion from court*, but this issue is less integrally linked to I.T., and it would take us too far afield to explore it here.

5 This is the so-called 'correctional curriculum'; see, for example, Denman (1983).

6 See Pratt (1983) for an analysis of the significance of this effective alliance between I.T. workers (the 'discontented radicals' of the social work profession: Millham, 1977), shaping and structuring everyday policy with the assistance of relatively generous financial support, at a time of severe cutbacks in other spheres of local authority expenditure, from a Conservative government with a

high profile on 'law and order'. For a commentary on how this alliance has been manufactured, see also Pratt (1986b).

7 As part of the national survey, interviews on I.T. policy were also conducted with probation services and voluntary agencies (see note 2); but data from these interviews have not been included in our preliminary analyses, either here or in Bottoms et al. (1986).

8 At the time when this paper was prepared, data on a total of 838 units of local I.T. provision (run by social services departments, probation services, or voluntary agencies) were available for analysis. (The eventual full total of units was just over 1,200.) For the purposes of preliminary analysis, a simple random sample of 200 of these 838 units was drawn (see Bottoms et al., 1986). For this chapter, it had been intended to use the same sample, but inspection showed that only 13 of the 200 units were for girls only. As this was insufficient for statistical analysis, the original sampling frame of 838 units was returned to, and all girls-only units among these 838 were selected: this yielded a total of 74 (including the original 13), which also showed that because of sampling error girls-only units had been slightly underrepresented in the original 200. (This point is relevant for the interpretation of Table 10.1(c), which uses data from the original random sample of 200.) Of the original 200 units, 108 were for boys only, 58 were mixed, 13 were for girls only, while in 21 units there was no information on the gender of clients *or* no clients in the unit at the specific date of the survey. In Tables 10.2 to 10.6, the 108 boys-only units, the 58 mixed units and the full sample of 74 girls-only units form the basic framework for analysis.

9 In this and all subsequent tables, no totals are given because of the different basis of selection of the girls-only units and the other units. For details see note 8 above.

10 Nevertheless, about half of all girls receiving I.T. are probably in mixed units: this can be seen from Table 10.5, bearing in mind that the girls-only units are a complete population, whilst the girls in mixed units are derived from a 1 in 4.2 sample of units.

11 This quotation, and all further quotations concerning specific I.T. projects given in the remainder of this chapter, is derived from material in an extremely helpful information pack on *Girls and I.T.* (National Youth Bureau, Leicester). For clarity, each such extract is marked 'NYB Pack'.

PART FIVE

. . . AND HOW TO CARE FOR GIRLS

11

Young female drug misusers

Towards an appropriate policy

Edna Oppenheimer

> I think it's a legend that half the population of the world is female: where on earth are they keeping them all?
>
> Joanna Russ, *The Female Man* (quoted in Oakley, 1981)

A drugs policy for women?

Despite the fact that in the United Kingdom, as in other countries, there has been over the last fifteen years or so a considerable increase in awareness of women's concerns and what are conveniently lumped together as 'women's rights', there has been a notable lack of concern about the specific needs of women and girls who misuse drugs, and the structural causes of their behaviour. Feminists writing about women have ignored drug abuse altogether and, by and large, people working on either analysis or policy in relation to drugs have ignored women.

Nevertheless, in recent years, there has been a progression, which perhaps to some observers seems glacial in speed, towards an increased awareness of women's needs in this field. No attention whatever has yet been paid specifically to girls other than in the context of concern for young people in general. In 1982, the UK government's Advisory Council on the Misuse of Drugs (ACMD) made no mention at all of girls or women drug misusers, nor of any other social grouping, and raised the question of distinguishing between addicts (in terms of drugs used and diagnosis) only to dismiss it:

> In the development of services we consider it counter-productive to identify more and more specific client groups (e.g. heroin addict, amphetamine addict etc.). This can give rise to the false assumption that

each category demands specific services, when experience and evidence show that all drug misusers share similar kinds of basic problems. (ACMD, 1982: 33)

However, it stressed that treatment and rehabilitation strategy had to be geared to individual needs: 'For some individuals a medical response will predominate . . . for others a social work response . . . for yet others, an educational and counselling approach will be best' (ACMD, 1982: 32).

A Medical Working Group on Drug Dependence which was set up following the Advisory Council's recommendation noted that 'drug users are a heterogeneous group' (1984: 5) and paid particular attention to the needs of pregnant opioid dependent women, stressing 'sympathetic understanding of the mother' and 'continuing support' (1984: 9).

A more positive step came with the ACMD's *Prevention* report in 1984, in which it stated:

> We are also concerned with other groups at risk of misusing drugs. In the 1960s and 1970s drug misuse amongst women was not considered an area of particular interest; researchers and policy makers have often assumed that hypotheses and policies drawn up in response to male drug misuse are equally applicable to women . . . the women's movement has drawn attention to the need to reconceptualize 'social problems' (such as the drug problem) from the point of view of women's interest and position in society . . . we consider that this literature raises important issues not adequately dealt with in earlier, male-centred work. (ACMD, 1984: 23)

In May 1985, the Social Services Committee of the House of Commons concluded a year-long enquiry into the misuse of drugs, 'with special reference to the treatment and rehabilitation of misusers of hard drugs'. In their report to the government, they noted that various witnesses, including doctors and social workers, testified to the special needs of women. Representative of that testimony was the criticism by the feminist oriented organization DAWN (Drugs, Alcohol, Women, Nationally) of the notion that drug misusers are a homogeneous group: 'the false assumption of a stereotypical drug user who is white, male, single, under 25, unemployed and rootless' (Social Services Committee, 1985: xi).

The Committee responded with the recommendation, *inter alia*, that women's needs should be given greater consideration by policy makers, and by those who are concerned with service delivery:

> An increasing proportion of hard drug misusers are women. We are particularly concerned at the number of young female addicts, some of whom are pregnant or have young children. It is essential that all agencies seeking to respond to drug misuse take greater account of this trend. (1985: lv)

This progressive awareness among policy makers has not been matched by action on the ground. Official government policy on drug misusers is primarily put into practice in the clinical system operated by the network of drug dependency units (DDU), which were set up in 1968 and in which free treatment is provided as part of the national health service. The clinics operate in partnership with non-statutory services which receive all or most of their funding from the public purse. These include a wide spectrum of treatment and rehabilitation models: street agencies providing points of contact and referral; day centres; counselling services; hostels and therapeutic communities for drug-free recovering addicts.

A recent survey of drug clinics found that 'Very few (13 per cent) of the DDUs offered women patients treatment differing from that offered to men and fewer still (3 per cent) offered different facilities such as separate waiting rooms or crèches' (Smart, 1985). The author notes that 'it is not possible to infer from our questionnaire whether this indicates a neglect of the special needs of women users, especially in relation to pregnancy and child care, or whether it represents a scarcity of resources' (Smart, 1985). Since that survey, one DDU has opened a day care centre which provides special facilities for parents (mostly women) and children. It is the only one.

Amongst the voluntary agencies there is also a sparseness in the facilities for women as women and not just as part of a generalized category of drug misusers. There are only two all-female residential rehabilitation centres in the UK out of more than twenty; both define themselves as operating by a Christian ethic. A few street agencies and some therapeutic communities operate women-only groups and in these feminism has been an important element. In London in 1987 a specialized family house opened catering primarily for mothers and their children and operating as part of a larger therapeutic community. Taken as a whole, the system in practice has hardly been touched by the new emphasis in policy.

Policy about drug misuse in Britain

The British system of dealing with the drug problem is, and has long been, a mixture of principles (sometimes in opposition) and pragmatism. It has been characterized by a sustained attempt to treat the drug addict as a patient to be helped rather than a criminal to be punished.

This approach was articulated as early as 1926 by the Rolleston Committee, which was set up by the Ministry of Health at the instance of the Home Office, and comprised members of the medical profession. It defined addiction as a problem for medical treatment, concluding: 'There was general agreement that in most well-established cases the condition must be regarded as a manifestation of disease and not as a mere form of vicious indulgence' (Departmental Committee on Morphine and Heroin Addiction, 1926: 11).

This emphasis on addiction as a medical problem did not mean that punishment as a control measure was discarded: in fact, the possibility of imprisonment and other punitive measures for possession of illicit drugs remained an important element in the State's apparatus of control. A complex relationship between two approaches to the problem was thus initiated and a pattern established for the future. As a 1982 study concluded, the British system 'has never been a purely penal or medical one. It has rather been a blend of two philosophies with one or other view dominating in different periods . . . The 1920s saw not a victory for medical dominance in the field of addiction, but an *entente* between doctors and the state' (Stimson and Oppenheimer, 1982).

In fact, this period from the mid-1920s to the mid-1960s can be seen as a sort of Golden Age in the history of drug control and treatment in the UK. The British method had a good press overseas. Some commentators, such as Edwin Schur (1963), claimed that Britain had no major drug addiction problem precisely because addiction was treated as a medical problem: addicts could get medical help and obtained legitimate supplies of their drug. There was therefore no need for addicts to meet each other and so there was no 'subculture of addiction'. This seemed a reasonable analysis at the time. In retrospect, though, it can be argued convincingly that the British method worked precisely because there was no major endemic drug misuse (for various historical and social reasons). For when drug misuse as a major problem did manifest itself, because of a supply situation that had not been anticipated, the system broke down.

By the mid-1960s it became apparent that the system was under stress. Reports of an epidemic of drug abuse appeared in the press, and the Home Office was becoming aware of a new type of addict – the young experimental drug user who had graduated into addiction (Spear, 1969). For the first time the numbers of men began seriously to overtake the number of women addicts known to the Home Office. The cause of this growth in addiction appeared to be, at least partially, an over-prescribing by a few irresponsible doctors, which created an overspill supply of drugs for the black market, and thus a milieu which recruited new addicts. The official response was to reconvene the Interdepartmental Committee on

Drug Addiction: the Brain Committee, which had been set up to advise the government on drug policy and which had last reported in 1961. Now, however, there was a change of emphasis. Addiction was described not as a disease but as a 'socially infectious condition' (1965: 8). Changes were recommended about the way treatment should be delivered. The aim of all the ensuing measures was to find a way of self-regulation for the medical profession and so avoid the overspill of drugs into the illicit market.

It was recommended that national health treatment centres (drug dependency units) should be set up in psychiatric hospitals or the psychiatric wings of general hospitals. Also, only licensed doctors, preferably those working in these treatment centres and assisted by an interdisciplinary team of nurses, social workers and psychologists, should be able to prescribe heroin and certain other listed drugs to addicts. General practitioners were still able to prescribe certain drugs containing opiates, such as Diconal and Palfium. The Brain Committee also recommended that there should be a system of notification of addicts similar to the notification of infectious diseases under the Public Health Act, to replace the existing system under which the Home Office collected information in a somewhat haphazard manner from routine inspection of chemists and informal notifications. These recommendations came into effect with the Dangerous Drugs (Notification of Addicts) Regulation 1968, and the Dangerous Drugs (Supply to Addicts) Regulation 1968 and were subsequently enshrined in the Misuse of Drugs Act 1971, which is still the basis of drug policy in the UK.

No mention was made of women as a special group and no thought was given to possible different approaches. The treatment offered by the new units was at first not substantially different from that previously offered by general practitioners. It took the form of the prescription of drugs, what is known as 'maintenance prescribing', that is, prescribing sufficient drugs to enable a person to lead a normal life in society without resorting to the black market. However, by the mid-1970s the task of balancing the supply of drugs in the community by 'judicious prescribing' became irrelevant. It was impossible to be scientific and precise in determining the dose or to ensure there was no excess prescribing. The therapeutic advisability of long-term maintenance prescribing was also questioned (Ashton, 1981; Ghodse et al., 1985), and crucially the proliferation of a black market in drugs meant that those who wanted it had easy access to illicit drugs (Lewis et al., 1985). The policy was seen to have been miscalculated.

In March 1985, a Home Office publication *Tackling Drug Misuse: a Summary of Government Strategy* (Home Office, 1985) emphasized the need to crack down on drug suppliers by international co-operation on measures of control and by severe sentencing and confiscation of drug suppliers' profits. The medical model of 'managing' addiction to which British policy had clung, and still clings, is being overshadowed by an attempt at prevention by policing. Nevertheless, the clinics are still extensively patronized by addicts and those facilities which cater particularly for detoxification and rehabilitation are more important than ever.

The recommendation in recent policy documents for an increased attention to women's needs has come at an awkward time. A new initiative in treatment and care is being suggested just when there is increasing emphasis on control measures and when, as a result of current government policy, funds are generally straitened for the whole national health service and other government-funded agencies.

None the less two factors give hope. As Edwards (1978) has argued 'the system has a degree of openness, that in changing circumstances it has a capacity for manoeuvre, that its very inconsistencies allow of evolution'. Another factor is the caring ethos in the system, the after-glow, as it were, of the medical approach. In 1926, the Rolleston Report recommended full use of therapeutic methods: '. . . education of the will . . . improvement of the social conditions of the patient' (Departmental Committee on Morphine and Heroin Addiction, 1926: 16). Since then, throughout the shifts of emphasis, from the concentration on prescribing to the involvement in control, that broad concept of treatment and care has remained. Indeed, in *Tackling Drug Misuse* the government was arguing that 'drug misusers have the same rights to appropriate provision for their needs as other people with health and social problems' (Home Office, 1985: 19).

Incentives for policy and action

As has already been noted, there have been two main factors which have influenced policy advisers recently. First, the alarming general increase in drug misuse in the UK and the increase in problems among women in particular. Secondly, the demands for attention and action by interested parties such as feminists, doctors and social workers.

Although the present extent of the drug misuse is not known one can discern the dramatic increase in the problem from a number of indications. Up until the mid-1960s the total number of known opioid addicts in the UK on the Home Office index was less than 1,000. In 1986 the total in the UK known to the Home Office was over 14,700 (Home Office, 1987), of whom a third were women.

However, the estimate of 60,000 (Hartnoll, 1986) to 100,000 (Social Services Committee, 1985) heroin addicts probably reflects more accurately the situation in the country; besides, there are many more 'recreational' users who are not yet addicted. There is also a mass of anecdotal evidence from the police, customs officers, families, researchers and clinicians that this is a boom time for hard drugs in the UK.

A particular spur to action is the soaring increase in drug taking among the young. Observation of official statistics shows that in 1986, 1,251 (25 per cent) of the new narcotic addicts notified to the Home Office were under 21 (Home Office, 1987). Coupled with what seems to be a real increase in use by young people, there is also something of a moral panic. The press devotes much space to drug addiction with such headlines as 'Hooked on heroin', 'Teenage epidemic hits council estates', 'Chasing the dragon' (*Sunday Times*, April 1984), and 'Heroin: stemming the tide' (*Sunday Times*, 19 August 1984). There have been numerous television and radio programmes on the problem and the government has initiated large-scale campaigns against drug taking aimed particularly at the young. The Home Affairs Committee of the House of Commons reporting to the government in May 1985 demanded '*immediate* and effective action'.

The number of women opioid misusers known to the Home Office has been rising yearly, and especially the number of young women who are newly notified. In 1975 there were 131 new females under 25 notified to the Home Office as opiate users; in 1986 the figure was 773 – a six-fold increase (Home Office, 1987). Results of a national survey of general practitioners in England and Wales found that 32 per cent of those who came for help with opiate-related problems in one month in 1985 were women (Glanz and Taylor, 1986). There are also many women who never approach treatment services and, therefore, are outside the official statistics. Another pointer to the extent of the problem is the number of women who were found guilty of, or cautioned or dealt with by compounding for, drug offences: in 1976 they numbered 1,851; in 1986 2,959. The proportion of female offenders has been between 10 and 15 per cent throughout the period 1976–86 (Home Office, 1987). Once again, these figures give a very incomplete picture of drug misuse amongst women because they reflect only those who have become addicted to heroin, and become known to the authorities by seeking help or becoming involved with the law. Many do not progress to becoming dependent, and many who misuse psychoactive substances do not continue to use heroin.

Despite the influence of feminist thought and of such action groups as DAWN, on official bodies such as the House of Commons Social Services Committee, most of the government's policy response to pressures and representations has been vague and general. It has been an expression of benevolent interest rather than concentrated attention to the problem. It also seems to hand over the consideration of what is to be done practically to help women to the existing structure of treatment and care: 'It is essential that all agencies . . . take greater account of this trend' (Social Services Committee, 1985). However, the 1984 government initiative to fund new projects on drug misuse treatment to the sum of £10 million does provide some hope that a favourable climate to initiatives on women's needs will prevail.

Drug-dependent women

'A career of narrowing options' is how the life outlook for an American woman who becomes addicted has been vividly summed up by Marsha Rosenbaum (1981) in her analysis of *Women on Heroin* in the United States. She notes that:

> Heroin expands her life options in the initial stages, and that is the essence of its social attraction. Yet with progressively further immersion in the Heroin world, the social, psychological, and physiological exigencies of Heroin use create an option 'funnel' for the woman addict. Through this funnel the addict's life options are gradually reduced until she is functionally incarcerated in an invisible prison. Ultimately, the woman addict is locked into the Heroin life and locked out of the conventional world. (Rosenbaum, 1981: 11)

The notion of 'a career of narrowing options' is particularly poignant when applied to the young or adolescent drug user. From the research literature a picture emerges of a stereotypical drug-dependent woman caught in this 'funnel', who is doubly disadvantaged because she is both a woman and an addict.

The story, as usually outlined, goes as follows. A girl begins to take drugs for fairly standard adolescent reasons (rebelliousness, experimentation, curiosity, boredom, searching for affiliation and peer group approval, etc.) and gradually becomes addicted to drugs. She then finds herself in a deviant culture from which she finds it difficult to escape, and in which she herself begins to engage in crime and prostitution in order to pay for her drugs. She is condemned by society for her behaviour more than a man would be. She forms a relationship with a person who almost inevitably is another addict. She falls pregnant and throughout her pregnancy endeavours to conceal the fact for fear of the reaction of the medical profession and the risk that her baby would be taken away from her. Later she becomes locked into a domestic situation, with one or more children and a strong possibility that the father of the children will not be around to support her because he has either left her or is in prison. She lives in constant fear that her children will be taken from her. In her contacts with treatment agencies she finds an ethos which is male-oriented. In particular she finds that there are few facilities to deal with her circumstances: no arrangements for child care while she attends a treatment centre; a rigid appointment system which takes little account of her difficulties with children; and no residential facilities where she can go with her children. Increasingly, her own coping strategies are weakened by lack of social support and by her growing feelings of guilt, anxiety and depression.

The stereotype both connects and disconnects with the real needs of women and this connection, which does not quite transmit the current, is also apparent in such limited practical provisions for women as have been made. Many drug-dependent women would recognize themselves in aspects of it, and the stereotype also exhibits many of the disadvantages to which the feminist movement has drawn attention, notably the woman's dependent role and the difficulties inherent in her need to adjust to a male-oriented society.

None the less, the stereotype, as my examination of practice will make more clear, embodies some of the very thinking about women that those who are particularly concerned for women's welfare would, it might be hoped, take care to avoid. In the first place, the theory of peer group influence is invoked, yet as Blom and van den Berg (this volume, Chapter 3) have argued, this theory is based on what is known about male rather than female adolescence. In the second place, and at a deeper level, the stereotype embodies a male view of woman as overdetermined by her identities as sexual partner and mother. This is the point at which the stereotype is both true and untrue: plausible and difficult to refute, yet uncomfortably ill fitting. Women are mothers, do love their children, dread their removal and need these responsibilities to be taken into account. Women have often followed their men through social as well as geographical space. So a theory and a set of practices which acknowledge these factors are better than a theory and a set of practices which treat women as the same as men. However, the disconnection comes because, whether with dim and lurking unease or with full feminist consciousness, many women are aware either that it is unfair that they are so bound or that they need not be so bound and that there ought to be a choice. Any theory which writes out this choice and how the ever-present potential for it is equally presently circumscribed will be both correct and false and will be limiting, as will any set of practices based on such a theory.

In the few comparative studies of male and female addicts which have examined the antecedents of an addiction career, the findings taken as a whole are far from conclusive. An early and classic study (Chein et al., 1964) which compared the families of male and female addicts found only small differences. Yet Binion (1979) concluded that women addicts came from more disturbed families and more frequently from 'broken homes'. In 1982, Binion suggested that among a sample of heroin addicts, there were sex differences in the perceptions of family interaction. Women were more likely than men to report negative impressions of their childhood and to have noticed differences in adults' treatment and expectation of boys and girls. Binion concluded that initial drug use for women was closely related to interpersonal affiliation issues and that women were more likely than men to seek out an addict peer group as a reaction to an unhappy family situation. Martin and Martin (1980) in their account of factors preceding and influencing the initiation into drug addiction also found that the differences between men and women were small: 'the personality characteristics of many female addicts are in most respects similar to those of male addicts. They exhibit sociopathic behaviour and may well have antisocial tendencies', but that: 'As a group, female addicts appear to be somewhat more neurotic and less psychopathic than male addicts'.

It seems that differences between male and female routes into addiction are not rooted in any specific 'pathology', but that the 'normal' socialization process which is applied to girls, with its powerful reinforcement of traditional female values and behaviours and especially its fostering of dependence amongst girls, underlies much of women's drug misuse and addiction to both legal and illegal drugs. This has led some observers to claim that addiction is a specific manifestation of women's general position in society: 'Dependency is an integral part of women's daily lives – use of substances is only the outward sign of it' (Merfert-Diete and Soltau, 1984).

It is this application to drug abuse of theories about women's designated role in society that is particularly sponsored by feminist opinion. In this context illegal drug use can at first represent a more active life, a revolt against woman's role. Chein et al. (1964) argue that the female addict is resisting the passive nature which is expected of her. Others argue that addiction represents a denial of woman's desire for passivity (Ball and Chambers, 1971). However, the addiction eventually leads to a depersonalized life-style which can be a gross form of dependency and, as already noted, 'the woman addict is locked into the heroin life and out of the conventional world' (Rosenbaum, 1981).

General treatment problems
One of the main complaints by women addicts, and they are backed up by researchers and feminist observers, is that *their problems of dependency and low self-esteem are exacerbated by the circumstances in which treatment and care are offered to them.* The whole treatment world is seen as thoroughly male-oriented:

> When conceived, Therapeutic Centres were an answer to an addiction problem that was primarily shared by men: *the needle world is a man's world*, in which three out of four users are male. The answer to the problem was given within the framework of the men's culture. (Nadeau, 1978)

The most blatant example of male-orientation in the treatment facilities is the neglect of women's emotional needs and of the special issues presented by pregnancy, motherhood and child care. The practical difficulties this causes can be daunting, as the testimony from a woman who attends a drug dependency unit in a hospital in London, illustrates:

> I found the male-oriented regime of the hospital extremely difficult to cope with. There's no provision for the care of children while you attend the meetings, and I found it impossible to have my children looked after for a couple of hours every week. This is not only completely disregarded, it's also considered an excuse for not being committed to the programme. If you miss three meetings in the six month period, your treatment is terminated. You also have to pick up your Methadone daily. In my case this involved a bus journey with two babies in tow – no mean feat when you're feeling like death until you've taken the Methadone. All this is supposed to give the patient a sense of being 'in control of her own care'. All it really comes down to is being manipulated with your life totally controlled by the clinic . . . the whole nasty patriarchal staff/junkie relationship reduced me to tears on many an occasion. (Jeffries, 1983)

These practical deficiencies are the most obvious symptoms of a pervasive attitude throughout the treatment and care system. The evidence for this comes mainly from American sources but seems to accord with what has been observed elsewhere.

American researchers (notably Cusky et al., 1981) argue that despite the growth of the problem, no adequate models of female addiction have yet been developed, and that the treatment models are still male-oriented. In some ways, by their very nature they discourage female addicts from entering into treatment programmes and lead to their early departure from them if they do enter. For instance, the so called *physiological* model, in which addiction is viewed as a narcotics-fuelled metabolic disorder, relies predominantly on Methadone maintenance for treatment. Such treatment, which is primarily aimed at reducing criminality and the use of illicitly obtained drugs, does not attempt to tackle the underlying problems which lead people to take drugs; it merely concentrates on achieving a status quo. There is evidence that women are not attracted to these programmes (Levy and Doyle, 1974).

The *social competence* model focuses on attending to functional problems such as unemployment and crime. Such an approach could help women to gain skills which would counteract the hopelessness of drug dependence and the 'career of narrowing options' but there is evidence that women want programmes which would attend first to psychological and emotional problems (Arnon et al., 1974), and anyway most programmes which foster education and retraining provide few real opportunities for women.

Both the *personality* model, which relates drug abuse to the user's personality problems, and the *socio-cultural* model, which pays attention to social environment (family, social development, etc.), are employed in residential treatment, notably in therapeutic communities. However, these communities were also found to be sometimes unsatisfactory on the grounds that women do not want to be resocialized on the programme's terms. In many of these communities, regimes of punishment and confrontation apply, using 'tearing down' sessions; so women with their low levels of self-esteem and lower assertiveness are at a disadvantage.

> For some individuals that come into treatment 'breaking one's image' is no problem: these persons come in already . . . having incorporated social guilt to its pathological limits . . . they need to anaesthetize, hopefully kill, their personal shame. There is nothing to break down and all to build up. The majority of women seeking admission fit in this category. (Nadeau, 1978)

In mixed-sex groups therapy employing 'encounter' sessions, it has been found that:

> The groups became settings for displays of power on the part of the males, who bonded together to form positions of dominance, and this drastically reduced the women's chances to be heard. When attention was directed towards the women it was in the form of recriminations and sexist attacks. (Soler et al., 1976)

Sexist discrimination has been found to be endemic in the system. For instance, in the organization of work in the therapeutic communities women are often assigned to traditional women's jobs and discouraged from learning 'male' skills. Promotion to a position of status is also more difficult. Women are less often directed towards educational and training opportunities (Cusky et al., 1981, various sources). In some therapeutic communities sexual harassment of women residents has been reported. One study in the

United States found that 'half the women interviewed had been propositioned by male staff members, and often were forced by circumstances to submit to their demands' (Soler et al., 1976). Having already broken the feminine stereotype, women find that a return to social acceptability of the sort envisaged is not a strong enough motive to radically change their pattern of living.

Although homosexuality among women addicts is considerably higher than in the general population, little attempt has been made so far to recognize this fact in a positive way in the treatment system. Indeed, those homosexual women who feel guilt or anxiety about their sexuality find that the attitudes of the treatment centres reinforce those feelings. Those who see their sexual orientation as part of their revolt against women's dependency role find themselves under pressure to change. Leaving the treatment programme is often the easiest option (Cusky et al., 1981).

However, there is some encouraging evidence from the UK that therapeutic communities have taken on board some of the criticisms which have emerged from American research. An attempt has been made in some communities to adopt non-sexist attitudes, for example in respect to work tasks in the house, and women's only groups have been established in some communities. On the whole the findings show the difficulty of proposing a satisfactory therapeutic model for women. But the problem appears to lie not in the contrariness of women, but rather in the ethos that lies behind all the models that were designed historically to cater for men's needs and not women's. That bias inevitably makes the drug-dependent woman the odd 'man' out in the system.

The special problems of a drug-dependent mother

DAWN's evidence to the Social Services Committee stated, 'Whenever we hold meetings for women using drugs, their problems and fears surrounding children form a major part of the discussion' (1985: xii, 20). The area in which drug-dependent women are most plainly disadvantaged because of their sex is, of course, motherhood, from pregnancy onwards. Even the fact of becoming pregnant and having a baby might well have a different resonance for a woman addict compared with other women. As Moriarty (1976) found, women addicts might be particularly gratified at being able to have a baby (some believe themselves to be barren because of their drug use and are surprised by pregnancy) as a contrast to their usual feelings of helplessness. Some might try deliberately to become pregnant to overcome isolation and to have someone to relate to: 'It gave them a role as mother to look forward to when they seemed to have nothing to live for' (Moriarty, 1976).

However, there were also negative reactions amongst women addicts. To the normal stresses of pregnancy, 'mood swings, doubts, fears, identity problems with body image and desirability', were added the particular stresses of the addict's life, 'poverty, lack of stable and supportive relationships and discrimination' (Moriarty, 1976). There is also the knowledge that the baby might be damaged or experience severe withdrawal. Added to this is an extremely widespread fear by women that the baby might be taken into care. A medical witness at an enquiry conducted by the Social Services Committee stated:

> I have had six patients who . . . when they had their babies they were so scared of the Social Services that they did not mention to any doctor or hospital or obstetrician or anyone that they were addicted . . . The husband would bring the drugs in when they were in hospital . . . and the babies had no special care. (1985: 119)

The very real possibility that a baby might be removed from an addict mother was recently emphasized in a report in *The Times* of 2 August 1985. Under the headline 'Mother loses plea over custody of drug addict baby' was the report of a case which made legal history because it was the first time that alleged ill-treatment of an unborn child was put forward as sufficient grounds for taking it away from its natural parents. The report also stated that the counsel for the local authority admitted 'that there was no evidence to suggest that the parents would ill-treat the child in the future and that it was not clear how much long term damage to the foetus had been caused by the mother's addiction to heroin and methadone'. On appeal, the House of Lords upheld the care order but stated that drug use in pregnancy cannot in itself constitute grounds for a care order: 'It seems then that the judgement is based on the common view that illegal drug users are necessarily chaotic, out of control of their own lives, and unfit to be in charge of anyone else's' (Perry, 1987).

The addict mother's anxiety that she might lose her children continues into the child-rearing stage, when she is virtually under surveillance by social welfare agencies. The British Association of Social Workers (BASW) reported to the Social Services Committee (1985) that in one Central London Authority 17 of the 66 cases on the Child Abuse Register were there because of drug abuse within the family, and of these half subsequently came into care. Some commentators (Densen-Gerber and Rohrs, 1973) have observed that adequate child care and addiction do not go very well together.

The addict mother previously quoted added a personal gloss to this:

The main reason I am finding it so hard to stop using drugs is the presence of the children. I can never relax my responsibility to them and that never ceasing guilt that comes with motherhood is exacerbated by the stigma of drug addiction. More and more I got to need the energy drugs gave me just to care for my children. (Jeffries, 1983)

Overall, society's condemnation of the female addict is a good deal more severe, and more emotional, than of the male addict.

Even in the drug culture itself, stigmatization by male users is rife. A woman staff member at City Roads (a crisis intervention centre in London) remarked that:

Men who are also using in that little circle really view these women as being pretty bad people . . . they want to be able to look after the woman because they feel they should be anyway, but . . . when it comes down to the nitty-gritty I think they view them pretty much as prostitutes if not in reality then certainly to some extent, they're not very complimentary towards women drug users once you actually get down and talk to them.

This, she had found, was particularly characteristic of young or adolescent drug circles.

Faced with this barrage of condemnation, one reaction of the female addict may be to accept it, and see herself through others' eyes, for example, 'through men's eyes as "low", "a tramp", "a whore" and as having lost her physical attractions' (Nurco et al., 1982). In the face of all these stereotypes, however, many observers have stated that addicts are often responsible and caring parents. For example:

The female Heroin addict tends to value her role as a mother very highly, and failure (as evidenced by the removal of her children from her care) is socially and emotionally devastating, often resulting in an attempt to terminate use of Heroin or, alternatively, in a further decline into heavy use. (Rosenbaum, 1979)

Towards an appropriate policy

It is commonplace to claim of any social issue that it requires more resources and more research. It is, however, self-evidently correct in the issue of female addicts' needs, which is in such an early stage of serious consideration. 'More resources' is usually taken to mean more money, but just as important as funding is how it should be allocated among the various services and facilities which seem to be important: how, for instance, it might be shared among the different phases in the recovery and rehabilitation process of a drug misuser, from detoxification to resocialization, and perhaps on to job training and rehousing. Also, more money spent on treatment and rehabilitation does not necessarily always mean more expense in the long term. For instance, the provision of mother–child facilities in treatment agencies could well lead to a reduction in the number of children taken into care, resulting in an economy to the state.

In the field of research, one of the main difficulties to date has been the lack of substantial evidence from the women themselves. As DAWN have written (1985): 'What company would market a service without proper market research?' The problem is that women have been 'invisible' in the system, not only because they are overlooked but also because they have a much lower rate of attendance than men at treatment agencies. If more women could be attracted to the agencies, then more subjects for research would be available, which might in turn modify the treatment system. In the meantime, research among women in the community at large is the only feasible way of identifying women at risk and establishing what services might be required.

However, although the research evidence is not large, it should not be dismissed. It is often illuminating and suggestive of possible lines of policy. At the least it is a basis for debate, which is how these suggested policy proposals are presented.

Prevention and education
The ACMD's *Prevention* report commended the idea of the 'potential contribution to drug prevention of women's consciousness-raising and self-help within the context of the women's movement' (1984: 36). Feminists see the female addict's problems as rooted in the problems of girls and women in society. Thus, education in schools and in the home should acknowledge the fact that, on approaching adulthood, girls face a narrower set of options than boys, and that there is a danger that they might perceive drug use at least initially as a way of broadening their horizon or achieving greater freedom (Rosenbaum, 1981).

Specifically, educators should be cognizant of the specific ways in which girls learn about drugs both in the family context (Vogt, 1985) and in their peer group (Dorn and Thompson, 1975). Considerable money and effort has been directed in the UK to mass media campaigns, despite warnings from the government's own advisory council that:

> We are concerned about measures which deliberately present information in a way which is intended simply to shock or scare. We believe that education programmes based on such measures on their own are likely to be ineffective, or, at worst, positively harmful. (ACMD, 1984: 35)

The harm, the ACMD believe, lies in the risk that 'ill-chosen educational methods . . . arouse in some people an interest which they would not otherwise have felt' (1984: 17). The ACMD's own recommendation was that drug education whether in the media or the schools should be 'de-emphasized as a separate topic' and integrated into broader frameworks of health and social education (1984: 39).

Early intervention
The most obvious way of limiting damage is to interrupt a young person's potential career from experimenter to addict. This often depends on people nearby such as teachers, youth workers, parents, being intelligently observant. In fact, the anecdotal evidence of drug addiction is full of parents who did not know that their daughter or son was taking drugs 'until too late'.

The importance of educating parents and other adults in positions of responsibility for children is evident. The minimal information should cover the nature and danger of drugs; detectable signs of use; the effects of their own alcohol or drug use on children; their own responsibilities for care; trying to ensure that children attend school and that supervised leisure facilities exist. In the UK information from government sources is available to advise parents about drugs, and there are signs of growing parental involvement. For instance, in some recent widely publicized outbreaks of drug misuse among the young on housing estates in industrial cities, parents have formed 'self-help' groups to try and counter the epidemic.

One of the ACMD's recommendations is for such self-help groups of 'ordinary people' in 'support services for children, and other groups at risk', and also for the social services departments to plan jointly with such community groups 'to provide a caring fabric in each neighbourhood' (1984: 39). The report goes further in its advocacy of increased awareness of drugs among supervisory elements in society, suggesting that 'teachers, youth workers, police officers, doctors and other health professionals, social workers, probation officers, health education officers', etc.; should have some training in 'preventive skills' (ACMD, 1984: 43).

The simple and useful level at which prompt observation can lead to early intervention is indicated in the case of children who truant from school. They are 'more likely to come into contact with those who misuse solvents' and often their first 'experiment' then, and 'persistent non-attendance . . . may predict maladjustment in later life, possibly including drug misuse' (ACMD, 1984: 22). Adult vigilance in such a social situation may be more productive of results than lurid warnings of the dangers of drugs.

Counselling by professionals for drug experimenters and their families as soon as difficulties become apparent is sometimes indicated. Reports from such family counselling programmes in the USA suggest that such an approach is an important contribution to prevention of addiction, as indicated by the Step One Programme, Phoenix, New York.

Relevant treatment and rehabilitation

One of the most persistent and strongly felt criticisms is that women are inevitably disadvantaged because the system is designed for men. Many proposals from interested parties therefore take the commonsense view that measures should be adapted to meet the specific needs of women. 'Positive discrimination in favour of women addicts', was recommended in the *Annual Report 1982–3* of the Standing Conference on Drug Abuse (SCODA) which represents over 30 voluntary agencies in the UK. This would include the provision of day care for children at centres where women attend for treatment; accommodation for mother and child at live-in agencies; the establishment of all-female therapeutic communities, with a predominance of female staff; and, at existing mixed-sex therapeutic communities, much greater emphasis on all-female therapy sessions.

There has also been a new emphasis on provisions for drug misusers who become pregnant, notably in the Report of the Medical Working Group on Drug Dependence for the Department of Health and Social Services (1984). This stresses the specialized medical care that is needed for both mother and child, before and after birth; also the psychological attention which includes a recognition and 'sympathetic understanding' of the mother's fears that her baby may be removed into care. Post-natal care, the report continues, should include 'the provision of adequate accommodation' and 'continuing support' by her GP in co-operation with the health visitor. In the field of medical care, quite apart from pregnancy, the woman addict living in the drug subculture often has many health problems. Agencies dealing with her should be conscious of her need for medical attention.

All-female rehabilitation facilities may seem an attractive measure to help women addicts. Testimony from women interviewed at the Addiction Research Unit in London suggests that women themselves are divided on this issue. Surprisingly most of the women in a mixed therapeutic community preferred to have 'women only' groups in a mixed milieu and felt that such an approach met many of their needs as women. There have been very few examples in operation from which any conclusions can be drawn. Two such projects are described below, one in the UK, one in the USA.

The Meta House project, a Christian rehabilitation centre which says no Christian commitment is required of applicants, has places for 16 women for periods from eight to fourteen months. It is funded by central and local government, and is one of the only two all-female communities in the UK. It believes that 'women coming off drugs have much more complex problems than men and need specialised care' (Meta House, 1985). Its rehabilitation programme covers individual, confrontational and group counselling. Amongst the rehabilitative goals are: building self-awareness and self-respect in a resident, creating a positive attitude in a resident, and reversing the addict's chaotic life-style through an ordered day. The two major goals in the final phase of the programme are: 'to move towards an independent life-style', and 'to make definite plans for the future'.

On the question of outcome of treatment the Meta House report is cautious as, at the time of writing, the house had only been operative for eighteen months, a fact which alone prevents an accurate measure of outcome. However, the house report states that approximately 60 per cent of those who have entered the programme are currently drug-free; approximately twice the national average. Meta House has recently launched an appeal for funds to enable them to open an additional facility for a 'drying-out' house for mothers and their babies (*Bournemouth Advertiser*, 6 January 1987). Other plans in Britain include a short-term crisis intervention facility for mothers and children and a family house which is to be part of a therapeutic community.

One of the few notable examples of a facility for mothers and children in the USA was in the Odyssey House Mabon Parents' Demonstration Programme, which was closely documented for the period 1974–7 (Cusky et al., 1979). This project accommodated 40 women and 40 children, and over 300 women were treated in the three-year period.

The programme paid particular attention to developing effective parenting. Initially they fostered a limited responsibility by the mother for her child, so as to 'break the intense, sometimes destructive, narcissistic bond between mother and child; to relieve the mother of the need to respond to the demands of the child at this early stage of treatment when she was likely to feel overwhelmed, inadequate and frustrated . . .' and to 'encourage the mother to view senior residents and staff as role models' (Cusky et al., 1979). For the women themselves, the programme followed a course of graduated responsibility for household tasks and graduated therapy sessions, so that in the final stage before re-entry into society education and vocational activities were available.

The researchers were able to re-interview only 97 of the 300 women in the programme after treatment. They found that over 80 per cent of the women had remained drug-free, but that only a small number were in work or involved in educational activities. Unfortunately, because only a third of the women were re-interviewed it is difficult to make an informed evaluation of the overall success of such a project, despite the evident help which it offered to some of its clients. Many women would no doubt welcome such an opportunity to be treated without being separated from their children.

Overall, feminist observers are justifiably critical of any treatment procedures that seem to reinforce the woman's dependency role. Feminist involvement is an important factor in keeping the issues of the female addict's problems on the agenda of public concerns. It is hoped that it will have its effects in changing attitudes within the system. On a practical level it can operate in a 'self-help' ethos, offering supportive services to women emerging from addiction, by way of women's groups or professionally staffed vocational counselling and help with accommodation.

In the range of possible 'solutions' surveyed above, can one look for priorities? Following Rosenbaum (1981) the two crucial issues of parenting and work should be stressed. British evidence too indicates the importance of agencies understanding the destructiveness of separating the mother and child. Also, it is essential that occupational opportunities and choices be provided through education and access to training for the development of skills. Employers might be given incentives to employ women ex-addicts: 'Such a programme would cost the government far less than treating and incarcerating addicts as well as providing foster care for their children' (Rosenbaum, 1981). However, even Rosenbaum, although *offering* help with real-life problems as well as a way out, does not offer us suggestions for the *young* user, or an understanding of how she may differ from her male counterpart in terms of personal space, needs, aspirations, and reasons for using.

In this survey of a subject in which the very limited British experience has been augmented by findings of not very extensive American research, it would be rash to be prescriptive about appropriate policy. But a fruitful approach to the problems of the female addict must surely lie in aiming at the restoration of vanished options and the creation of new ones.

12

'Troublesome girls'

Towards alternative definitions and policies

Annie Hudson

She is a very promiscuous girl and, if all that she tells the other girls is to be believed, *then no young man is safe.* (Residential Social Worker, my emphasis)

Embedded at the heart of contemporary British welfare practice with adolescent girls is an almost psychic fear of a predatory female sexuality. The irony of this should be obvious: it is men who rape and the sexual abuse of children is almost entirely perpetrated by men. Yet, perhaps highest on the professional agenda is the assumption (and concomitant practices) that girls in trouble fundamentally have problems with *their* sexuality. Whilst welfare professionals frequently legitimate their intervention with girls as 'for their protection', the quote from the social worker above (made in a report for a case conference) prizes open the complexity of the 'welfare as protector' discourse. It suggests that, hidden beneath, lies an almost inarticulated but profound fear of the young woman who is sexually active, sexually explicit, and who is not actually possessed by any one male. This conceptualization of adolescent girls as 'property' (of men, of the family, of the dominant social order) will be a key thread to much of this discussion. It helps explain why some girls are defined as 'troublesome'; it is also a crucial component of any attempt to conceptualize different welfare strategies for responding to their needs.

This chapter focuses on girls who are seen, often very generally and vaguely, as manifesting some kind of social or emotional trouble. The apparently loose concept of 'troublesome girls' allows for a discussion of girls who are not necessarily delinquent (in the sense of committing criminal offences). Statistics (DHSS, 1986) suggest that the majority of girls do not get drawn into the complex web of the British personal social services because they have committed offences. It is more likely to be because of concerns about their perceived sexual behaviour and/or because they are seen to be 'at risk' of 'offending' against social codes of adolescent femininity.

Work with girls in trouble has, in terms of explicit policy, been marginalized and rendered almost invisible. Because girls do not so publicly resist the normative order (McRobbie and Garber, 1976) because there is not much political capital to be gained by developing strategies for responding differently to their modes of rule-breaking, and because it has been assumed that girls' deviant behaviour will be normally dealt with from within the boundaries of the family, policies have been ad hoc, framed in vague and diffuse language and lacking in imagination. This, of course, does not mean that the net result has had any less of an impact upon the experience of girls deemed to require state intervention, whether controlling or apparently benign. In fact, the reverse has often been true; the assumption that extant policies and practice are 'in their best interests' adeptly conceals a complex fabric of control and subordination (for example, see Casburn, 1979; Campbell, 1981).

The ideas presented below have in part emerged out of my own empirical research[1] into the decision-making processes concerning adolescent girls in an English inner-city social services department, together with consultancy work in a variety of social work agencies. However, an alternative way of working is shown by the apparent success of some youth and social work projects (Mountain, 1988; Yeung, 1985) and of work in the voluntary sector with girls who have been sexually abused (National Association of Youth Clubs, 1984). Such initiatives provide a source of optimism in the possibility of working in ways which are explicitly geared towards giving power back to young women.

The first section of this chapter reviews some of the broad issues involved in developing welfare strategies for responding to the needs of 'troublesome' girls. The socio-political terrain of life in the United Kingdom in the late 1980s is given particular consideration, as this will form the backdrop of any alternative strategy. The second section explores dominant definitions of 'troublesome girls' and considers ways of beginning to redraft the agenda. Attention will be given not only to the role of welfare professionals but also to the relationship between girls, their families and the State. Much of the debate about troublesome girls has occluded the politics of family life as a fundamental influence on girls' careers through the criminal justice and welfare systems. This particular part of the jigsaw is seen as crucial in moving away from the current myopia pervading welfare practice with girls in trouble. The third section identifies some core principles for moving forward and considers the viability and problems inherent in implementing different policy strategies.

Underpinning the discussion throughout is a concern to move

away from a deficit model of the needs and problems of adolescent girls in trouble (for example that they are 'insufficiently feminine' or 'out of control'). Proposing a positive model for work with girls may sound relatively simple. But we are all caught up in well-trodden ways of sexually stereotyping young women; it is thus crucial that we all continuously examine our assumptions and beliefs. Moreover, manifestations of girls' troubles and subordination are very real; to deny that they sometimes experience individual stress and personal difficulties is not only naive, it also does them an injustice in their (sometimes quite literal) fight for survival.

Developing alternatives: some problems and contradictions

It is usually easier to be critical of the status quo than to develop alternative and concrete proposals and strategies. Moreover, 'radical' critiques are, sometimes quite validly, criticized for their lack of realism and for their tendency to leap dramatically from talking about 'what's wrong now' to presenting blueprints for that moment 'after the millennium' when all social injustice has somehow, almost magically, been eradicated. The middle ground, which is explored here, is much messier, more contradictory and arguably more littered with the potential for liberal-reformist 'debris'.

However, there are innumerable problems in endeavouring to move towards some alternative definitions and strategies. Most profoundly problematic perhaps is the idea of academics and welfare professionals attempting to develop policies based around concepts such as 'participation' and 'empowerment'. To state this more baldly, there is a danger of replacing one set of 'top down' definitions with another (if perhaps a more liberal variety). In both sets of circumstances a powerful group is defining the shape and contours of the debate.

Another problem besetting any attempt to generate new agendas revolves around welfare's firmly embedded patriarchal traditions; they are not likely to give way easily (Dale and Foster, 1986). Feminism's critique of the values and operations of social work, for example, continues to be met with, at best, polite avoidance or, at worst, outright hostility (Hudson, A., 1985). The organization of welfare has been structured, in a competitive and bureaucratic society, around hierarchical and masculine styles of management (Hale, 1983). Such a style of management not only pushes consumers away from the locus of decision making but it also marginalizes the influence of those who work directly with the consumer group in question. The disproportionate male presence in the upper reaches of British social work agencies, for example, emphasizes the enormity of the challenge provoked by feminist critiques; male managers certainly have a lot of power and prestige to lose. It is not sufficient merely to articulate policy proposals, it is as crucial to develop strategies for their implementation.

Steering a middle course is also problematic in terms of its inherent vulnerability to charges of reformism and incorporation. We must undoubtedly keep sharp the cutting edge of radical/ alternative approaches (Hearn, 1982) but, as feminist praxis has demonstrated, there are risks in colluding with the culture of fatalism ('the tasks are so enormous that there's no point in struggling to change things'). Feminists (Rowbotham et al., 1979; Stanley and Wise, 1983) have pointed out how crucial it is to question and challenge the taken-for-granted, the apparently mundane and everyday representations of sexism. The work of Women's Aid and Rape Crisis Centres is testimony to the possibilities of doing something now and, at the same time, beginning to change ideas and practices.

Prevailing social and political conditions can give us some grounds for optimism; the development of the women's movement and of feminist perspectives has undoubtedly had some purchase on the practice of some social workers in the UK (Hanmer and Statham, 1988). There is now an increasingly burgeoning interest in developing work with girls in trouble within a perspective which actively acknowledges some of the contradictions of adolescent femininity. Such interest has been reflected in practice initiatives, workshops and conferences, and in general professional debate (Mountain, 1988; Rainer Foundation, 1986). However, any acknowledgement of the socio-political climate of the UK in the 1980s also generates considerable pessimism; the 'rolling back' of some of the more benign aspects of the Welfare State and the related reassertion of women's traditional roles as homemakers grounds any discussion of alternative policies in depressing and everyday economic and political realities.

The legal challenge in the mid-1980s by a Roman Catholic mother, Victoria Gillick, to the authority of doctors to prescribe contraceptives to girls under 16 without their parents' consent was a significant marker buoy in the apparently ever-quickening drift to the moral right (All England Law Reports, 1985). Whilst the House of Lords eventually found against Gillick, the tale is clearly not finished. The case touched some of the central nerves in the relationship between the state, the family, and adolescent girls and so can serve as a valuable template in analysing certain aspects of the social and political climate that are likely to have a bearing on any new policy developments.

First, at the nub of the moral right's arguments to prohibit girls from having access to contraceptives without their parents' consent are calls for the reassertion of family values. There has been little discussion in such quarters about girls' rights or indeed about the concrete realization of parental responsibilities. Lord Denning, speaking about the issue on television in 1983, commented: 'I should have thought it more important, even though she may fall pregnant, that we should maintain the family relationship' (quoted in *The Guardian*, 5 December 1983). Giving daughters any rights to self-directed sexuality is clearly seen as potentially disuniting for families. In the USA calls to return to a more traditional, 'more stable' order have similarly resulted in the gradual constraining of girls' rights in the name of 'familialism'. The 'teenage chastity programme' which received approval in 1982 now means that family planning agencies are only eligible for federal funds if they adopt a 'family-centred approach' (Petchesky, 1984).

The Gillick case also brings into focus the denial of girls' capacities or rights to determine their own sexuality. Lord Templeman (one of the judges who dissented from the majority House of Lords judgment) stated: 'There are many things which a girl under 16 needs to practise, but sex is not one of them' (quoted in *Daily Express*, 18 October 1985). The notion of girls having an autonomous sexuality is clearly anathema to many. In contrast, boys are allowed free rein and do not become the spotlight for censure and regulation; sexual activity is seen as all part and parcel of their 'normal' growing up to be men.

After the House of Lords judgment, Gillick rounded on the judges with: 'We now have contraception on demand from doctors – a male charter to abuse the female population' (quoted in *The Daily Mail*, 18 October 1985). Of course, in one sense, she has a point; girls are indeed vulnerable to sexual abuse and exploitation from men, not least, however, from their fathers. It has been estimated, for example, that between one in 10 and one in 3 adult women in the UK have been sexually abused as children, most commonly by someone they know and almost invariably by men (Glaser and Frosh, 1988). However, like other ideologues of the new right, Gillick and her supporters have adeptly appropriated an aspect of feminist 'wisdom' for their own purposes. Male abuse and exploitation should indeed be part of the political agenda. But defining the solution in terms of intensifying the control of girls and young women is, at best, naive and, at worst, highly damaging of the rights of young women to define their own sexuality.

The renewal of interest in asserting the 'rightfulness' of familialism emerges out of and reflects the concern to construct a morality which meets the needs of a monetarist economic strategy. However, the ascendancy of familialism generates its own contradictions (Barrett and McIntosh, 1982), for how can the family be celebrated as a source of stability when there is also irrefutable evidence of the violence and abuse experienced by women and girls within this sacrosanct institution? Only by neatly cordoning off 'pathological' families for treatment (they are the 'sick' and the 'aberrant') can the image of the family as a 'haven in a heartless world' be left intact.

Because girls are usually seen as having troubles related to their roles and place within the family nexus, they are particularly susceptible to interpretations that their problems relate to their individual, or their family's, psychopathology. There is a significant disjunction, moreover, between the frames of reference employed in relation to girls in trouble and those more commonly employed with boys. The wealth of empirical material which has testified to the significance of subculture, labelling and social disadvantage has forced policy makers and practitioners to take more account of such factors in their assessments and in their intervention with boys in trouble with the law.

Finally, there are certain risks in focusing public attention on 'troublesome' and delinquent girls. First, such attention may well fuel moral panics that girls are becoming 'as bad as boys' or indeed that 'bad girls are badder than boys'. There are also other attendant, if less prominent, risks. Cohen (1985) has drawn attention to the need of 'social control' professionals to expand constantly the ambit of their legitimacy. Cohen argues that in order to do this professionals have engaged in either endogenous (filling in or creating categories) or iatrogenic (mopping up the casualties created by their own operations) system expansion. The repercussions of endogenous system expansion are demonstrated in the diffuse and unspecific categories employed to define the needs and problems of girls in trouble. The term 'at risk' is frequently employed to legitimate intervention (through the courts, voluntary care or 'preventive' casework); the use of such an ambiguous and shifting category means that girls identified as having the characteristics of becoming a 'problem' can be drawn into a net of increasingly intense contact with welfare and juvenile justice agencies.

Similarly, we can see iatrogenic system expansion at work in the less statistically amenable, but nonetheless powerful process of girls being taken into care (either through the courts or 'voluntarily', under Section 2 of the Child Care Act 1980) and then being placed in establishments which fail to address their needs and instead create problems which the system had supposedly been designed to remedy. Absconding, for example, may force a girl into situations (living rough and having to live off older men) where she may indeed be vulnerable to male exploitation. As one social worker in my study commented: 'We forced her into a position where she has been absconding and . . . therefore possibly at risk of some sort of abuse.'

Redrafting the agenda: whose troubles, whose definitions?

The somewhat skewed triangular relationship between adolescent girls, their families and welfare professionals forms the axis around which definitions, policies and practices have evolved. In prizing open some of the implicit assumptions and ideologies embedded in such definitions, we can begin to redraft a somewhat different agenda for policy and practice.

Social historians such as Weeks (1981) have suggested that the 1880s were a particularly significant moment when the dichotomy between the private/decent and the public/unrespectable was firmly established. But whilst women and girls are supposed to keep to the former area, men are free to travel between the two without fear of social sanction. Moreover, in their zeal to protect working-class girls from prostitution, late nineteenth-century reformers created new objects for control. Simultaneously they also established an explanatory code that portrays girls as passive and in need of protection, but also as potentially socially dangerous if they do not conform to codes of sexual respectability and domesticity. Such codes are clearly still firmly entrenched (Hutter and Williams, 1981). But it is girls from specific social groups who are particularly vulnerable to state intervention. Working-class and black girls have to walk a particularly shaky tightrope between demonstrating both their respectability and their sexual attractiveness. Black girls for example may be perceived as contesting not only codes of femininity but also white norms; they may thus be on the receiving end of a double dose of disapproval. One residential social worker commented about a Rastafarian girl in a report in my study: 'Her hair is the one thing which she resents us criticizing and it is this which spoils her otherwise attractive appearance.'

The overt moral tone of the late Victorian era was gradually eroded by the ascendancy and increasing attachment to psycho-analytic paradigms which meant that an apparently plausible veneer of scientism could occlude latent values. Girls who got into trouble (criminal or otherwise) could be confidently defined as 'neurotic', 'hysteria prone' and so on. Such scientism continues to legitimize welfare professionals' assessments not just about current behaviour but, more significantly, about anticipated future behaviour. Such persistence in maintaining the validity and viability of 'the tutelary complex' (Donzelot, 1979) in such a full-blown form is perhaps particularly striking when we consider that welfare's management of boys in trouble has increasingly been subjected to scepticism about the capacity (let alone the morality) of making judgments about future conduct.

Discussions elsewhere (Campbell, 1981; Casburn, 1979; Gelsthorpe, 1981; Hudson, A., 1983) provide substantive accounts of the dominant ideologies influencing the careers of adolescent girls through the welfare and justice systems.

Four key precepts form the kernel of the discussion that follows and provide the basis for the alternative practices suggested in the final section:

1   girls as the 'property' of the family: is the home so safe?
2   adolescent female sexuality as a barometer of 'womanhood': the need to problematize gender relations;
3   'troublesome girls' as victims of psychological inadequacies: reclaiming emotionality;
4   normalizing girls' troublesome behaviour: collective similarities and differences.

Girls as the 'property' of the family: is the home so safe?

There is more than a note of truth in the assumption that girls' troubles are often related to family problems and their position in the family. However, such 'family problems' have been viewed in an apolitical way: the power dynamics between parents and daughters (most crucially those between fathers and daughters), and those between women and men in the family have been completely obscured by traditional commentators. Yet it is the family which is one of the key sources of the social control of women (Barrett and McIntosh, 1982; Segal, 1983). The under-reporting of child sexual abuse together with the blaming of mothers for such abuse is obviously one of the most blatant ways in which the politics of family life is pushed aside as 'irrelevant' (Ward, 1984). Moreover, whilst the Cleveland child sexual abuse 'crisis' provoked an enhanced consciousness of the extensiveness of child sexual abuse, the terms in which that debate is developing suggest that there continues to be a reluctance both to acknowledge that child sexual abuse occurs in otherwise seemingly 'normal' families and that it is predominantly a crime perpetrated by adult men towards children whom they know and are supposed to protect. (For an excellent discussion of the Cleveland 'crisis', see Campbell, 1988.)

Child sexual abuse is thus a powerful mechanism by which girls and young women are maintained within the institution of the family. Physical violence and threats from abusers that disclosure will lead to 'breaking up the family' added to girls' internalized feelings that they are guilty and responsible for the crimes of adult men ensure that the costs of disclosure of abuse frequently seem greater than the benefits.

However, in other more subtle ways, girls are subjected to an unspoken but relentless subordination. For daughters, like their mothers, are essentially seen as the 'property' of 'the family'. Adolescent girls are controlled by the idea that they 'belong' to the home, unlike their brothers whose rights to be 'on the street' are unquestioned. Girls are expected to act like 'little housewives' and to service the family (and particularly their fathers and brothers) both emotionally and materially (Griffin, 1985). Such beliefs affect families as much as welfare professionals. When the family's regulation of girls seems to be breaking down parents can easily construe that their daughters are 'beyond their control' and demand that 'something is done'; over a quarter of the cases in my study fell into this category. What is perhaps of equal significance is that it was usually the mother who was most active in expressing such concerns to welfare agencies. This reflects, I suggest, the role of mothers as 'emotional housekeepers' which demands that they nurture and cosset the family's emotional life. If conflicts arise, they are expected to act to resolve and smooth them over.

Like their daughters, mothers are in a double bind; they are vested with a duty and responsibility to be concerned about their daughters' behaviour, to be worried if they do not return at night or when they seem depressed. But they also frequently get blamed when things go wrong inside the family. Given the lack of emotional support from fathers in many families it is perhaps not surprising that some mothers turn to welfare agencies for help and support. Blaming mothers for their daughters' problems leaves unchallenged the inequitable division of emotional labour in families.

It is important to point out here that girls themselves (unlike the majority of boys who are referred to the personal social services) often request to be taken into care. The emotional (and sometimes physical) struggle for survival at home becomes too much for some girls to cope with. They have few accessible or legitimate 'escape' routes and so care may be viewed as a preferable, if not ideal, alternative. Sometimes therefore welfare agencies do need to offer girls a refuge from the family; such provision, however, needs to be based around different assumptions and methods of practice than residential care is at present.

The constant sexualizing of the 'troublesome' behaviour of girls by welfare professionals has meant that they have often avoided looking at a further contradiction of familialism: the extensiveness of sexual abuse of girls in their families. In a fifth of the cases I studied the girl had been sexually abused by her father or stepfather, but in only a small percentage had this been a factor influencing the decision to take her into care. It was normally only much later that the abuse had come to light.

In refusing to recognize the deeply entrenched power inequalities between male and female members of families, social workers have thus colluded with the assumption that 'the home is a safe place' (Hudson, A., 1985). When girls are 'signalling' that they are being abused (for example by constantly running away or by taking overdoses) their behaviour is reinterpreted as evidence of their 'uncontrollability' and of their pathology, rather than as a manifestation of the results of their father's abuse of power and trust. Moreover, in tacitly accepting a variety of myths, for example that girls are 'seductive', social workers have thereby reinforced the moral and emotional guilt felt by girls who have been sexually abused.

The girl as property of the family ideology is carried on into the workings of welfare establishments. For not only are girls' residential establishments often based around the objective of re-establishing femininity (Ackland, 1982), but if girls in care do become pregnant then this is often viewed in a positive light. It is as if pregnancy symbolically represents a girl's return to 'the family' and her apparent acceptance of traditional femininity. This is somewhat ironic given that fears of unmarried teenage motherhood are usually high on the list of the perceived risks of adolescent girls becoming 'beyond control'.

When girls reject or refuse to take on their responsibilities as 'dutiful daughters' they are viewed as problematic and 'disloyal'; in short, they are not 'good little girls'. As long as welfare policies collude with such definitions there will be little possibility of diminishing the unequal power differentials in families; as long as they remain, adolescent girls are the losers.

Adolescent female sexuality as a barometer of 'womanhood':
the need to problematize gender relations
The development of a more critical and feminist influenced analysis of young women's deviance (see, for example, Casburn, 1979; Heidensohn, 1985; Smart, 1976) has demonstrated how girls who appear before the juvenile court for criminal offences are subject to a 'double penalty'. They are punished both for the offence itself and for the 'social' crime of contravening normative expectations of

'appropriate' female conduct via 'promiscuity', 'wayward' behaviour, 'unfeminine' dress and so on. Similarly, my study found that the most common cause of anxiety at the point of referral was that the girl was 'beyond control' and/or at risk morally. The centrality of sexuality in welfare's definitions of 'troublesome' girls reflects three key taken-for-granted assumptions.

First, it is assumed that girls' sexuality, once 'unleashed' is uncontrollable and not bound by any sense of self-responsibility or self-control. As Bland (1983) has argued, the instincts of women have traditionally been viewed as focused on her reproductive capacity, on her potential for maternity. The prostitute or the adolescent girl whose behaviour is interpreted as potentially like that of a prostitute is seen as representative of an active female sexuality, of a sexuality which may threaten the girl's interest and capacity to be a 'good wife' and mother and therefore her future 'womanliness'.

Secondly, a girl's apparent sexual behaviour is seen as a barometer for testing her capacity to learn the appropriate codes of social (but particularly sexual) conduct with men (Lees, 1986). One of the contradictions of the double standard revealed time and time again in this volume is that it implies that boys need to have access to different sexual experiences; yet the girls who presumably are supposed to 'meet' such needs are stigmatized and punished.

As long as boys' sexual behaviour is heterosexual their sexuality remains unproblematic; it is 'natural' and thus does not merit attention. But my own research highlighted how a girl's sexual 'reputation' is often a determining factor in shaping her career through the personal social services. In over a quarter of the cases examined, social workers acknowledged that their decision making was a function of what other people (particularly the police and parents) were alleging. Moreover, once an opinion had been formed, it was easy for the label of 'promiscuity' or 'being on the game' to stick, with all the negative connotations that such labels imply. Labels based on shifting and unsubstantiated opinions are particularly hard to shed; as one social worker commented about one of her young female clients: 'Once (she) had developed a "reputation" (for sexual activity), it became very easy to say that she was actually involved in prostitution.' Once created, such reputations, with all their attendant anxieties, seem to have pushed many of the social workers in my study (if sometimes quite reluctantly) to regard many of their adolescent female clients as in need of the 'protective' care and attention of a residential placement. This was despite the fact that many social workers acknowledged that care is hardly an effective contraceptive.

There was also evidence that the police similarly act on a girl's 'reputation' in this way. They were involved in almost half of the referrals in my study and in more than half of these they obtained place of safety orders (these give police or social workers the power to remove children and young people). Police involvement in these situations was only very rarely because a girl had committed a criminal offence. Moreover, there were disproportionately more police place of safety orders taken on girls living in an area with a significant Afro-Caribbean population and also with a local 'reputation' as a 'red-light district'. The other area studied was comparable in terms of many indices of social disadvantage but did not have such a reputation; the Afro-Caribbean population was also much smaller. This suggests that the level of police (and possibly social work) control may increase according to the social composition and 'reputation' of the neighbourhood. Although as yet not empirically tested, it would seem that certain groups of black adolescent girls (most particularly Afro-Caribbean girls) are especially vulnerable to perceptions by the police and possibly social workers that their behaviour warrants special scrutiny and policing.

The research also highlighted other ways in which racist stereotypes can affect police and welfare practice. One social worker said of her white adolescent female client, who had run away from home and was detained by the police on a place of safety order: 'People think that as she has got black boyfriends, she must be promiscuous, she must be on the game, or she is being used'. The association in some people's eyes between black men and 'unrespectable' sexuality suggests that the fears of racial miscegenation which were so prevalent in the 1950s and 1960s in the UK (Gilroy, 1987) continue to have purchase on the relationship between working-class white girls and welfare agencies. In short, white girls' relationships with black male youth may conjure up images of the potential 'descent of white womanhood' (Gilroy, 1987: 80) and thereby further 'legitimate' the intensification of state intervention.

Whilst it is increasingly accepted that girls (like adult women) are informally disciplined through concepts of acceptable sexuality, what is undoubtedly more contentious is what should be done. It would be naive to suggest that girls are not vulnerable to male sexual exploitation but balancing 'here and now' realities with visions of what the future could and should be like poses acute problems. To date the problem has always been framed as a problem of and for women; male power and responsibility barely enter the discussion. Bringing gender relations onto the agenda allows us instead to see cultural definitions of male sexuality as problematic.

We must take seriously girls' rights as well as their responsibilities and the risks to which they are subject. One such right must surely be to informed contraceptive advice and practice; there is, moreover, as yet little evidence that AIDS health education programmes are altering young male heterosexual practices. Another right should be to an adequate understanding of gender and familial relations. Finally, there are issues concerning girls' rights to choose their sexual identity. Social work agencies should be more conscious of the extent to which policy and practice is predicated upon an assumption of heterosexuality as both the norm and as the most 'desirable' form of sexual expression. The option of lesbianism is almost invariably closed off in discussions between welfare professionals and adolescent girls. If it is part of the discussion it is invariably cloaked with negative connotations. Some girls may want to choose lesbianism as their preferred sexual identity; to deny them this as an option is once more to misrecognize and render invisible the real needs of individual girls.

We need also to unlatch the association of adolescent female sexuality from its connotation of potentially sullying a girl's prospects of a 'happy and satisfying' womanhood. There is no reason why either having had several or no sexual partners in adolescence should prejudice a girl's enjoyment of adult life. Her enjoyment and satisfaction as an adult woman is much more likely to be related to other factors such as decent housing, employment, and adequate child-care provision.

At a more concrete level, the influence of girls' reputations in the decision-making processes affecting them should be critically monitored. Welfare professionals need to take a much stronger stand, vis-à-vis the police, their own organizations and girls' families, in seeking out actual evidence of the risks which a girl is alleged to be under. Similarly, court reports and case conference discussions should be more thoroughly scrutinized as a way of beginning to minimize the power of the 'give a dog a bad name' process that clearly operates against the interests of many girls.

'Troublesome girls' as victims of psychological inadequacies: reclaiming emotionality

The dominance of psychopathological paradigms in welfare professionals' assessments of the needs of adolescent girls has been emphasized elsewhere (Hudson, B., 1984b; Campbell, 1981). The persistence, in my study, of such explanations as 'bizarre family relationships', 'missing out on affection' and 'insufficient parental control' testifies to the continued adherence to a family pathology model.

I would not want to contest unequivocally the notion that girls manifest some of the social contradictions of adolescent femininity in emotional ways; many girls referred to welfare agencies often do feel depressed, suicidal and have very poor self-images. But the assumption that emotional expression is intrinsically negative and that emotional responses are unaffected by social and material processes has to be challenged. Perhaps it is rather the lack of overt emotionality amongst boys and men which should be problematized. The rational, masculinist British culture generally denigrates emotional expression as a sign of weakness; moreover, whilst British culture rewards men for certain forms of emotionality (aggression is the most obvious example), it punishes girls for the same kind of behaviour.

The emotionality of 'troublesome girls' is usually problematized and even feared. Certainly, many social workers take for granted the assumption that girls are 'more difficult to work with'; their apparent mood swings, non-rationality, outbursts of aggression and internalization of emotional discontents often act to make welfare professionals feel impotent, uncertain of their skills and at a loss for what to do. So when girls step outside the bounds of expectation that they should be self-controlled and passive, it is not wholly surprising that they meet with panic, disapproval, and assessments that they need 'treatment'. For, after all, they are implicitly challenging normative codes of emotional conduct. Two shifts in thinking are required. First, adolescent girls' emotional responses need to be seen as a form of resistance or struggle against 'the inner hold' of their oppressive circumstances. Their responses should be legitimated as not 'unnatural' but as quite rational ways of surviving. To psychopathologize their emotions is to perpetuate the belief (one that is often internalized by girls themselves) that their troubles are their fault. Secondly, emotionality as a means of social communication and expression should be seen not as a sign of a deficient personality but rather as a positive resource. It is only by affirming girls' emotional responses as a comprehensible and positive means of coping with their experience of social injustice that they are likely to begin to feel any sense of autonomy in their lives. As long as they are effectively told that their emotional responses are 'crazy' their confidence in their right to express themselves will be undermined.

Normalizing girls' troublesome behaviour: collective similarities and differences

It has become obvious that the dominant definitions and assumptions of troublesome girls are essentially social constructs. What is also striking is how many of these 'troubles' are experienced, in some way or other, by the majority of adolescent girls. Certainly one of the most constant characteristics of my personal contact with girls 'in trouble' is how very many of their dilemmas, problems and needs connect with my own memories of growing up 'to be a woman'.

This leads to the central imperative, in addressing alternative definitions and policies for 'troublesome girls', of developing a framework which normalizes their behaviour. Linked to this is the parallel urgency to analyse and act towards girls' troubles from a perspective which actively acknowledges the cultural, ideological and material pressures on adolescent girls, and most particularly those which black and working-class girls face. The bifurcation of adolescent girls into the 'respectable and decent' and the 'promiscuous and dangerous' creates socially constructed categories which are both rigid and ambiguous. They deny the fact that most girls experience the need to demonstrate respectability and sexual attractiveness. Such a dichotomizing of young women also denies that girls might be interested in things other than the opposite sex, such as work, politics, music, female friends, social adventure and excitement.

My own experience of working with adolescent girls has consistently highlighted how they are invariably extremely aware (in both a personal and political sense) of many of the contradictions of adolescent femininity. Whilst some girls cope with such contradictions and injustices in an overtly rebellious and public way, others internalize them as 'their fault'. Still other girls accept their 'lot' apparently stoically and fatalistically but recognizing, at the same time, that there are personal costs (for example, 'tolerating' violence from boyfriends because 'I love him'). Girls who have particularly restricted access to society's material and social 'goodies' (employment, education, decent housing and so on) perhaps have less to lose by their active resistance than their more privileged counterparts.

The principle of defining girls' needs, problems and resources in collective terms could facilitate a depathologizing of their particular predicaments, whether those be as survivors of sexual abuse, arguments with parents or delinquency. It could also encourage a recognition of the possibility of girls providing more effective support to one another than huge armies of professional 'helpers'. The concern with collective consciousness raising in the contemporary women's movement evolved out of the need to enable women to name more publicly what were previously private experiences. Certainly, welfare agencies could learn much from the work of feminist groups such as Women's Aid and Rape Crisis Centres in asserting the possibility of the support and concrete action that can emerge out of challenging traditional maxims about how people are best 'helped' (Pahl, 1985).

Alternative approaches to welfare practice with adolescent girls must thus be based upon an active acknowledgement both of their socially constructed similarities and of the differences mediated by class, race and sexual identity. The hegemony of casework in social work has inhibited the possibility of recognizing similarities which, whilst mediated through individuals, are none the less socially and culturally constructed. There are, however, certain inherent dangers in shifting from an individualistic paradigm to one which places 'blame' on external social forces. Very few radical perspectives on social relations have explored the ways in which social circumstances distort and appropriate the individual's needs and capacities. In contrast, feminists have politicized subjectivity and highlighted the reciprocal relationship between individual identity and the material world (see, for example, the work of Eichenbaum and Orbach, 1984). Girls' apparently personal troubles should be viewed through a perspective which recognizes that girls' experiences are both unique and linked inextricably to their status as young women.

Towards alternative policies and practice

Welfare tasks in the UK, as elsewhere in northern Europe at least, tend to be boxed into supposedly linked, but in reality often isolated, compartments such as health, housing, education and personal social services. Needs and problems are seen as 'belonging' to a particular agency's sphere of responsibility. For example, 'problem' young people in the school system are referred to 'disruptive units' or to the personal social services, thereby inhibiting a critique of the school's deficiencies and failure to cope with non-conforming youngsters. Only by looking at welfare's management of girls in trouble from within a systems perspective can alternative policies be effectively implemented. Although any of these services could provide a starting point, I shall concentrate here on the personal social services.

The development of equal opportunities policies in many British local authorities could be a useful lever in getting the needs of 'troublesome' girls on policy agendas. But services for 'troublesome' adolescent girls continue to be marginalized and undebated. Generally, only front-line workers are actively questioning how policy definitions are put into operation. However, their capacity to influence decision making is circumscribed by the structures of the organizations in which they work. Policy makers (elected members and senior officers) should take positive action in initiating more equitable and comprehensive strategies for intervention with girls in trouble. Of equal importance is the need to begin to develop anti-sexist strategies for work with boys and young men in trouble. For to concentrate concerns about gender solely on girls and young women is to imply that the male half of the population is unaffected by sexism. Yet as we have seen only by problematizing gender relations generally is it likely that welfare agencies can begin to respond to the needs of adolescent girls in trouble in a sensitive and equitable manner. Male welfare professionals have a particular responsibility to scrutinize critically the ways in which masculinist assumptions shape their work with boys in trouble (Hudson, A., 1988).

But what do we mean by 'alternative policies' and how can these evolve so that 'top down' definitions are not perpetuated? Social policies generally have tended to be constructed around the needs of the economy; such needs focus on the relations between labour and capital rather than on relations in the family and the community (Coote, 1984). No doubt this is one of the reasons why male delinquency is seen to warrant the attention and resources it commands (young males being viewed as the future army of waged labour). It is perhaps not surprising that social policies relating to 'troublesome girls' have failed to acknowledge how family and community relations shape both the 'problems' girls present and the welfare responses which they precipitate.

In considering some concrete proposals for policy and practice with girls in trouble, there are three key and interrelated issues:

1 empowerment and participation;
2 welfare or justice: is least always best?
3 a separatist strategy: possibilities and problems.

Empowerment and participation
A fundamental prerequisite of any attempt to grapple with the complex task of evolving alternative policies for girls in trouble (criminal or otherwise) is to eradicate the victimology which underpins the status quo. Rowbotham et al. (1979) have reminded us of the importance of seeing disadvantaged groups not as 'passive victims' but as people who do have the means and wherewithal for generating the power which all groups create as a means of survival and resistance. Girls are no more passive victims of their oppressive circumstances than are waged labourers, battered women or black youth.

'Empowerment' and 'participation' can, however, be deceptively simple slogans. What they might mean in practice is much more difficult to articulate; not least because girls and welfare professionals alike have been socialized to assume that 'adults know best'. Certainly the educational system disinclines us to contemplate young people as active contributors to their own learning.

A very basic way of beginning to give girls in trouble some power is to involve them more readily in defining their needs. Whilst, for example, girls (like boys) are now more likely to be allowed access to case conferences, anyone who has attended such meetings will testify to the frequent marginalization of their voices: 'Yes, dear, but you know you do really need to learn to be more self-controlled/less aggressive/more mature before . . .' Such patronizing of girls in trouble denies that they might have any conception of what they want and need. As long as girls expect their needs and strengths to be misinterpreted or denied they are unlikely to feel that it is worthwhile discussing them with professionals.

The emphasis here on girls' capacities is important. Because social work deals with society's 'problem' groups, modes of intervention have focused on remedying deficits rather than building on the resources of such groups. The professional–client relationship reinforces the idea of the 'expert' having something to offer with the client as the passive recipient of the 'goodies'.

None the less some positive developments have recently been taking place in the corners of some welfare agencies. Drawing upon a social education model some social workers have taken creative initiatives in working collectively with girls in trouble. Empowering young women and giving them the confidence to participate are central tenets of such schemes (Mountain, 1988). As one social worker has commented:

> Our agenda is to provide an opportunity for young women to explore issues that are important to them, to provide a forum whereby they can develop some confidence in their own power and to act as facilitators in the group, taking action on their own behalf. (National Association of Youth Clubs, 1985: 13)

That girls do indeed want to talk about and do something about the issues affecting their lives (family, school, friendships, experiences of male violence) has been similarly underlined by my contact with other, similar schemes in social services departments. Giving girls access not only to different activities but also to different roles and assumptions about femininity can give girls an opportunity to work out, with girls in a similar situation, everyday strategies for coping with sexism.

Yet there are certain in-built difficulties. Women's Aid has been able to challenge the 'traditional charitable relationship of helped and helper' (Hanmer, 1977) in part because of its relative autonomy from the State and also because adult women are involved. But State welfare agencies endeavouring to implement even a very watered-down empowerment philosophy are likely to be doubly constrained first, by their statutory roles (which can inhibit a sense of safety and confidentiality for any girls who are involved) and, secondly, by legal and social considerations of the rights and capacities of adolescent girls 'to have a say'. Whilst the work of the National Association of Young People in Care (Stein, 1983) has undoubtedly forced some agencies to reconsider their assumption that they 'know what's best', the reluctance to give young people any rights remains firmly entrenched.

This points us to another important aspect of empowerment oriented policies: girls in trouble could be encouraged to have closer contact with non-statutory women and girls' groups and organizations. Girls in residential care are particularly likely to be 'cordoned off' not only from their 'normal' peers but also from women and girls' groups and organizations which might be able to help them increase their confidence. There could also be greater collaboration with some of the more constructive policies and practices in youth work (see Yeung, 1985, for a 'route map' of such work with girls). The fears of 'contamination' which continue to perpetuate many statutory-based agencies and which mean that much youth provision is still effectively for 'good' girls (and boys) are, however, likely to brake such possibilities.

Fears of 'contamination' also work the other way around; feminist influenced organizations are not infrequently seen by welfare professionals as potentially 'damaging' for their female clients. There is still a widespread belief that women-only and girls-only groups will be used to reinforce their clients' 'distrust' and 'hatred' of men and, moreover, that feminists will use such groups to further their own philosophies. Apart from this being a gross misunderstanding of the objectives of feminism, such fantasies also inhibit women and girls from having the opportunity to enhance their sense of personal worth and confidence with women who may have been through similar experiences, such as sexual abuse.

Given that welfare professionals are likely to resist the viability and desirability of 'empowerment' philosophies, *their* education should perhaps be highest on the agenda. Perhaps because so many welfare professionals (at least in the lower ranks) are female, there has been no wholesale commitment to tackle the endemic sexism of welfare practice. Indeed suggestions that there is a problem are frequently met with denial or patronizing humour. Social workers who are committed to developing more gender-sensitive perspectives and skills for working with girls in trouble are therefore marginalized and isolated. Support from management, in terms of resources and supervision, is usually, at best, non-existent, or, at worst, quite hostile.

Managers and practitioners alike should be forced to look at their attitudes, assumptions and values in this sphere of welfare practice. The allocation of resources demands critical scrutiny but so too should recruitment policies be reviewed. This latter point is especially important for residential-based posts where the power of managers to determine the regimes of their establishments is relatively unfettered.

Welfare or justice

In many respects the re-ascendancy of a justice model for the management of juvenile delinquency can be responded to quite positively. For it has redressed some of the excesses of a 'welfarist' paradigm whereby social work's 'needology' has pulled an increasing number of male and female juveniles into the system through definitions of their need for 'treatment' (Thorpe, 1978). However, the fact that the critique of welfarism has coalesced around an uneasy alliance of the left (who see it as an erosion of civil liberties) and the right (who view it as 'soft and ineffective') should make us more hesitant before accepting the justice orientation, lock stock and barrel. In the current political climate the latter perspective is likely to have a more powerful purchase.

Barbara Hudson has pointed to some of the endemic problems of transferring girls to a pure justice model; they would still be subjected to 'the double condemnation as offenders and as flouting the values of femininity' (Hudson, B., 1985: 16). She argues that only a change in social attitudes will give girls any real chance of justice. This is undoubtedly the case. However, it is worth considering ways in which we might begin to loosen the grip of the assumption that girls become criminal because of welfare problems. The current muddling of welfare and justice needs pushes girls up the tariff, in many cases, more quickly and for more trivial offences than boys (Harris and Webb, 1987). The writing of court reports gives social workers a not inconsiderable power to influence the courts in disposing of offenders. They should desist from using girls' appearances on criminal offences to justify supervision or care for welfare needs and instead use the tariff in stricter, justice terms. This might lead to more civil proceedings (for supervision and care) under the Children and Young Persons Act 1969. But at least there would be a greater degree of clarity and honesty about the objectives of welfare intervention rather than the double messages and standards which now prevail.

Perhaps 'least is best' as far as criminal justice considerations are concerned (not least because the vast majority of juveniles 'grow out of' offending). But such a principle is more problematic when considering the majority of girls who come into care essentially for 'welfare' reasons (in 1983 only 24 per cent of girls who came into care on a statutory order were there under criminal offence clauses of the 1969 Act; this contrasts with 67 per cent of boys). We have already seen how the politics of family life renders girls vulnerable to exploitation. Some girls want and have a right to an alternative to the home. When kith and kin are not available or willing to provide such an alternative, welfare agencies may need to step in. For girls who have had to run away from home to escape the abuse of their fathers, care will be preferable to sexual molestation.

Moreover, when families are rejecting their daughters some form of interim 'breathing space' provision is required. Once in care it is often difficult for girls to be extricated not least because behaviour in care can be used to rationalize the original decision to receive her into care ('she's running away and aggressive and obviously "out of control"'). Smaller neighbourhood-based and explicitly 'transitional' units could do much to provide the 'breathing space' that girls and their families may need. Finally, the structures and workings of many residential establishments are based on familial ideas about the gender division of labour; indeed many attempt explicitly to offer 'alternative families'. They are certainly not often organized to encourage adolescent girls' personal autonomy and rights to participate in the decisions affecting them. They are often large institutions, situated away from the girl's community; generally they are very second-rate alternatives. A range of provision that is both less stigmatizing and more flexible is undoubtedly required, as well as provision that does not idealize a specific cultural form of domestic and familial arrangements by a self-conscious and self-proclaimed 'second bestness' to it.

A separatist strategy

Social work, in common with most other welfare professions, has always been reluctant to acknowledge, in its methods of work, the collective similarities between some of its individual clients. The deeply enshrined principle of 'individualizing the client' has kept sociological contributions at the threshold of intervention. Moreover, social work's liberal democratic origins and self-image has always enabled it to rebuff charges of discrimination: taken-for-granted principles of 'client self-determination' and 'objectivity' have prompted the rhetoric that 'we respond to clients on the basis of individual need'. The needs of social minorities such as black people and girls have thus been denied.

Those involved with girls in trouble could usefully learn from the experiences of some women youth workers who have fought (sometimes quite successfully) for the establishment of girls' projects (Yeung, 1985). A similar separatist strategy is also warranted inside personal social service agencies; it could begin to reduce the marginality of work with girls in trouble and support those who are endeavouring to work in different ways. Many of those social workers (mostly women) who are endeavouring to establish work with girls as a legitimate 'specialism' undoubtedly do have a clear commitment to challenge the status quo; they are also well aware of the invisibility and misrecognition of girls' needs by the agency in which they work. However, many still feel at a considerable loss as to how to proceed; in contrast with their relative confidence when working with boys they often feel uncertain as to the kind of approach and activities which girls will both enjoy and find useful.

Reference has been made throughout this chapter to the differences as well as the similarities of the needs of girls in trouble. The needs of black and Asian girls particularly are currently denied and misinterpreted. Workers involved in working with girls in trouble thus need to have a more critical understanding of exactly how the system currently responds to the needs of girls from minority groups. The negative evaluation of black and Asian family structures means, for example, that assessments are loaded not only with sexist but also racist stereotypes (Bryan et al., 1985). White feminists, in particular, may need to examine the extent to which they frame the predicaments of Afro-Caribbean and Asian girls as emanating from sexism within their cultures rather than as emerging out of the culture of racism in Britain. Such perspectives implicitly affirm the superiority of Western social arrangements where girls are concerned (Ahmed, 1986). Only if resources are specifically allocated both for the training of workers and for need-responsive services will the complexity of the differences between girls' needs and their 'careers' through welfare agencies develop with any principled and strategic rigour.

Some will protest that a separatist strategy will either further ghettoize adolescent girls or that it will prevent girls from becoming more confident and assertive with boys and men; the assumption presumably being that you need boys or men to increase your assertive powers. Such arguments can be countered by pointing to the necessity of creating a social and political space in which work with girls can develop. Managers must be persuaded of the legitimacy of creating such a space. Whilst there is a risk that a separatist strategy might encourage 'endogenous' system expansion, carefully constructed, it would at least amount to putting girls in trouble on to a social policy agenda. Until that task is tackled, girls in trouble will continue to be at the receiving end of a system imbued with values which render it dubiously able to cope with their needs.

Note

1 The research was a largely qualitative study of forty-five adolescent girls referred to two area-based English inner city social services department teams specializing in work with adolescents. The research focused on the ideologies and factors influencing social work decision making and intervention. Field-based social workers were interviewed about their interventions; case files were also examined. The full research results will be published in my forthcoming book: *Troublesome Girls: Adolescence, Femininity, and the State* (London: Macmillan).

Appendix

Girls in the European criminal courts

A Comparative View

Participants in the Florence Conference

Approaching a comparative project in full knowledge of all the theoretical difficulties of comparison itself, let alone of comparing official statistics (Hindess, 1973; Cain, 1983, 1985, 1986a; Finch, 1986) is perhaps foolhardy. We know that direct empirical comparison is not possible for people who, like us, regard knowledge of the social world as problematic and that world itself as constantly changing. We know that subjectivities cannot be compared either, or even with certainty (that chimerical objective) the processes of the social construction of the data. Moreover, comparison in terms of theorized categories can have its dangers too: women are notoriously and regretfully aware that the categories of 'malestream' sociology do not apply comfortably to the world as they tentatively think they experience it. So what on earth are we doing comparing official statistics? Is it a possible task and what is it for?

The question of 'why comparison?' has already been in large part answered by Maureen Cain in the Introduction to this volume. It encourages the already present healthy awareness among women and feminists that they are not one, and likewise that there is not one politics. But it also sharpens the theoretical and critical awareness to see how different processes can produce the same (all too often) or different results. A mobile, complex, tolerant and altogether more convincing theory should result. Also, our evaluations of other theoretical positions are affected. It is hard to see the sex/gender structure as an effect or function of capitalism when similarities in the positions of women emerge in countries as diverse in political economic terms as Portugal and Ireland and Denmark or the Federal Republic of Germany. Finally, there is the down-to-earth point that we can get ideas from each other about what to do and what is not worth trying. This perhaps is the best thing that happens.

We attempt in this concluding discussion to address three questions to the official data, each of which questions has a bearing on our theory of how the pervasive discourse of the couple is reinforced within and by the criminal justice system. Statistics of what the criminal justice system records itself as doing are a crucial part of an answer to this question, although they cannot answer it sufficiently. The three questions are: do girls and boys receive different sentences for the same kinds of offences? Are sentences for girls and boys getting more severe or more lenient through time? What are the employment prospects for girls and boys in the different EEC countries?

The contributors to this appendix are Maria-Teresa Beleza, Maureen Cain, Mary Eaton, Anne Elzinga, Caterina Fanfani-Bühler, Claude Faugeron, Gabriella Ferrari-Bravo, Nell Rasmussen, Pilar Rivilla,[1] Jean Tansey and Lode Walgrave.

We have kept the three questions simple because each country has a different penal system. The statistical categories of offences, the age groups used for classification, the sentences available and so on vary from place to place, and not all EEC countries prepare juvenile justice statistics in a routine or systematic way. We do not want to claim more in terms of results from this exercise than so theoretically shaky and empirically incomplete a data base will bear. But we do claim to have collated some materials in a form that women can make use of in constructing and developing their theories of gender and the impact of courts and of jobs and unemployment upon it.

Sentencing of girls and boys

We first considered whether or not the more severe treatment of girls for status offences applied in all European countries. This practice strongly supports the argument of the book that growing up good, for a girl, means developing approved sexual practices. Status offences are actions which can only be sanctioned if the offender is young, such as licentious behaviour (Portugal), running away from home (Belgium) or, a passive 'offence', being in moral danger (England and Wales). Three of us compiled secondary sources to reveal the national pictures in Belgium, England and Wales, and the Netherlands.[2] These accounts support the argument that girls at risk of having a sexual encounter (the theme in common between the diverse status offences) are penalized more severely than boys. But the Belgian analysis reveals the complexities of the processes which underlie the broad finding, and provides a caution against simplistic interpretations. We therefore present the Belgian findings in full as an extended example.

The Belgian findings
In Belgium there is a unified procedure for juveniles so that not only 'incriminable acts' but also welfare matters pass through the prosecutor's office. Between 1974 and 1982 the numbers of people under 18 brought to the attention of the prosecutor increased for each of the five 'status offence' categories, as well as for incriminable acts, and for girls as well as boys. A simplified table is presented in Table A.1 (see also Walgrave, 1987: Table 1). First note that almost a third of the girls were reported for traffic offences (32.8 per cent in 1981). As Cipollini et al. (1987) argue, researchers should perhaps begin to pay more attention to these first penal experiences.

It should also be noted that slightly more boys than girls are reported for status offences.

Table A.1 *Reason for referral to the prosecutor's office in Belgium*

Reason	1974		1981	
	Male	Female	Male	Female
Incriminable acts	34,659	9,012	56,484	13,904
Status offences[1]	14,171	11,286	18,732	15,296

[1] These include: misconduct, in danger, running away, truancy, moral protection.

Source: Adapted from Walgrave, 1987

However 'when reported to the public prosecutor girls "in danger" and runaways have more chance of being referred to court than boys have. On the other hand, girls reported for "incriminable acts" are less likely to be referred to court than boys'. Citing Junger-Tas and Van Bosstraeten, Walgrave argues also that the 'in danger' category for girls includes many reclassified delinquent acts, and girls who had run away, had sexual intercourse, or gone out to dances or cinemas without permission (Walgrave, 1987).

Once in court judges more frequently make a provisional control measure against girls than boys (these are almost all carceral, and can last up to two years) but 'the type of control is more protective and less explicitly repressive' (Walgrave, 1987).

When the definitive measures are considered, the adage 'when she was good she was very very good, but when she was bad she was horrid' applies to girls who are sentenced for violent offences, whereas boys' sentences span the middle ranges of seriousness, and girls are also penalized more severely for 'misconduct' (Table A.2). For other status offences the disparities are not large, but should be read in the context of a higher proportion of girls having been referred to the court on these grounds in the first place.

Portugal and Spain

Juvenile court figures, hitherto unpublished, are also available for Portugal and Spain and these seem to suggest an extreme form of penalization for girls convicted of status offences, since in Portugal 41.0 per cent of them as opposed to only 16.8 per cent of boys so convicted were incarcerated in 1984 (Table A.3). In the Madrid juvenile court in Spain in 1984 internment was used for 22.2 per cent of the girls convicted of status offences, and only 6.4 per cent of the boys (Table A.4).

Statistics are not available for the other five countries in this comparative survey, usually because status offences are dealt with as welfare matters, lost to all but ethnographic research by the encompassing penumbra of discretion.

Recarceration

Our second question is whether the situation for young people in general and for girls in particular has been getting worse or better, whether, that is, court sentencing has been getting more severe or not. (We all regarded carceral sentences as 'worse' than non-carceral ones). Such a question can only be answered by an examination of official statistics, although even here there are uncertainties in relation to those sentences which create discretion to incarcerate, and some countries (e.g. Ireland) produce no statistics of court decision making. Here we had to make do with statistics of prison populations, which of course made it impossible to situate imprisonment in the context of the courts' changing patterns of choice between a range of sentences. However, we do have more complete data than we were able to bring to bear on our previous question.

The comparative data reveal that girls' chances of being incarcerated by the courts are clearly worse than they were in the decade preceding the conference in four of the ten nations reviewed, namely England and Wales, France, Italy and Spain. Further evidence of deterioration comes from Ireland, where sentences for young people are getting longer, while in Portugal more young people are held in prison at any one time than ever before, before or after the Revolution, although the proportion of girls in that larger total is declining. (We do not know proportions to population.) In Belgium, our statistics reveal few changes over time but there has

Table A.2 *Sentence by offence or activity in Belgium, 1982*

	Procedure stopped				Sent to penal court				Simple reprimand				Kept under control (non-custodial)				To family home				To private institution				To state institution				Totals	
	M	%	F	%	M	%	F	%	M	%	F	%	M	%	F	%	M	%	F	%	M	%	F	%	M	%	F	%	M	F
Against the person	19	5.6	5	26.3	18	5.3	2	10.5	158	46.5	3	15.8	108	31.8	3	15.8	3	0.9	—	0.0	21	6.2	6	31.6	13	3.8	—	0.0	340	19
Against property	97	7.3	11	9.1	55	4.1	1	0.8	598	45.2	52	43.3	329	24.9	25	20.8	16	1.2	5	4.2	151	11.4	19	15.8	77	5.8	7	5.8	1323	120
Sex offences	10	10.7	2	6.9	3	3.2	—	—	32	34.4	13	44.8	31	33.3	9	31.0	1	1.1	—	0.0	12	12.9	4	13.8	4	4.3	1	3.4	93	29
Traffic offences	1	2.6	2	66.6	—	0.0	—	—	31	79.5	1	33.3	7	17.9	—	0.0	—	0.0	—	—	—	0.0	—	—	—	0.0	—	0.0	39	3
Others	3	5.1	2	11.1	—	0.0	—	—	30	50.8	5	27.8	14	23.7	8	44.4	2	3.4	—	0.0	6	10.2	3	16.7	4	6.8	—	0.0	59	18
Misconduct	12	8.0	3	2.9	5	3.4	1	0.9	25	16.8	16	15.4	51	34.2	32	30.8	10	6.7	4	3.8	35	23.5	41	39.4	9	6.0	7	6.7	149[1]	104
In danger	74	6.4	109	8.8	—	0.0	—	—	99	8.5	55	4.5	338	29.0	344	27.9	187	16.1	241	19.5	450	38.7	461	37.4	15	1.3	23	1.9	1163	1233
Running away	—	0.0	1	2.8	—	0.0	—	—	4	25.0	6	17.1	2	12.5	8	22.8	—	0.0	1	2.8	8	50.0	19	54.3	2	12.5	—	0.0	16	35
Truancy	1	50.0	1	50.0	—	0.0	—	—	1	50.0	—	0.0	—	0.0	1	50.0	—	0.0	—	0.0	—	0.0	—	0.0	—	0.0	—	0.0	2	2
Moral protection	—	0.0	—	0.0	—	0.0	—	—	—	0.0	—	—	—	0.0	—	0.0	—	0.0	—	0.0	—	0.0	1	100.0	—	0.0	—	0.0	—	1

[1] Two cases not accounted for.

Source: Walgrave, 1987, Table 8

Table A.3 *Sanctions applied by juvenile courts (Tribunals de Menores)[1] by offence, by sex in Portugal, 1984*

Offences	Reprimand				Education, professional training				Placement in an institution				Family placing				Other				Total			
	M	%	F	%	M	%	F	%	M	%	F	%	M	%	F	%	M	%	F	%	M	%	F	%
Status off.	256	68.5	60	38.5	32	8.6	24	15.4	63	16.8	64	41.0	8	2.1	3	1.9	15	4	5	3.2	374	16.3	156	24.7
Off. against the person	238	83.5	87	97.8	3	1	—	—	2	0.7	1	1.1	4	1.4	—	—	38	13.4	1	1.1	285	12.4	89	14.1
Off. against property	1199	85.6	286	91.1	21	1.5	4	1.3	97	6.9	17	5.4	6	0.4	1	0.3	78	5.6	6	1.9	1401	60.9	314	49.8
Drug off.	6	100.0	—	—	—	—	—	—	—	—	—	—	—	—	—	—	—	—	—	—	6	0.3	—	—
'Political' offence[2]	13	92.9	5	100	—	—	—	—	1	7.1	—	—	—	—	—	—	—	—	—	—	14	0.6	5	0.8
Other[3]	24	77.4	16	45.7	5	16.1	9	25.7	2	6.5	10	28.6	—	—	—	—	—	—	—	—	31	1.3	35	5.5
Traffic offence[4]	186	99	32	100	1	0.5	—	—	—	—	—	—	—	—	—	—	1	0.5	—	—	188	8.2	32	5.1
Total	1922	83.6	486	77	62	2.7	37	5.9	165	7.2	92	14.6	18	0.8	4	0.6	132	5.7	12	1.9	2299	100.0	631	100.0

[1] Or by the other courts, in the districts where juvenile courts have not yet been created. Juvenile jurisdiction extends to before 16 years of age, on to 18 if the minor commits a not very serious offence and has already been subject to a judicial measure. Only status and criminal offences are considered here (i.e. decisions about abandoned children are not included).

[2] Illegal possession of weapons, threatening/injuring a policeman or other public authority or not obeying their order, perjury.

[3] Unspecified offences, illegal hunting and fishing, food or medicine altering.

[4] And other misdemeanours (*transgressões*).

Source: M.-T. Beleza, Original data compiled for the project by staff of the Ministry of Justice (Gabinete de Estudos e Planeamento)

Table A.4 *Sanctions applied by juvenile courts (Tribunal Tutelar de Menores) in Madrid, 1984*

Offence	Caution M	%	F	%	Provisional freedom M	%	F	%	Short internment (under 30 days) M	%	F	%	Internment M	%	F	%
Against the person[1]	113	66.5	21	75.0	6	3.5	—	0.0	1	0.6	—	0.0	3	1.8	—	0.0
Against property[2]	626	56.3	53	41.1	72	6.6	9	7.0	44	4.0	5	3.8	25	2.2	4	3.1
Drug offences	12	52.2	1	00.0	—	0.0	—	0.0	1	4.3	—	0.0	2	8.7	—	0.0
Status offences[3]	13	27.7	3	11.1	9	19.1	5	18.5	1	2.1	—	0.0	3	6.4	6	22.2
Miscellaneous[4]	9	75.0	—	0.0	—	0.0	—	0.0	1	8.3	—	0.0	2	16.7	—	0.0
Minor violations[5]	11	84.6	—	0.0	1	7.7	—	0.0	—	0.0	—	0.0	—	0.0	—	0.0
Total	784	57.0	78	41.7	88	6.4	14	7.4	48	3.5	5	2.7	35	2.5	10	5.3

Table A.4 *continuation*

Offence	Recorded or 'archived' M	%	F	%	No record: absolute discharge M	%	F	%	Case dismissed M	%	F	%	Others M	%	F	%	Total M	%	F	%
Against the person[1]	19	11.2	4	14.3	6	3.5	—	0.0	21	12.3	3	10.7	1	0.6	—	0.0	170	0.0	28	100
Against property[2]	191	17.2	45	34.9	80	7.2	9	7.0	58	5.2	—	0.0	15	1.3	4	3.1	1111	100.0	129	100
Drug offences	1	4.3	—	0.0	7	30.4	—	0.0	—	0.0	—	0.0	—	0.0	—	0.0	23	99.9	1	100
Status offences[3]	16	34.0	8	29.6	3	6.4	3	11.1	2	4.3	1	3.7	—	0.0	1	3.7	47	100.0	27	99
Miscellaneous[4]	—	0.0	2	100.0	—	0.0	—	0.0	—	0.0	—	0.0	—	0.0	—	0.0	12	100.0	2	100
Minor violations[5]	—	0.0	—	0.0	—	7.7	—	0.0	—	0.0	—	0.0	—	0.0	—	0.0	13	100.0	—	0.0
Total	227	16.5	59	31.6	97	7.0	12	6.4	81	5.8	4	2.1	16	1.2	5	2.7	1376	99.9	187	99

[1] Includes: menaces; insults; injuries; homicide.

[2] Includes: theft; larceny; misappropriation; fraud; damage; dishonest abuses.

[3] Includes: misbehaviour; irregular behaviour; licentious behaviour; running away from home; not submitting to parents' authority.

[4] Includes: violations; public disorder.

[5] Includes: infringement of railway regulations; hunting regulations, and road traffic regulations.

Source: Pilar Rivilla, original data compiled for the project

Table A.5 *Belgian people under 18 incarcerated in 1974 and 1982*

Sentence	1974				1982			
	M	%	F	%	M	%	F	%
Provisional measures								
Under control (non-custodial)	751	17.7	564	17.9	986	24.3	513	21.4
Family home	461	10.9	496	15.6	426	10.5	443	18.5
Private institution	2079	49.0	1865	58.5	1644	40.6	1303	54.4
State institution	534	12.6	146	4.6	499	11.1	43	1.8
House of detention	413	9.7	116	3.6	544	13.4	91	3.8
Definitive measures								
Prosecution stopped	260	6.3	189	7.7	217	6.8	136	8.7
Sent to penal court	108	2.6	31	1.2	81	2.5	4	0.2
Reprimand	1026	24.9	266	10.8	980	30.8	151	9.6
Under control (non-custodial)	1218	29.5	714	29.0	880	27.6	430	27.5
In family home	278	6.7	296	12.0	219	6.9	251	16.0
In private institution	1057	25.6	904	36.7	683	21.4	554	35.4
In State institution	176	4.3	61	2.5	124	3.9	38	2.4

Source: Walgrave, 1987

Table A.6 *Numbers of boys and girls (by age) imprisoned in Denmark after sentence (absolute numbers)*

		Lenient imprisonment		Imprisonment	
		15–17	18–20	15–17	18–20
1979	M	16	633	73	499
	F	1	19	1	21
1980	M	16	739	80	565
	F	—	19	7	14
1981	M	17	434	68	507
	F	—	7	—	14
1982	M	11	411	64	415
	F	—	5	1	14

Source: Oversigtstabeller, Table 1.6; data provided and translated for the project by Nell Rasmussen

Table A.7 *Numbers of people receiving custodial sentences (in thousands) in England and Wales*

| | 1973 | | | | 1983 | | | |
| | 14–16 | | 17–20 | | 14–16 | | 17–20 | |
	M	F	M	F	M	F	M	F
Care order (discretion to incarcerate)	3.6	0.6	N/A	N/A	1.2	0.2	N/A	N/A
Detention centre	3.0	—	4.7	—	4.8	—	6.7	—
Borstal	1.4	—	5.2	0.2	0.6	—	2.8	0.1
Youth custody	N/A	N/A	N/A	N/A	1.3	0.1	9.6	0.4
Prison (suspended)	N/A	N/A	2.3	0.2	N/A	N/A	2.1	0.2
Prison (unsuspended)	N/A	N/A	2.7	0.1	N/A	N/A	3.3	0.2

N/A = sentence not available.

Source: Eaton, 1987

been a continuing debate about the introduction of more punitive legislation. Only for Denmark and the Federal Republic of Germany is there evidence from the official statistics that sentencing was not getting worse as the decade progressed. Joachim Kersten warns, however, that the figures presented from Germany do not include welfare statistics, and 'it is in the welfare system where girls, given the same . . . backgrounds . . . are more likely to be institutionalized, spend longer periods in secure accommodation, are more often put into the "cooler", etc.' (personal letter 3 February 1988; see also this volume, Chapter 8). Pratt (1986a) offers a useful explanation for the unique liberality of Denmark, in terms of their 'no alternatives' decarceration policy. We did not obtain Dutch data.

The statistics presented are not directly comparable: each of us has had to make the best use possible of the available data in order to address this profoundly serious issue. The evidence in Tables A.5–13 supports our argument.

Employment and unemployment

Our point about employment can be made rather briefly. Our thesis as stated in the introduction was that the transitions to adulthood of girls and young women are doubly disrupted in a time of economic recession, by not finding employment themselves at the approved life stages and by the unemployment of their prospective marriage partners. In five of the countries examined (Belgium, Denmark, France, Italy, Portugal) girls' employment prospects were worse than boys'. In Belgium and France this is so despite the fact that more girls than boys participate in higher education. The data also reveal that girls are unemployed for longer (Walgrave, 1987; Faugeron, 1985; Eurostat, 1983). (These Eurostat figures are for 1981. At the time of Maureen Cain's visit to the Division of Social Affairs in 1985, later figures were not subdivided by gender.)[3]

Table A.8   Trends in the sentencing of young people[1] in the Federal Republic of Germany, 1976–82

		1976		1977		1978		1979		1980		1981		1982	
		Number	%	Number	%	Number	%	Number	%	Number	%	Number	%	Number	%
Total corrective measures	M	7,999	8.4	9,546	9.3	11,236	10.1	12,033	10.6	13,739	11.6	16,377	12.9	19,618	14.7
	F	1,962	16.0	2,208	17.0	2,504	18.7	2,663	19.6	2,838	20.3	3,263	22.2	3,923	24.5
Total disciplinary measures	M	70,088	73.9	76,358	74.4	82,613	74.2	84,784	74.4	88,031	74.3	91,692	72.3	93,247	69.7
	F	9,189	74.9	9,528	73.5	9,766	72.8	9,711	71.5	10,059	71.9	10,163	69.3	10,889	67.9
Suspended sentences	M	9,667	10.2	9,837	9.6	10,588	9.5	10,468	9.2	10,329	8.7	11,499	9.1	12,606	9.4
	F	817	6.7	907	7.0	839	6.3	866	6.4	863	6.2	938	6.4	907	6.5
Indeterminate sentences	M	496	0.5	454	0.4	397	0.4	311	0.3	291	0.2	317	0.2	274	0.2
	F	10	0.1	6	0.1	10	0.1	7	0.1	6	0.0	8	0.1	13	0.1
Determinate sentences	M	6,647	7.0	6,405	6.2	6,544	5.9	6,380	5.6	6,071	5.1	6,972	5.5	7,979	5.9
	F	292	2.3	310	2.3	295	2.2	331	2.4	222	1.6	288	2.0	306	1.9
Total of these measures	M	94,897	100.0	102,600	99.9	111,378	100.0	113,994	100.0	118,461	99.9	126,857	100.0	133,724	99.9
	F	12,270	100.0	12,959	100.0	13,414	100.1	13,578	100.0	13,988	100.0	14,660	100.0	16,038	100.0

[1] All aged 14–17. Some 18–20, i.e. includes all those prosecuted under the juvenile code.

Source: Statistisches Bundesamt, Wiesbaden, *Strafverpolgungsstatistik (Ausfürliche Ergebnisse)*, Table 10

Table A.9 *Trends in imprisonment in France for people under 18*

		Suspended sentences	% of total penal sanctions	Unsuspended sentences	% of total penal sanctions	Total penal sanctions
1979	M	9,170	50.2	3,901	21.3	18,266
	F	651	47.7	224	16.4	1,364
1980	M	8,810	44.1	4,911	24.6	19,990
	F	636	42.3	319	21.2	1,505
1981	M	9,824	46.5	5,176	24.5	21,141
	F	658	40.2	413	25.2	1,638
1982	M	10,024	51.4	4,696	24.1	19,487
	F	684	44.5	388	25.3	1,534

Source: Faugeron (1985), recalculated from Table VII

Table A.10 *Length of sentence of those 15–20 committed to prison in Ireland by year of committal*

		Less than 6 months		6–11 months		12–23 months		2 years or more		Total	
		Number	%	Number	%	Number	%	Number	%	Number	%
1973[1]	M	286	50.3	186	32.7	96	16.9			568	99.9
	F	66	81.5	12	14.8	3	3.7			81	100.0
1974[1]	M	231	49.4	140	29.9	97	20.7			468	100.0
	F	38	74.5	9	17.6	4	7.8			51	99.9
1975	M	197	44.5	156	35.3	72	16.3	17	3.8	442	99.9
	F	54	77.1	12	17.1	3	4.3	1	1.4	70	99.9
1976	M	226	41.5	201	36.9	111	20.4	7	1.3	545	100.1
	F	49	68.1	16	22.2	7	9.7	—	—	72	100.0
1977	M	177	40.8	140	32.3	97	22.3	20	4.6	434	100.0
	F	33	62.3	14	26.4	6	11.3	—	—	53	100.0
1978	M	169	38.9	161	37.1	73	16.8	31	7.1	434	99.9
	F	25	59.5	14	33.3	3	7.1	—	—	42	99.9
1979	M	153	39.1	117	29.9	88	22.5	33	8.4	391	99.9
	F	41	67.2	11	18.0	9	14.8	—	—	61	100.0
1982	M	143	31.2	119	25.9	139	30.3	58	12.6	459	100.0
	F	20	35.1	27	47.4	9	15.8	1	1.7	57	100.0

[1] All sentences of 12 months or more are combined in 1973 and 1974.

Source: Department of Justice, *Annual Reports on Prisons*, cited in Tansey, 1985: 25–5.

Table A.11   *Numbers detained in penal institutions in Italy aged 14–17, 1973–84*

	1973	1974	1975	1976	1977	1978	1979	1980	1981	1982	1983	1984
Male	11,307	11,120	10,044	10,636	10,477	9,193	8,602	9,019	11,098	9,847	9,732	7,480
Female	123	135	322	371	471	359	690	632	920	958	1,008	732
Total	11,430	11,255	10,366	11,007	10,948	9,552	9,292	9,657	12,018	10,805	10,740	8,212
% Female	1.1	1.2	3.1	3.4	4.3	3.8	6.9	6.6	7.7	8.9	9.39	8.8

Source: original data compiled by Gabriella Ferrari-Bravo

Table A.12   *Numbers of young people imprisoned by sex, in Portugal 1970–82*

Year	Young people (age 16–29)	% of total prisoners	M	%	F	%
1970	1,990	39.1	1,838	92.4	152	7.6
1972	1,721	42.3	1,619	94.1	102	5.9
1974	1,441	67.6	1,403	97.4	38	2.6
1975	2,375	68.4	2,309	97.2	66	2.8
1976	2,485	68.4	2,430	97.8	55	2.2
1977	2,955	68.8	2,860	96.8	95	3.2
1978	3,162	67.1	3,060	96.8	102	3.2
1979	3,402	66.9	3,302	97.1	100	2.9
1980	3,494	65.3	3,498	97.3	96	2.7
1981	3,409	63.1	3,308	96.9	103	3.1
1982	3,167	63.9	3,090	97.6	77	2.4

Source: D.G. Serviços Prisionaïs, in Cruz and Reis, 1983: 36

In Portugal, not at that time included in EEC records, the unemployment rate for girls in the 15–19 age range was markedly higher than that for boys (Table A.14). However, 'in the Federal Republic of Germany, the Netherlands, the United Kingdom and Ireland the young women's unemployment rate was lower than that for a young man' (Eurostat, 1983). No data were gathered from Spain.

When males are taken as a yardstick nothing can be said about the unemployment of girls. Once again, who is worst off is not a helpful question unless theoretically guided. More studies exploring the impact of teenage unemployment on gender relations are urgently required.

Table A.13 *Trends in sentencing for boys and girls in the Tribunal Tutelar de Menores (Facultad Reformadora) in Madrid, 1977-83*

Sentence	1977		1978		1979		1980		1981		1982		1983	
	M	F	M	F	M	F	M	F	M	F	M	F	M	F
Admonition	51.2	37.9	24.0	14.6	17.8	6.2	40.9	21.9	50.5	40.3	50.6	39.3	57.6	37.8
Supervision	4.5	12.9	2.1	10.6	1.4	8.2	6.7	11.2	4.9	13.6	6.6	18.3	6.6	6.2
Internment under 30 days	19.2	4.0	2.5	2.0	3.4	—	7.6	0.6	6.6	—	5.1	0.5	2.9	—
Internment	3.0	5.7	1.3	4.6	0.8	5.2	2.1	3.9	2.0	7.2	2.9	6.8	2.2	9.1
(total interned)	(22.2)	(9.7)	(3.8)	(6.6)	(4.2)	(5.2)	(9.7)	(4.5)	(8.6)	(7.2)	(8.0)	(7.3)	(5.1)	(9.1)
Case dismissed	12.4	16.1	54.8	37.1	54.9	11.3	20.5	20.8	17.5	24.3	18.8	23.7	17.8	21.1
Unsettled	9.7	23.4	15.3	31.1	21.7	69.1	22.2	41.6	18.5	14.6	16.0	11.4	12.9	25.8
Total	100.0	100.0	100.0	100.0	100.0	100.0	100.0	100.0	100.0	100.0	100.0	100.0	100.0	100.0
N^1	1417	124	1500	151	2095	97	1589	178	1842	206	1743	219	1700	209

[1] Total includes those for charges lodged in previous years.

Source: Data compiled for the project by Pilar Rivilla

Table A.14 *Unemployment rates in Portugal for young people aged 15–19 years, 1977–81*

Unemployed (second semester)	1977	1978	1979	1980	1981
Male	14.7	16.3	13.4	10.2	9.8
Female	26.5	33.3	31.3	31.1	27.6

Source: IPE/INE in Seruya, 1983: 61

Conclusion

We have attempted to depict, in this survey of court practices and employment prospects, the tips of icebergs hinting at very complex social processes which produce these results.

First, there is evidence that girls are still punished more severely than boys for activities which put them at risk of an unauthorized sexual encounter, for status offences, although boys engage in these activities at least as often as girls. This last point is evidenced by self-report studies from the United Kingdom, Belgium, the Federal Republic of Germany, the Netherlands, and Spain, not reproduced here.[4]

More serious is the finding that girls' chances of being incarcerated at all, and for longer, appear to be rising in seven of the ten European countries studied.

It does seem, then, that the doubly disrupted transition of girls into adult life when both employment and marriage to a good wage earner became problematic, is being policed with an increasingly punitive response by our European penal systems.

Notes

1 We have not been able to contact Pilar Rivilla. Her work cited here was, however, prepared for this volume.
2 See Eaton, 1987; Elzinga and Naber, 1987; Walgrave, 1987.
3 Our thanks are particularly due to the staff of this Division, who gave generously of their time.
4 *El Menor Marginado*, 1979: 247; Junger-Tas, 1977, 1984; Junger-Tas and Kruissink, 1987; Schwind, 1986.

References

Acker, S. (1988) 'Teachers, gender and resistance', *British Journal of the Sociology of Education*, 9(3): 307.

Ackland, J. (1982) *Girls in Care*. Aldershot: Gower.

Adler, F. (1975) *Sisters in Crime*. New York: McGraw-Hill.

Advisory Council on the Misuse of Drugs (1982) *Treatment and Rehabilitation*. London: Department of Health and Social Security.

Advisory Council on the Misuse of Drugs (1984) *Prevention*. London: Home Office.

Ahmed, S. (1986) 'Cultural racism with Asian women and girls', in S. Ahmed, J. Cheetham and J. Small (eds). *Social Work with Black Children and their Families*. London: Batsford.

All England Law Reports (1985) 'Gillick *v* West Norfolk and Wisbech Area Health Authority and Another', *1 All ER:* 553–9.

Andrieu-Sanz, R. and Vasquez-Anton, K. (1987) 'A description and interpretation of prostitution of young women in Bilbao', in 'Becoming a Teenage Prostitute in Spain and the USA', EUI Working Paper 304/87. San Domenico, Florence: European University Institute.

Angelou, M. (1984) *I Know Why the Caged Bird Sings*, London: Virago Press.

Arnon, D., Kleinman, M.H. and Kissin, B. (1974) 'Psychological differentiation in heroin addicts', *International Journal of the Addictions*, 9(1): 151–9.

Ashton, M. (1981) 'Theory and practice in the new British system', *Drug Link*, 16 (1–5).

Austin, J. and Krisberg, B. (1981) 'Wider, stronger and different nets: the dialectics of criminal justice reform', *Journal of Research in Crime and Delinquency*, 18 (1): 165–96.

Austin, J. and Krisberg, B. (1982) 'The unmet promise of alternatives to "incarceration"', *Crime and Delinquency*, 3 (July): 374–409.

Badinter, R. (1982) Speech to the Commission de Réforme du Droit Penal des Mineurs. Vaucresson.

Ball, J.C. and Chambers, C.D. (1970) *The Epidemiology of Opiate Addiction in the US*. Springfield, IL: Thomas.

Barrett, M. and McIntosh, M. (1982) *The Anti-Social Family*. London: Verso.

Bertelli, B. (1979) 'Analisi di un campione di 500 fascicoli', in A. Balioni et al. (eds), *Devianza e giustizia minorile*. Milan: Angeli.

Binion, V.J. (1979) 'A descriptive comparison of the families of origin of women heroin users and non-users', in NIDA, *Addicted Women, Family Dynamics, Self Perception and Support Systems*. Washington DC: National Institute on Drug Abuse.

Binion, V.J. (1982) 'Sex differences in socialisation and family dynamics of female and male heroin users', *Journal of Social Issues*. 38(2): 43–57.

Bland, L. (1983) 'Purity, motherhood, pleasure or threat', in S. Cartledge and J. Ryan (eds), *Sex and Love*. London: Women's Press.

Bottoms, A.E., Brown, P., McWilliams, B., McWilliams, W. and Pratt, J. (1986) 'The national picture: preliminary results of the national survey of I.T.', paper presented at the annual conference of the National Intermediate Treatment Federation, Sheffield, 1985. Shortened version from I.T. Evaluation Project, Institute of Criminology, University of Cambridge as *Research Bulletin*, 2 (1986).

Bourricaud, F. (1968) 'Conformité et déviance', *Encyclopedia Universalis*, Vol. IV. Paris.

Box, S. (1981) *Deviance, Reality and Social Control*. London: Holt, Rinehart & Winston.

Brake, M. (1980) *The Sociology of Youth Culture and Youth Subcultures*. London: Routledge & Kegan Paul.

Bryan, B., Dadzie, S. and Scafe, S. (1985) *The Heart of the Race: Black Women's Lives in Britain*. London: Virago.

Büttner, P. (1982) *Der Psychologe in der Heimerziehung*. Frankfurt: Internationale Gesellschaft für Heimerziehung.

Cain, M. (1983) 'Quantity and quality: the future of the comparative method', in M. Cain and K. Kulcsar (eds), *Disputes and the Law*. Budapest: Academiai Kiado.

Cain, M. (1985) 'Delinquent girls in Europe: towards a comparative perspective'. EUI Conference Paper 396/85, San Domenico, Florence.

Cain, M. (1986a) 'Realism, feminism, methodology and law'. *International Journal of the Sociology of Law*, 14(3) and (4).

Cain, M. (1986b) 'Socio-legal studies and social justice for women: some working notes on a method'. Paper presented at Law and Society Association of Australia Annual Conference, Brisbane, 5–7 December.

Cain, M. (1987) 'Realist philosophy, social policy and feminism: on the reclamation of value-full knowledge', paper presented to the annual conference of the British Sociological Association, Leeds, Easter.

Cain, M. and Finch, J. (1982) 'Towards a rehabilitation of data', in P. Abrams (ed.), *Practice and Progress: British Sociology 1950–1980*. London: Allen & Unwin.

Campbell, A. (1981) *Delinquent Girls*. Oxford: Basil Blackwell.

Campbell, B. (1988) *Unofficial Secrets: Child Sexual Abuse – the Cleveland Case*. London: Virago.

Carlen, P. (1985) *Criminal Women*. Cambridge: Polity Press.

Casburn, M. (1979) *Girls will be Girls: Sexism and Juvenile Justice in a London Borough*. London: Women's Research and Resources Centre.

Chein, I., Gerald, D.L., Lee, R.S. and Rosenfeld, E. (1964) *The Road to Heroin*. New York: Basic Books.

Chesney-Lind, M. (1973) 'Judicial enforcement of the female sex role', *Criminology*, 8 (Fall): 51–69.

Chesney-Lind, M. (1977) 'Judicial paternalism and the female status offender', *Crime and Delinquency*, 23: 121–30.

Chesney-Lind, M. (1978) 'Chivalry re-examined: women and the criminal justice system', in L. Bowker (ed.), *Women, Crime and the Criminal Justice System*. Massachusetts: Lexington.

Cipollini, R., Faccioli, F. and Pitch, T. (1986) 'Aspetti dell'intervento penale sulle minorenni a Roma', *Dei Delitti e delle Pene*, 4(3): 501–32.

Cohen, S. (1979) 'The punitive city: notes on the dispersal of social control', *Contemporary Crises*, 3: 339–63.

Cohen, S. (1985) *Visions of Social Control*. London: Polity Press.

Conen, M.-L. (1985) *Mädchen flüchten aus der Familie*. München: Minerva Publikation.

Connell, R. (1983) 'Men's bodies', in *Which Way is Up?* London: Allen & Unwin.

Cooper, J. (1970) 'Social care and social control', *Probation*, 16(1): 22–5.

Coote, A. (1984) 'A new starting point', in J. Curran (ed.), *The Future of the Left*. London: Polity Press and New Socialist.

Cousins, M. (1980) 'Men's rea', in P. Carlen and M. Collison (eds), *Radical Issues in Criminology*. Oxford: Martin Robertson.

Covington, C. (1979) *The British Juvenile Justice System – a Historical Perspective*. London: Justice for Children.

Cruz, M.B. and Reis, M.L. (1983) *Criminalidade e Delinquência Juvenil em Portugal*. Lisbon: ICS.

Curran, D.A. (1983) 'Judicial discretion and defendants' sex', *Criminology*, 21(1): 41–58.

Cusky, W.R., Richardson, A.E. and Berger, A.B. (1979) *Specialized Therapeutic Community Programme for Female Addicts*. Washington DC: National Institute on Drug Abuse/Department of Health, Education and Welfare.

Cusky, W.R., Berger, L.H. and Densen-Gerber, J. (1981) 'Issues in the treatment of female addiction: a review and critique of the literature', in E. Howell and M. Boys (eds), *Women and Mental Health*. New York: Basic Books.

Dale, J. and Foster, P. (1986) *Feminists and State Welfare*. London: Routledge & Kegan Paul.

Datesman, S. and Scarpitti, F. (1980) 'Unequal protection for males and females in the juvenile court', in S. Datesman and F. Scarpitti (eds), *Women, Crime and Justice*. New York: Oxford University Press.

Davies, M. (1985) 'Determinate sentencing reform in California and its impact on the penal system', *British Journal of Criminology*, 25(1): 1–30.

Davis, K. (1937) 'The sociology of prostitution', *American Sociological Review*, 2(5).

De Leo, G. (1981) 'Devianza, personalità e risposta penale: una proposta di ricon-cettualizzazione', *La Questione Criminale*, 7(2): 219–43.

Delphy, C. (1977) 'The main enemy: a materialist analysis of women's oppression', *Explorations in Feminism*, 3.

Delphy, C. (1984) *Close to Home*. London: Hutchinson.

Denman, G. (1983) *Intensive Intermediate Treatment with Juvenile Offenders: a Handbook on Assessment and Groupwork Practice*, Lancaster: University of Lancaster Centre for Youth, Crime and Community.

Densen-Gerber, J. and Rohrs, C. (1973) 'Drug addicted parents and child abuse', *Contemporary Drug Problems*, 2(4): 683–95.

Department of Health and Social Security (DHSS) (1972) *Intermediate Treatment: a Guide for Regional Planning*. London: HMSO.

Department of Health and Social Security (DHSS) (1977) *Intermediate Treatment: 28 Choices*. London: DHSS.

Department of Health and Social Security (1986) *Personal Social Services: Local Authority Statistics*. London: DHSS.

Departmental Committee on Morphine and Heroin Addiction (1926) *Report*. London: HMSO.

Dobash, R.E. and Dobash, R. (1979) *Violence against Wives*. New York: Free Press.

Donzelot, J. (1979) *The Policing of Families*. London: Hutchinson.

Dorn, N. and Thompson, A. (1975) *A Comparison of 1973 and 1974 Levels of Mid-Teenage Experimentation with Illegal Drugs in some Schools in England*. London: Institute for the Study of Drug Dependence.

Eaton, M. (1983) 'Mitigating circumstances: familiar rhetoric', *International Journal of the Sociology of Law*, 10(3): 385–400.

Eaton, M. (1986) *Justice for Women? Family, Court and Social Control*. Milton Keynes: Open University Press.

Eaton, M. (1987) 'Descriptive material from Great Britain', EUI Working Paper 303/87, San Domenico, Florence.

Edwards, G. (1978) 'Some years on: evolutions in the "British System"', in D.J. West (ed.), *Problems of Drug Abuse in Britain*. Cambridge: Cambridge University Press.

Eichenbaum, L. and Orbach, S. (1984) *What do Women Want?* London: Fontana.

El Menor Marginado (1979) Madrid.

Elzinga, A. and Naber, P. (1987) 'Girls and the Dutch juvenile justice system: the judicial control of sexuality', EUI Working Paper 300/87. San Domenico, Florence: EUI.

Emerson, R. (1968) *Judging Delinquents*. Chicago: Aldine.

Eureka (1983) 'Girls and juvenile justice', *Journal of the London Intermediate Treatment Association*, 4 (special issue).

Eurostat (1983) 'The employment and unemployment of young people under 25 years old', *Employment and Unemployment* (Statistical Bulletin) April. Luxembourg.

Farrington, D.P. and Morris, A. (1983) 'Sex sentencing and reconviction', *British Journal of Criminology*, 23(3): 229–48.

Faugeron, C. (1985) *Quelque Données pour la France*. EUI Conference Paper 390/ 85, San Domenico, Florence.

Ferrari-Bravo, G. (1982–3) 'The penal institutionalisation of juvenile female offenders'. Thesis, University of Rome.

Finch, J. (1986) *Research and Policy*. London: Falmer Press.

Foucault, M. (1977a) *Discipline and Punish: the Birth of the Prison*. London: Allen Lane.

Foucault, M. (1977b) *Überwachen und Strafen*. Frankfurt: Suhrkamp.

Garland, D. (1985) *Punishment and Welfare*. Aldershot: Gower.

Gelsthorpe, L. (1981) 'Girls in the juvenile court: defining the terrain of penal policy'. *Justice for Children,* no. 23.

Gelsthorpe, L. (1985) 'Normal, natural trouble: girls and juvenile justice', *Lay Panel Magazine* (Northern Ireland Courts Association, Belfast), pp. 1–9.

Ghodse, H.A., Sheehan, M., Taylor, C. and Edwards, G. (1985) 'Death of drug addicts in the United Kingdom 1967–1981', *British Medical Journal*, 290: 425–8.

Giller, H. and Morris, A. (1983) *Providing Juvenile Justice for Children*. London: Edward Arnold.

Gilligan, C. (1982) *In a Different Voice*. Cambridge, Mass.: Harvard University Press.

Gilroy, P. (1987) *There ain't No Black in the Union Jack*. London: Hutchinson.

Girtler, R. (1984) *Der Strich*. Vienna: Age d'Homme.

Glanz, A. and Taylor, C. (1986) 'Findings of a national survey of the role of general practitioners in the treatment of opiate misuse: extent of contact with opiate misusers', *British Medical Journal*, 293: 427–30.

Glaser, D. and Frosh, S. (1988) *Child Sexual Abuse*. London: Macmillan.

Gouldner, A. (1973) *For Sociology*. London: Allen Lane.

Greenberg, D. and Humphries, D. (1980) 'The co-optation of fixed sentencing reform', *Crime and Delinquency*, 26 (April): 206–25.

Griffin, C. (1985) *Typical Girls?* London: Routledge & Kegan Paul.

Hale, J. (1983) 'Feminism and social work practice', in B. Jordan and N. Parton (eds), *The Political Dimensions of Social Work*. Oxford: Basil Blackwell.

Hall, S., Clarke, J., Erichter, C. and Jefferson, T. (1977) *Policing the Crisis: Mugging, the State and Law and Order*. London: Macmillan.

Hancock, L. (1980) 'The myth that females are treated more leniently than males in the juvenile justice system', *Australian Journal and New Zealand Journal of Sociology*, 16(3): 4–13.

Hanmer, J. (1977) 'Community action, women's aid and the women's liberation movement', in M. Mayo (ed.), *Women in the Community*. London: Routledge & Kegan Paul.

Hanmer, J. and Statham, D. (1988) *Women and Social Work*. London: Macmillan.

Harding, S. (1983) 'Why has the sex gender structure become visible only now?', in S. Harding and M. Hintikka (eds), *Discovering Reality*. Boston: D. Reidel.

Harris, R. and Webb, D. (1987) *Welfare, Power and Juvenile Justice*. London: Tavistock.

Harrison, E. (1985) 'Sexism and sex roles in I.T.' *I.T. Mailing*, 20: 8–9.

Hartnoll, R. (1986) 'Recent trends in drug abuse in Britain', *Drug Link*, 1(2): 13.

Hartsock, N. (1983) 'The feminist standpoint: developing the ground for a specifically feminist historical materialism', in S. Harding and M. Hintikka (eds), *Discovering Reality*. Boston: D. Reidel.

Hearn, J. (1982) 'Radical social work: contradictions, limitations and possibilities', *Critical Social Policy*, 2(1): 19–34.

Heidensohn, F. (1985) *Women and Crime*. London: Macmillan.

Hindess, B. (1973) *The Use of Official Statistics in Sociology*. London: Macmillan.

Home Office (1985) *Tackling Drug Misuse: a Summary of the Government's Strategy*. London: HMSO.

Home Office (1987) *Statistical Bulletin*, Sept., 1987; issue 28/87. London: HMSO.

Hudson, A. (1983) 'The welfare state and adolescent femininity', *Youth and Policy*, 2(1): 5–13.

Hudson, A. (1985) 'Feminism and social work: resistance or dialogue?', *British Journal of Social Work*. 15: 635–55.

Hudson, A. (1988) 'Boys will be boys: masculinism and the juvenile justice system', *Critical Social Policy*, 21 (Spring): 30–48.

Hudson, B. (1984a) 'The rising use of imprisonment; the impact of "decarceration" policies', *Critical Social Policy*, 11: 46–59.

Hudson, B. (1984b) 'Adolescence and femininity', in A. McRobbie and M. Nava (eds), *Gender and Generation*. London: Macmillan.

Hudson, B. (1985) 'Sugar and spice and all things nice?', *Community Care*, 4 April: 14–17.

Hutter, B. and Williams, G. (eds) (1981) *Controlling Women: the Normal and the Deviant*. Bromley: Croom Helm.

Ingham, M. (1985) *Men*. London: Century.

Institut de Criminologie (1982) *Etudes Statistiques*. Paris.

Interdepartmental Committee on Drug Addiction (1965) *Second Report*. London: HMSO.

ISTAT (1982–3) *Annuario di statistiche giudiziarie*, Vol. 29. Rome: Istituto Centrale di Statistica.

Jackson, S. (1980) 'Girls and sexual knowledge', in D. Spender and E. Sarah (eds), *Learning to Lose*. London: Women's Press.

James, J. (1978) 'Adaptive strategies and self-destructive behaviors in female prostitution'. Unpublished manuscript, Seattle.

Janssen, O. and Swierstra, K. (1982) *Heroinegebruikers in Nederland: een Typologie van Levensstulen*. Groningen: Kriminologisch Instituut Rijksuniversiteit Groningen.

Jeffries, S. (1983) 'Heroin addiction: beyond the stereotype', *Spare Rib*, 132 (July): 6–8.

Jones, R. (1979) *Fun and Therapy*. Leicester: National Youth Bureau.

Jones, R. and Kerslake, A. (1979) *Intermediate Treatment and Social Work*. London: Heinemann.

Junger-Tas, J. (1978) 'Hidden delinquency and judicial selection in Belgium', in P. Friday and V. Stewart (eds), *Youth, Crime and Juvenile Justice*. New York: Praeger.

Junger-Tas, J. (1984) *Juvenile Delinquency: Background of Delinquent Behaviour*. The Hague: Ministry of Justice.

Junger-Tas, J. and Kruisink, M. (1987) *The Evolution of Juvenile Delinquency* [in Dutch]. WODC.

Kersten, J. (1982) 'Auf den ersten Blick ein braves Mädchen', in H. Schüler-Springorum (ed.), *Mehrfach auffällig*. München: Juventa.

Kersten, J. (1986) 'Zum Vollzug der Freiheitsstrafe an Jugendlichen', in S. Müller and H.U. Otto (eds), *Damit Erziehung nicht zur Strafe wird*. Bielefeld: KT Verlag.

Kersten, J. and Wolffersdorff, C. (1980) *Jugendstrafe*. Frankfurt: Fischer.

Kersten, J., Kreissl, R. and Wolffersdorff, C. (1983) 'Die sozialisatorische Wirkung totaler Institutionen', in P.A. Albrecht and H. Schüler-Springorum (eds), *Jugendstrafe an 14- bis 15-Jährigen*. München: Fink.

Kersten, J., Sprau-Kuhlen, V. and Wolffersdorff-Ehlert, C. v. (1987) *Arbeitsgruppe Geschlossene Unterbringung: Geschlossene Unterbringung in Heimen-Untersuchungen zu einem Streitfall der Jugendhilfe (Diskussionsfassung)*. München: Deutsches Jugendinstitut.

Kieper, M. (1980) *Lebenswelten 'verwahrloster' Mädchen*. München: Juventa.

Konopka, G. (1966) *The Adolescent Girl in Conflict*. New Jersey: Prentice-Hall.

Kreissl, R. (1985) 'Gender and genius', Unpublished mimeograph, Melbourne.

Lagrée, J.-C. and Lew Fai, P. (1985) *La Galère: marginalisations juveniles et collectivités locales*. Paris: Editions CNRS.

Laing, R. and Esterson, A. (1960) *Sanity, Madness and the Family*. Harmondsworth: Penguin.

Lakoff, R. (1975) *Language and Women's Place*. London: Harper & Row.

Lalive d'Epinay, C. and Kellerhals, J.H. (1985) 'Paroles de vieux: la place des récits de vie dans une recherche sur l'intégration et la mise à l'écant des personnes âgées', in *Life Stories/Récits de Vie*. Colchester: Oral History Society and Paris: Maison des Sciences de l'Homme, Vol. I, pp. 29–40.

Lamott, F. and Andriessen, M. (1985) 'Weiblichkeitsmythen zur Erklärung männlicher Delinquenz?' *Monatsschrift für Kriminologie und Strafrechtsreform*, 68: 311–12.

Lamnek, S. (1982) 'Sozialisation und Kriminelle Karriere', in H. Schüler-Springorum (ed.), *Mehrfach auffällig*. München: Juventa.

Lee, C. (1983) *The Ostrich Position*. London: Writers & Readers.

Lees, S. (1986) *Losing Out: Sexuality and Adolescent Girls*. London: Hutchinson.

Leonard, D. (1980) *Sex and Generation*. London: Tavistock.

Levy, S.J. and Doyle, K.M. (1974) 'Attitudes towards women in a drug abuse treatment programme', *Journal of Drug Issues*, 4(4): 428–43.

Lewis, R., Hartnoll, R., Bryer, S., Davioud, E. and Mitcheson, M. (1985) 'Scoring smack: the illicit heroin market in London 1980–83'. *British Journal of Addiction*, 80(3): 281–90.

Lombroso, C. and Ferrero, W. (1900) *The Female Offender*. New York: Appleton.

Ludwig, W. (1982) 'Mehrfachtäter im Kontext gesellschaftlicher Produktion von

Jugendkriminalität', in H. Schüler-Springorum (ed.), *Mehrfach auffällig*. München: Juventa.

Ludwig, W. (1983) 'Strukturmerkmale institutioneller Rekrutierung', in P.A. Albrecht and H. Schüler-Springorum (eds), *Jugendstrafe an 14- bis 15-Jährigen*. München: Fink.

McLeod, E. (1979) *Working Women: Prostitution Now*. London: Croom Helm.

McRobbie, A. (1985) 'Working class girls and the politics of glamour: the prevention and treatment of juvenile delinquency among girls in the EEC – towards an evaluation'. Unpublished talk, EUI, San Domenico, Florence.

McRobbie, A. and Garber, J. (1976) 'Girls and subcultures', in S. Hall and T. Jefferson (eds), *Resistance through Rituals*. London: Hutchinson.

Magistrates' Association (1975) *Evidence to the House of Commons Public Expenditure Committee on the Workings of the Children and Young Persons Act 1975*. London: HMSO.

Marsh, P. et al. (1978) *The Rules of Disorder*. London: Routledge & Kegan Paul.

Martin, C.A. and Martin, W.R. (1980) 'Opiate dependence in women', in O.J. Kalant (ed.), *Alcohol and Drug Problems in Women*. New York: Plenum.

Mathieson, T. (1980) *Law, Society and Political Action*. London: Academic Press.

Mattioli, M.T. (1985) 'Gypsy girls in the penal . . . institution of Casal del Marmo', EUI Conference Paper, November, San Domenico, Florence.

Matza, D. (1964) *Delinquency and Drift*. New York: John Wiley.

Medical Working Group on Drug Dependence (1984) *Guidelines of Good Clinical Practice in the Treatment of Drug Misuse*. London: DHSS.

Merfert-Diete, C. and Soltau, R. (eds) (1984) *Die Alltägliche Verstickung in Abhangigkeit* Hamburg: Rowohlt.

Merton, R.K. (1983) *Eléments de théorie et de méthode sociologique*. Brionne: Gérard Monfort.

Meta House (1985) *Information Sheet*. Bournemouth Project, Dorset.

Miller, E.M. (1987) 'Routes to hustling careers in the U.S.: generalizations from a study of hustling in Milwaukee, Wisconsin', in 'Becoming a Teenage Prostitute in Spain and the USA', EUI Working Paper 304/87. San Domenico, Florence: EUI.

Millham, S. (1977) 'I.T. – symbol or solution?', *Youth in Society*, 26: 22–4.

Moriarty, J. (1976) 'The psychological understanding and treatment of pregnant drug addicts', in NDAC, *Critical Concerns in the Field of Drug Abuse*. New York: National Drug Abuse Conference Inc.

Morris, A. (1987) *Women, Crime and Criminal Justice*. Oxford: Basil Blackwell.

Morris, A. and McIsaac, M. (1978) *Juvenile Justice: the Practice of Social Welfare*. London: Heinemann.

Mountain, A. (1988) *Womanpower: a Handbook for Women Working with Young Women in Trouble*. Leicester: National Youth Bureau.

Nadeau, L. (1978) 'Women's issue in T.C.: patriarchy and male protection as counter therapeutic', *Addiction Therapist*, 2(3–4), Pt 1: 71–3.

Nagel, I. (1981) 'Sex difference in the processing of criminal defendants', in A. Morris and L. Gelsthorpe (eds), *Women and Crime*. Cambridge: Cambridge University Institute of Criminology.

Nagel, I.H. and Hagan, J. (1983) 'Gender and crime: offence pattern and criminal court sanctions', in M. Tonry and N. Morris (eds). *Crime and Justice*, Vol. 4. Chicago: University of Chicago Press.

National Association for the Care and Resettlement of Offenders (1985) *Monitoring the Criminal Justice Act*. London: NACRO.

National Association of Youth Clubs (NAYC) (1984) 'The best kept secret', *Working with Girls Newsletter*, 23.

National Association of Youth Clubs (NAYC) (1985) 'Feedback', *Working with Girls Newsletter*, 29.

National Youth Bureau (NYB) (1978) *A Bibliography of Intermediate Treatment 1968–1976*. Leicester: NYB.

Nurco, D.N., Wegner, N. and Stephenson, P. (1982) 'Female narcotic addicts: changing profiles', *Focus on Women*, 3(2): 62–96.

Oakley, A. (1974) *The Sociology of Housework*. Oxford: Martin Robertson.

Oakley, A. (1981) *Subject Women*. Oxford: Martin Robertson.

Pahl, J. (1985) 'Refuges for battered women: ideology and action', *Feminist Review*. 19: 25–43.

Paley, J. and Thorpe, D. (1974) *Children: Handle with Care*. Leicester: National Youth Bureau.

Parker, H., Casburn, M. and Turnbull, D. (1981) *Receiving Juvenile Justice*. Oxford: Basil Blackwell.

Perry, L. (1987) 'Fit to be parents?', *Drug Link*, 2(1): 6.

Petchesky, R. (1984) *Abortion and Women's Choice: the State, Sexuality and Reproductive Freedom*. Harlow: Longman.

Pitts, J. (1974) 'Preventive work in the school', *Youth Social Work Bulletin*, 1(2): 3–8.

Pizzey, E. (1974) *Scream Quietly or the Neighbours will Hear*. London: Penguin.

Platt, A.M. (1969) *The Child Savers*. Chicago: University of Chicago Press.

Pouget, B. du (1977) *Adolescents de Banlieue*. Lyon: Fédérop.

Pratt, J. (1983) 'Intermediate treatment and the normalisation crisis', *Howard Journal*, 22:19–37.

Pratt, J. (1986a) 'A comparative analysis of two different systems of juvenile justice: some implications for England and Wales', *Howard Journal*, 25(1): 33–51.

Pratt, J. (1986b) 'A revisionist history of "intermediate treatment"'. Unpublished paper, University of Cambridge. [Now published, *British Journal of Social Work*, 17 (1987).]

Rainer Foundation and CCETSW (1986) 'Girls in trouble: whose problem?' Conference papers, London: Rainer Foundation.

Reicher, H. (1904) *Die Fürsorge für die verwahrloste Jugend*. Vol.: *Deutsches Reich: die Zwangserziehung im Grossherzogtum Baden*. Vienna: Manzsche.

Richardson, H.J. (1969) *Adolescent Girls in Approved Schools*. London: Routledge & Kegan Paul.

Roach, P. (1983) 'Where have all the young girls gone?' *Eureka*, 4:9–11.

Robbins, D. and Cohen, C. (1978) *Knuckle Sandwich*. London: Penguin.

Robert, P. (1966) *Les bandes d'adolescents*. Paris: Editions Ouvrières.

Rosenbaum, M. (1979) 'Difficulties of taking care of business: women addicts as mothers', *American Journal of Drug and Alcohol Abuse*, 6: 431–46.

Rosenbaum, M. (1981) *Women on Heroin*. New York: Rutgers University Press.

Rowbotham, S., Segal, L. and Wainwright, H. (1979) *Beyond the Fragments*. London: Merlin.

Rush, F. (1982) *Das bestgehütete Geheimnis: sexueller Kindesmissbrauch*. Berlin: Sub rosa Frauenverlag.

Rutherford, A. (1986) *Growing out of Crime*. Hardmondsworth: Penguin.

Schultze, E. (1910) *Die jugendlichen Verbrecher im gegenwärtigen und zukünftigen Strafrecht*. Wiesbaden: Bergmann.

Schur, E.M. (1963) *Narcotic Addiction in Britain and America*. London: Tavistock.

Schwind, H. (1986) *Kriminologie*. Heidelberg: Kriminalistik Verlag.

Segal, L. (ed.) (1983) *What is to be Done about the Family?* Harmondsworth: Penguin.

Selosse, J. (1976–7) 'Les recherches de Vaucresson: conceptions, objectifs et méthodes', *Annales de Vaucresson*, 147–67.

Seruya, J.M. (1983) *Desemprego Juvenil em Portugal*. Lisbon: ICS.

Shacklady Smith, L. (1978) 'Sexist assumptions and female delinquency', in C. Smart and B. Smart (eds), *Women, Sexuality and Social Control*. London: Routledge & Kegan Paul.

Skinner, A. (1985) *A Bibliography of Intermediate Treatment 1968–1984*. London: National Youth Bureau.

Smart, C. (1976) *Women, Crime and Criminology: a Feminist Critique*. London: Routledge & Kegan Paul.

Smart, C. (1985) 'Drug dependence units in England and Wales: the results of a national survey', *Drug and Alcohol Dependence*, 15: 131–44.

Smith, D. (1980) 'A sociology for women', in J. Sherman and E. Beck (eds), *The Prism of Sex*. Wisconsin: University of Wisconsin Press.

Social Services Committee (1985) *Misuse of Drugs with Special Reference to Treatment and Rehabilitation of Misusers of Hard Drugs (4th Report)*. London: HMSO.

Soler, E., Ponsor, L. and Abod, J. (1976) 'Women in treatment: client self-reports', in NDAC, *Women and Treatment. Issues and Approaches*. Arlington, VA: National Drug Abuse Centre for Training and Resources Development.

Spear, H.B. (1969) 'The growth of heroin addiction in the United Kingdom', *British Journal of Addiction*, 64: 245–55.

Spear, M. (1985) 'Teachers' attitudes towards girls and technology', in J. Whyte, R. Deem, L. Kant and M. Cruickshank (eds), *Girl Friendly Schooling*. London: Methuen.

Spencer, B. (1984) 'Young men: their attitudes towards sexuality and birth control', *British Journal of Family Planning*, 10: 13–19.

Standing Conference on Drug Abuse (SCODA) (1985) *Annual Report*. London: SCODA.

Stanley, L. and Wise, S. (1983) *Breaking Out: Feminist Consciousness and Feminist Research*. London: Routledge & Kegan Paul.

Steffensmeir, D.J., Steffensmeir, R.H.S. and Arblatt, R. (1982) 'Sex-based differences in the sentencing of adult criminal defendants: an empirical test and theoretical overview', *Sociology and Social Research*, 66 (3): 289–304.

Stein, M. (1983) Protest in care', in B. Jordan and N. Parton (eds), *The Political Dimensions of Social Work*. Oxford: Basil Blackwell.

Stimson, H.B. and Oppenheimer, E. (1982) *Heroin Addiction: Treatment or Control in Britain*. London: Tavistock.

Summers, A. (1975) *Damned Whores and God's Police*. Sydney: Penguin.

Sumner, C. (1983) 'Rethinking deviance: towards a sociology of censures', *Research in Law, Deviance and Social Control*, 5: 187–204.

Syndicat de la Magistrature (1982) *Evidence to the Commission de Réforme du Droit Penal des Mineurs*. Paris: Ministry of Justice.

Tansey, J. (1985) 'Data and information for the project (Ireland)', EUI Conference Paper 389/85, San Domenico, Florence.

Thomas, W.I. (1967) *The Unadjusted Girl*. New York: Harper & Row. (First published, 1923.)

Thorpe, D. (1978) 'Intermediate treatment: problems of theory and practice', in R. Bailey and P. Lee (eds). *Theory and Practice in Social Work*. Oxford: Basil Blackwell.

Thorpe, D. (1983) 'Deinstitutionalisation and justice', in A. Morris and H. Giller (eds), *Providing Criminal Justice for Children*. London: Edward Arnold.

Thorpe, D., Smith, D., Green, C.J. and Paley, J.H. (1980) *Out of Care: the Community Support of Juvenile Offenders*. London: Allen & Unwin.

Vasquez, K. and Andrieu, R. (1986) *Prostitution: from the Margins of Society to Integration*. Madrid: Grupo Cultural ZERO.

Visher, C.A. (1983) 'Gender, police arrest decisions and notions of chivalry', *Criminology*, 21(1): 5–28.

Vogt, I. (1985) *Für alle Leiden gibt es eine Pille: über Psychopharmatztionium und das Geschlechtrollenspezifische Gesundheits Konzept bei Mädchen und Frauen*. Opladen: Westdeutscher Verlag.

Walgrave, L. (1987) 'Girls in the Belgian judicial system', EUI Working Paper 303/87. San Domenico, Florence: EUI.

Walker, A. (1982) *The Color Purple*. New York: Pocket Books.

Ward, E. (1984) *Father–Daughter Rape*. London: Women's Press.

Warren, J. (1977) 'Provision for naughty boys', *I.T.*, 4:1–2.

Weeks, J. (1981) *Sex, Politics and Society*. Harlow: Longman.

Willis, P. (1977) *Learning to Labour: How Working Class Kids get Working Class Jobs*. London: Saxon House.

Wilson, D. (1978) 'Sexual codes and conduct', in C. Smart and B. Smart (eds), *Women, Sexuality and Social Control*. London: Routledge & Kegan Paul.

Yeung, K. (1985) *Working with Girls: a Reader's Route Map*. Leicester: National Youth Bureau.

Index

Index compiled by Peva Keane